BEACON
BIBLE
EXPOSITIONS

BEACON BIBLE EXPOSITIONS

BEACON BIBLE EXPOSITIONS

VOLUME 10

THESSALONIANS
TIMOTHY
TITUS

by

SYDNEY MARTIN

Editors
WILLIAM M. GREATHOUSE
WILLARD H. TAYLOR

BEACON HILL PRESS OF KANSAS CITY
Kansas City, Missouri

Permission to quote from the following copyrighted versions of the Bible
is acknowledged with appreciation to the publishers:

New English Bible (NEB), © The Delegates of the Oxford University
Press and the Syndics of the Cambridge University Press, 1961, 1970.

The Bible: A New Translation (Moffatt), by James Moffatt. Copyright
1954 by James Moffatt. By permission of Harper and Row, Publishers, Inc.

New International Version of the New Testament (NIV), copyright ©
1973 by The New York Bible Society International.

The New Testament in Modern English (Phillips), copyright © by J. B.
Phillips, 1958. Used by permission of the Macmillan Co.

Revised Standard Version of the Bible (RSV), copyrighted 1946 and 1952.

The Living Bible (TLB), copyright © 1971, Tyndale House Publishers,
Wheaton, Ill.

Contents

Editors' Preface

No Christian preacher or teacher has been more aware of the creating and sustaining power of the Word of God than the Apostle Paul. As a stratagem in his missionary endeavors, he sought out synagogues in the major cities where he knew Jews would gather to hear the Old Testament. No doubt he calculated that he would be invited to expound the Scriptures, and so he would have a golden opportunity to preach Christ. That peripatetic preacher was confident that valid Christian experience and living could not be enjoyed apart from the Word of God, whether preached or written. To the Thessalonians he wrote: "And we also thank God constantly for this, that when you received the word of God which you heard from us, you accepted it not as the word of men but as what it really is, the word of God, which is at work in you believers" (1 Thess. 2:13, RSV). Strong Christians—and more broadly, strong churches—are born of, and nurtured on, authentic and winsome exposition of the Bible.

Beacon Bible Expositions provide a systematic, devotional Bible study program for laymen and a fresh, homiletical resource for preachers. All the benefits of the best biblical scholarship are found in them, but nontechnical language is used in the composition. A determined effort is made to relate the clarified truth to life today. The writers, Wesleyan in theological perspective, seek to interpret the gospel, pointing to the Living Word, Christ, who is the primary Subject of all scripture, the Mediator of redemption, and the Norm of Christian living.

The publication of this series is a prayerful invitation to both laymen and ministers to set out on a lifelong, systematic study of the Bible. Hopefully these studies will supply the initial impetus.

—WILLIAM M. GREATHOUSE AND
WILLARD H. TAYLOR, *Editors*

Introduction to the
Epistles to the Thessalonians

There has sometimes been a tendency to treat 1 and 2 Thessalonians more or less as suppliers of proof texts. These Epistles could fill such a role admirably, and any preacher preparing sermons on entire sanctification and the Second Advent would readily acknowledge this. For instance, within these eight brief chapters there is an unusual abundance of eschatological material. In 1 Thessalonians every chapter ends with a reference to the Second Coming, while the Second Epistle contains a wealth of information on some relatively unfamiliar aspects of the last things. As might be expected, there is no less emphasis upon the necessity for, and the availability of, that holiness without which no man shall see the Lord.

Nevertheless, these Epistles deserve to be loved for their own sakes, and the student who is willing to spend time in their company will prove that within their broader compass lie insights of rich theological and practical value. As an additional bonus it will be seen that those homiletical gems already mentioned—the proof texts—will take on an added lustre when viewed against their contextual backgrounds.

But before dealing with the Epistles, as such, it might be well to briefly consider their author and some of the events leading up to the formation of the church to which they were written.

The Apostle to the Thessalonians

Much has rightly been made of Paul's evangelistic strategy. He has been called the missionary counterpart of

Alexander the Great; for, like him, the apostle was quick to mark the tactical value of the great metropolitan centres. In this connection Thessalonica was a prize indeed. Cicero described it as "lying in the lap of the Roman Empire," and its abiding geographical importance is well proven by the fact that, as modern Salonika, it is still the second largest city in Greece. It is a focal centre of industry and commerce, boasting a population of a quarter of a million.

But Paul's strategy was cast in a mould infinitely superior to that of his imperial counterpart, for in every well-ordered step of his the apostle was acutely sensitive to the Holy Spirit's guidance. For this reason, to the uninitiated, it must have seemed as if many of his decisions were taken without rhyme or reason. Moore, standing in the shoes of a superficial observer, can say that "Paul, Silas and Timothy entered Thessalonica more by accident than by their design."[1] At this point we might note some of those diversions and apparent frustrations that would have daunted a man of less spiritual stature and discernment than the apostle.

In the first place we learn from Acts 15:36 that what we have come to know as Paul's second missionary journey actually began as an exercise for the strengthening of the existing churches in western Asia. In this connection the choice of Barnabas, the son of encouragement, was a happy one. Yet, before the chapter closes, the partnership is broken, Barnabas is replaced by Silas, and, at Lystra, Timothy is recruited in place of Mark who had been the bone of contention between the two senior missionaries.

Then we encounter further unexpected events. Because of that economy of words so typical of the New Testament narratives, sequences and details are not always easy to follow. However, we may gather from Paul's own personal reference in Gal. 4:13 how, in one instance, the Spirit communicated His will. Here we read of no mystical experience of guidance but, in the words of the NEB, "As you know, it was bodily illness that originally led to my bringing you the Gospel." By such means, apparently, was the apostle forbidden of the Holy Spirit to preach the Word in Asia (Acts 16:6). As he recovered, he seems to have become increasingly drawn by the lure of Bithynia. Once again, though by what means we are not told, he is made aware of the restraint of the Spirit and, instead of proceeding northwards, he and his colleagues turn their faces once more westward, arriving in due course at Troas.

It must indeed be confessed that an observer of these delayings and diversions would not be overly impressed by the Pauline strategy, particularly since this latest manoeuvre appeared to lead up to the blank wall of a dead-end street. Yet it was to this man, so finely susceptible to divine promptings and pressures, that God gave a vision which was to result in the Church breaking clean through a continental barrier. The apparent dead-end street suddenly opened up into what could rightly be called a global main street, for Thessalonica was a city built astride the Egnatian Way, that great imperial highroad of the Roman world. So was born the European Church.

The Epistles to the Thessalonians

Authorship. It was not until the mid-19th century that the Pauline authorship of these letters was seriously questioned. Those responsible were mainly of the Tübingen school and, as William Neil laconically observes, these scholars were prone to overturn any established conclusion on principle. That they did not always act on firm evidence is clear from the fact that almost every current standard work considers that the weight of both internal and external evidence brings the scale firmly down on the side of the Pauline authorship of both Epistles.

Date and Place of Origin. In establishing these, we again find clues both within the Epistles themselves and in the Acts. From 1 Thess. 3:6 we conclude that the First Epistle was written shortly after Timothy had brought back to Paul his report of the Thessalonian situation. We may assume that the writing took place in Corinth, at which city the apostle had arrived via Berea and Athens after his hasty retreat from Thessalonica. It was at Corinth that Paul was rejoined by Silas and Timothy, and we may presume that the Epistle was penned after Timothy's report had been received (Acts 18:1-5). But the date may be fixed with some precision by relating Paul's movements at this time to a well-documented event. As we know from Acts 18:11, Paul spent 18 months in Corinth. This extended sojourn was justified in view of the encouraging Gentile response but, true to type, the envious Christ-rejecting Jews again stirred up violent opposition, subsequently accusing Paul before Gallio (Acts 18:12). Knowing the date of Gallio's proconsulship, we have a means of determining with fair accuracy that 1 Thessalonians was written at the very latest in A.D. 51, and possibly as early as A.D. 50.

What of the Second Epistle? Again both internal and external evidences point to an early date. Acts 20:1 ff. would seem to lend support to this view, for these verses show that Paul returned to Macedonia, probably not too long after his first visit. Thus it is hardly likely that he would have written such a second letter *after* having paid this second visit. Such persistent problems as this letter discusses would already have been dealt with face-to-face. As regards the place of writing there is evidence leading us to believe that this again was Corinth. We know from 2 Thess. 1:1 that Paul, Silas, and Timothy were together at the time and, according to Acts 18:5, Corinth appears to have been the only place where the three colleagues were in company in the interim between Paul's first and second visits to Macedonia.

This question of date is of more than academic importance, for it means that if A.D. 50 to 51 is accepted, then, with the possible exception of Galatians, we have here the earliest of all New Testament documents. To quote Arnold Airhart, "Written barely 20 years after the resurrection of Christ, these letters provide us with an important picture of the Early Church. The curtain is pulled aside on that

Church's problems, hopes, fellowship, discipline, and standards."[2]

Content and Purpose. Doubtless Morris' comment that the Thessalonian Epistles "lack the theological profundity of Romans and the exciting controversy of Galatians"[3] is warranted; but he rightly points out that most, if not all, of the great Pauline doctrines are present, either by implication or direct mention. This is significant, for some have too readily assumed that because, in these Epistles, the great evangelical doctrines are not discussed at length, they have evidently not yet "evolved" in the mind of the apostle. Admittedly, such doctrines as the atonement, the Lordship of Christ and His equality with God, the person and work of the Holy Spirit, and, in effect, the Trinity, are mostly indirectly introduced. But the fact that they appear with that naturalness born of long acquaintance would give the lie to the notion that they had just begun to emerge in Paul's thinking.

Nevertheless, it is one of the major virtues of such writings as these that they are not primarily didactic but rather intensely personal in character. As such they present to us a priceless view of the inner heart of the great apostle. Here we see, blended with the vision and passion of the Church's foremost missionary, the warm compassion of its truest of pastors. Because these are essentially Epistles of the heart, they do not lend themselves readily to neat analysis. But what love letter ever did? Other preachers too, when writing to their dearly beloved, have been known to break the pattern of "firstly, secondly, thirdly"!

Yet while the passion of the writer may be more in evidence than the pattern of the writings, it is possible to discern a broad design. This may be seen as twofold. On the one hand we see concern for the *protection* of the beloved Thessalonians, and on the other an equal concern for their *perfection.* Around these dual concerns there revolves much of the content of these letters.

Paul's protective instinct is expressed in words of exceeding tenderness, as in 1 Thess. 2:7 and 11, and was provoked partly because of outside pressures upon his readers. These arose from two sources. First, from the continuing machinations of those Jews who, by slander and insinuation, were seeking to undermine the character of the apostle and the loyalty of his converts. And secondly, bitter persecution by their pagan compatriots was a sore trial. But there were inside pressures too. In the main these arose out of an imperfect understanding of Paul's teaching, particularly with reference to the Second Coming. While the First Epistle seems to have largely taken care of the external problems, these internal difficulties persisted. In fact, the problems remaining in regard to certain implications of the Second Advent were a major reason for the apostle taking up his pen again (2 Thess. 1:7—2:17).

Out of Paul's concern for the perfection of his readers have come those gems of holiness truth already referred to, truth that reflects the ardent longing of Christ himself (cf. Eph. 5:25-27 and 1 Thess. 5:23). But, as always, Paul sees beyond the merely cosmetic value of sanctity. He sees holiness not only as an exquisite adornment but as an essential armament against all that threatens the well-being and effectiveness of a church so lately hewn out of heathenism. What is more, he sees the experience of entire sanctification and readiness for the Second Coming as twin truths, indeed as "Siamese twin" truths. They cannot be separated without serious damage ensuing to the one, or the other, or both.

It is such emphases that invest these Epistles with perpetual significance, "and so much the more, as [we] see the day approaching."

The First Epistle
to the
THESSALONIANS

Topical Outline of First Thessalonians

Introduction and Salutation (1:1-3)
   A Gracious Greeting (1:1)
   The Grace of Gratitude (1:2)
   The Triad of Graces (1:3)

The Evidence of True Election (1:4-10)
   The Fact Stated (1:4)
   The Fact Demonstrated (1:5-10)

The Defence of the Apostolic Method (2:1-12)
   Charges Answered Negatively (2:1-6)
   Charges Answered Positively (2:7-12)

The Response to the Apostolic Message (2:13-16)
   The Reception That the Message Was Given (2:13)
   The Recognition That the Message Was God-given (2:13)
   The Opposition That the Message Received (2:14-16)

The Expression of Apostolic Concern (2:17—3:13)
   The Reason for Paul's Absence (2:17-20)
   The Reason for Timothy's Presence (3:1-5)
   The Nature of Timothy's Report (3:6-9)
   Paul's Response and His Prayer (3:10-13)

Instructions to Those Who Live in Christ (4:1-12)
   Given by Divine Authority (4:1-2)
   Given in the Interests of Sexual Purity (4:3-8)
   Given in the Interests of God's Family (4:9-10)
   Given in the Interests of Christian Industry (4:11-12)

Encouragement to Both the Living and the Dead in Christ (4:13-18)
   The Provision for Those Asleep in Christ (4:13-14)
   The Priority of Those Asleep in Christ (4:15-18)

Exhortations to Those Who Live in Expectation of the Day (5:1-22)
   Live Consistently as Children of the Day (5:1-11)
   Live Congregationally as Children of the Day (5:12-22)

Final Prayer, Charges, and Benediction (5:23-28)
   A Prayer to God (5:23-24)
   Charges to the People of God (5:25-27)
   A Benediction upon the People of God (5:28)

Introduction and Salutation

1 Thessalonians 1:1-3

1 THESSALONIANS 1

A Gracious Greeting

1 Thess. 1:1

> 1 Paul, and Silvanus, and Timotheus, unto the church of the Thessalonians which is in God the Father and in the Lord Jesus Christ: Grace be unto you, and peace, from God our Father, and the Lord Jesus Christ.

As already stated, there is decisive evidence in favour of Pauline authorship, and even though the names of Silvanus (the Latinized form of Silas) and Timotheus are appended, this is no indication of a composite Epistle. Both colleagues had accompanied Paul on his second missionary journey, both were probably by his side as he wrote this letter, and Silvanus might well have acted as his amanuensis. The fact that the apostle here refers to himself simply as "Paul," without any mention of his apostolic status, may be noteworthy. This omission could be a subtle hint of that relationship of mutual trust and esteem which soon becomes apparent as the letter proceeds. So far as he is concerned, Paul appears to assume that his readers are well enough disposed towards him that they will interpret the fruits of his ministry among them as being sufficient proof of his apostleship.

In this opening verse an important doctrine is suggested, for the combination of the terms *God the Father* and *the Lord Jesus Christ* is twice presented. This strongly indicates the essential unity of Father and Son. Yet it should be kept in mind that, first and foremost, this Epistle is truly a letter and by no means a theological treatise. William Neil has called it a "short, simple letter from a great missionary to a young Church struggling to keep its feet—and its head—in difficult and trying times."[4] Yet this unpretentious document, and similarly the second, help us the better to understand the personality and methods of Paul and to sense the atmosphere and temper prevailing within a developing primitive church.

Paul addressed his readers as *the church of the Thessalonians.* Why did he employ this unusual designation in preference to the more familiar form "the church at (or in) Thessalonica"? George Milligan thinks that the reason may have been that the apostle wished to draw special attention to his concern for the local body of believers. Such an emphasis would be appreciated, for there is reason to believe that their numbers were small. Neil suggests that the fellowship might have resembled the old Scots "kitchen meeting," with the company gathered in the living room of Jason's house (Acts 17:5 ff.), and composed largely of so-called working-class folk. Acts 17:4 informs us that, apart from a number of influential women, the church consisted mainly of Greek proselytes, and A. L. Moore feels that the *great multitude* of these, as mentioned in the text, should probably be understood relatively.

Yet Paul had no hesitation in declaring these Thessalonian believers to be truly *in God the Father and in the Lord Jesus Christ.* It has been well said that a preposition makes all the difference to a proposition. This is very much the case when that preposition is "in"; and when this word is used within its present context, it makes a mighty difference to the morale of such a little, obscure, persecuted "home mission" church like these Thessalonians!

The Grace of Gratitude

1 Thess. 1:2

> 2 We give thanks to God always for you all, making mention of you in our prayers;

We give thanks (2). The Greek verb so translated derives from the same root as *grace* in v. 1. This common origin is suggestive for two reasons: First, because everything that was thankworthy in the Thessalonians was the product of God's grace. It was the result of what He had graciously done through them rather than what they had done for Him. Secondly, Paul's warm commendation of his readers reflects God's own graciousness. God is gladdened when He beholds His people's wholehearted service, imperfect though it appear to Him. In v. 3 Paul recognized a threefold cause for thankfulness; yet while he was unstinting in his praise, he was not blind to the need for continuing progress. The Thessalonians' *faith* still needed to be perfected (3:10), their *love* still needed to increase and abound (3:12), and their *hope* needed to become more enlightened (4:13 ff.). So did the apostle exemplify his own dictum that perfect love is always "eager to believe the best" (1 Cor. 13:5, Moffatt).

The Triad of Graces

1 Thess. 1:3

> 3 Remembering without ceasing your work of faith, and labour of love, and patience of hope in our Lord Jesus Christ, in the sight of God and our Father;

The phrase *your work of faith, and labour of love, and patience of hope* (3) Calvin describes as "a short definition of true Christianity."

1. The NEB renders the first section as "your faith has shown itself in action," and several of the newer versions have similarly placed prior emphasis on faith. This is consonant with Pauline thought in which, first:

a. Faith precedes works. Faith is not in itself a "work" except in the sense that it is a work of *God.* (See in John

6:29—"This is the work of God, that ye believe on him whom he hath sent.") C. H. Dodd has made the remark that "to Paul faith is that attitude in which, acknowledging our complete insufficiency for any of the high ends of life, we rely utterly on the sufficiency of God." But secondly:

b. Faith produces works. Paul wrote to the Galatians of *the faith which worketh* (5:6). Hence the Reformers reminded us that, while we are saved by faith alone, the faith which saves is never alone. True faith is productive. Precisely what kind of work the apostle had here in mind we are not told, though some commentators link *your work of faith* with *ye turned to God from idols* in v. 9. This is assuredly the initial product of saving faith, though it seems more likely that what Paul had most in mind was the Thessalonians' magnificent work of witness (v. 8). That he had little time for those who were idlers is evident from his later rebuke administered to the work-shy minority, in 2 Thess. 3:10-12.

2. Just as work is produced by faith, so is "labor prompted by love" (NIV), but note the progression from *work* to *labor.* The latter word (Gk., *kopos*) denotes that arduous, unremitting toil which involves sweat and fatigue, such as Paul himself had so often experienced (see 2:9; 3:5; 2 Thess. 3:8; and elsewhere). If such labor is to be promoted, it is essential that love (Gk., *agapē*) be allied to faith, for in effective service to God and man such love is the indispensable dynamic. It alone enables one to seek the highest good of others, in spite of opposition and indifference. It alone empowers the Christian worker to persevere even when those to whom he ministers neither deserve nor desire what he offers. As Sangster has said in his *Pure in Heart,* "The saint never gives up. He goes on serving, loving, helping . . . He aches for souls. Neither indifference, nor slander, nor injury can stop him for he does not make a motive of gratitude. His great motive is his utter love of God."[5]

3. *Patience of hope.* V. 3 contains Paul's first reference to the triad of Christian graces. To many readers the Corinthian sequence is the more familiar, but as Eadie finely puts it in his commentary on this Epistle, the sequence in Corinthians proceeds from "the faith that is child-like, through the hope that is saint-like, to the love that is God-like."[6] for at Corinth such love was the prime need. But as Lightfoot observes in his comment on Col. 1:4-5, where the Thessalonian sequence occurs, "while faith rests on the past, and love works in the present, hope looks to the future." This climactic of hope was particularly relevant to the Thessalonian situation, for it focussed their vision upon Christ's return. This blessed hope had already inspired them to endure sore trial, and the clearer understanding of the implications of this event, yet to be ministered to them by Paul, would strengthen still further their patient endurance.

The Evidence of True Election
1 Thessalonians 1:4-10

The Fact Stated

1 Thess. 1:4

> 4 Knowing, brethren beloved, your election of God.

During the Hebrides Revival the main opposition to Duncan Campbell's preaching did not arise from his emphasis on holiness so much as his claim that a believer could know that he was a true child of God. For preaching such a truth he incurred the wrath of certain Hebridean ministers, one of whom wrote a tract warning his parishioners against the revival movement, and against this "heresy" in particular. The tract bore the title *Arminianism Exposed!* But here Paul goes far beyond Duncan Campbell's claim, for he declared that *he* knew that the Thessalonian believers were true children of God. James Denney observed that the doctrine of election has often been taught as if the one thing that could never be known about anybody was whether he was or was not elect, but he added that this assumed impossibility does not square with New Testament ways of speaking. That is abundantly confirmed by the teaching in this verse.

1. Paul stated that the Thessalonians were "brothers beloved by God" (NEB), which is the more correct translation. No less than 21 times in the Thessalonian correspondence did Paul use this word translated "brothers," but here he speaks of "brothers beloved," a double term of endearment very rarely used elsewhere. And as Barclay points out in his *Daily Study Bible,* "'beloved by God' was applied by Jews only to supremely great men like Moses and Solomon, and to the nation of Israel itself."[7] What but the miracle of grace could have inspired Paul, this once bigoted Pharisee of the Pharisees, to greet once despised Gentiles as brothers beloved of God, part of His very elect?

2. Paul stated that his readers were the chosen of God. Here again we quote the more recent versions which invariably use "chosen" in preference to "elect," for the former term preserves the simplicity of this important New Testament doctrine. And election is essentially simple. Here Paul, by his quite casual use of the word, implies that his readers understood its meaning, even though they were by no means theologically erudite. John McNeill, the Scots evangelist, was once approached by a young, newly inducted minister who expressed his fear that he "might have offered free grace to some who were not of the elect." The veteran evangelist replied, "Son, Ah wouldna worry. If ye happen to get the wrang man saved the Lord'll forgive ye."

This is not to imply that the doctrine is easy to comprehend in all of its ramifications. Indeed Paul himself confesses that it is a "mystery" (Eph. 1:14), a mystery all the more profound in the light of this verse which reveals that God chose His people, not only before they existed, but before the world itself existed. Yet, as with other New

Testament "mysteries," while this one cannot be fully explained, it can be wonderfully experienced. Let any man make the response that God has ordained, and that man will awake to the fact that his salvation was preordained, that before he chose Christ he was chosen by Christ. So here Paul stresses the truth in respect to his readers. "Brothers loved by God, we know that he has chosen you" (NIV). Yet,

a. God's choosing does not preclude the necessity of man's response. Jesus himself said, *Ye have not chosen me, but I have chosen you* (John 15:16); yet John also announced that *as many as received him, to them gave he power* [right] *to become the sons of God* (John 1:12). For, as Agar Beet has said in his Romans commentary, "God resolved to save not all men promiscuously, but only those who should believe the Gospel."[8]

b. God's choosing does not deny the possibility of all men responding. "For the grace of God has appeared for the salvation of all men" (Titus 2:11, RSV). And if saving grace has appeared for all men, then believing grace must of necessity have been included, for the one is of no use without the other.

The Fact Demonstrated

1 Thess. 1:5-10

> 5 For our gospel came not unto you in word only, but also in power, and in the Holy Ghost, and in much assurance; as ye know what manner of men we were among you for your sake.
> 6 And ye became followers of us, and of the Lord, having received the word in much affliction, with joy of the Holy Ghost:
> 7 So that ye were ensamples to all that believe in Macedonia and Achaia.
> 8 For from you sounded out the word of the Lord not only in Macedonia and Achaia, but also in every place your faith to God-ward is spread abroad; so that we need not to speak any thing.
> 9 For they themselves shew of us what manner of entering in we had unto you, and how ye turned to God from idols to serve the living and true God;
> 10 And to wait for his Son from heaven, whom he raised from the dead, even Jesus, which delivered us from the wrath to come.

1. *The subjective evidence experienced by the preachers* (5), that is, the inner consciousness that, as they had

preached, their hearers were even then *being born again . . . by the word of God* (1 Pet. 1:23).

a. The preaching had not been merely verbal. Samuel Chadwick used to say that some preaching is like sheet lightning, it shines but it does not strike. Paul recoiled from such preaching. He deliberately refrained from employing the vain arts of rhetoric and empty eloquence.

b. The preaching had been vital. Paul and his co-workers had proclaimed the living Word of God which had gone forth with *power* (Gk., *dynamis*). Such preaching had exposed the falsity of the idol-gods and had inspired the service of the living and true God. The Word had also gone forth with *full assurance* (conviction). There is some difference of opinion among scholars as to whether this conviction related to preachers or hearers. The context would seem to favour the former, but the fact is that where the preacher enjoys the Spirit's anointing, the conviction with which he speaks invariably communicates itself to his hearers.

Perhaps one cautionary word may be added here. We can be certain that, while Paul's preaching was simple, it was not superficial. The Word must be rightly divided if it is to be divinely anointed. The Spirit falls only upon a prepared offering.

2. *The objective evidence of election exhibited in the hearers* (6-10).

a. Ye became followers (imitators) *of us, and of the Lord* (6). This is the first but by no means the last time that Paul encouraged his readers to imitate himself (see 1 Cor. 4:16; 11:1; Phil. 3:17). If this sounds oddly self-righteous and even conceited, it should be remembered that the preachers of that day could not exhort their hearers as we might do, "Don't copy us, copy Christ." How were they to know what Christ was like? They had no New Testament. They were busy writing it. Yet, as Neil comments, this was not an evidence of "Pauline megalomania . . . [Paul and his fellow-workers] were able to speak of

Christ and themselves in the same breath because they were Christ-men."[9]

b. The Thessalonians became themselves pattern believers (7). The word translated *ensample* (Gk., *typos*) was used, among other things, to denote a stamp made by a die. The use of the word here suggests, therefore, that these believers, having been stamped with the authentic Christian likeness, had now become dies for stamping that likeness upon others. It was this that earned for them the title of a model church, an honour conferred upon no other congregation. Yet this is surely what every church is meant to be. In the second century, when men began to ask for an explanation of the incredible growth of the Christian Church, it was Justin Martyr who gave the answer that wherever the gospel had gone, you were likely to run across a new kind of people. They could be trusted, they lived purely, they were ready to help others and to share what they had. They were people of peace, goodwill, and contentment. They obviously knew God.

The Church must restore such an image. For too long she has assumed that the secret of communication lies in indoctrination, whereas it lies much more in incarnation. Twentieth-century Christians must see that, in a world that is increasingly dependent on visual aids, a merely verbal witness must remain unconvincing. Let this lesson be learned and the Church will prove that, without the need for gimmicks, she will have far more vital contacts than she can reasonably handle. But like the Thessalonian Church she will prove that such a vital, visible witness will incur opposition; yet where this is borne *with joy of the Holy Ghost* (6), she will prove that affliction, instead of stultifying the witness, will actually amplify it until it resounds far and wide (8).

c. The Thessalonians became a "sort of sounding board," which is how Phillips paraphrases v. 8. In his commentary, William Hendriksen has shown that here the Thessalonians "are compared to a parabolic arch or a sounding-board which reinforces sounds and cause them to travel in various directions."[10] In these days when electronic amplification usually takes care of the acoustical defects in our church buildings, the old sounding board is rarely seen. This was in the form of a wooden roof or canopy fitted above the preacher's head to prevent his words being lost among the rafters. But there ought still to be a sounding board in every church, not above the pulpit but in the pews, in the form of a receptive, communicative people ready to echo the Word of the Lord in every place.

d. The Thessalonians furnished the incontrovertible evidence of both being and doing. They were Christians indeed because they were Christian in deeds. This was shown by their separation—they *turned to God from idols;* in their ministration—*to serve the living and true God;* and in their expectation—*to wait for his Son from heaven* (9-10). This is full-orbed, three-dimensional Christianity. Those who practised it were very evidently of the elect.

e. The Thessalonians enjoyed deliverance from future wrath. Here *wrath* is quite clearly associated with the time of the end. This gives it more than the somewhat impersonal aspect that C. H. Dodd seems to have in mind when he speaks of divine wrath as an inevitable process of cause and effect in a moral universe. Certainly there is a present and continuing divine judgment in the world (see Rom. 1:18), but to so limit judgment is to give insufficient consideration to two important aspects of the truth. One of these is explicit in v. 10, namely, that there is a truly eschatological judgment, yet future and climactic.

The other is implicit, namely, that we must consider this to refer to the wrath of God, in a personal sense. For if this is God's universe, and if one element in His moral law is that judgment follows upon sin, then it is impossible to conclude that this takes place independently of Him. James Denney once said that to take the condemnation out of the Cross was to take the nerve out of the gospel. It was no nerveless gospel that Paul had brought to Thessalonica.

The Defence of the Apostolic Method

1 Thessalonians 2:1-12

1 THESSALONIANS 2

Charges Answered Negatively

1 Thess. 2:1-6

> 1 For yourselves, brethren, know our entrance in unto you, that it was not in vain:
> 2 But even after that we had suffered before, and were shamefully entreated, as ye know, at Philippi, we were bold in our God to speak unto you the gospel of God with much contention.
> 3 For our exhortation was not of deceit, nor of uncleanness, nor in guile:
> 4 But as we were allowed of God to be put in trust with the gospel, even so we speak; not as pleasing men, but God, which trieth our hearts.
> 5 For neither at any time used we flattering words, as ye know, nor a cloak of covetousness; God is witness:
> 6 Nor of men sought we glory, neither of you, nor yet of others, when we might have been burdensome, as the apostles of Christ.

Timothy's report on the Thessalonian situation had been, in the main, reassuring (3:6-10), though apparently it had carried some disturbing undertones. The first of these related to the smear campaign being conducted in Paul's absence. That this was something to be reckoned with is evident from the fact that, having already defended his ministry in Thessalonica (1:5, 9), the apostle now deemed it essential to return to his defence in considerable detail.

Chiselled into the stonework of one of our older halls of learning is the legend which, translated, reads, "They say. What do they say? Let them say!" That could serve as a motto for all who are dedicated to the fearless proclamation of truth. Yet the preacher of the gospel must apply such sentiments with due discretion. He certainly cannot afford the luxury of self-pity, for he who is dedicated to tending the wounds of others will have little time to spend upon his own. But he must not imagine that this gives him the right to exhibit a jaunty disregard for the opinion of others. He must realize as Paul did, that if the traducer succeeds in destroying the reputation of the messenger, then the message is in danger of dying a natural death. It would be well, therefore, to examine the charges levelled against Paul and his companions, and to note how he refutes them. We may gather from Paul's defence that, in all, seven accusations were being brought against him and his colleagues.

1. *Their ministry had been empty* (1-2). The word translated *vain* (Gk., *kenos*) has the primary meaning of "void," or "empty" (see Mark 12:3), while its secondary meaning, "wasted" or "fruitless," is found in 1 Cor. 15:58. Which meaning applies in this case is in some dispute, though some scholars have suggested that its ambiguity may have been intentional. In any case Paul had his answer. On the one hand, the catalogue of results issuing from his preaching, already listed in chapter 1, more than answered any charge of fruitlessness. On the other hand, far from the missionaries having come empty-handed—and here is probably the first intimation that their accusers had denounced them as parasites—they had brought with them a gospel full of power. What was more, the declaration of that gospel had been full of risk and potential suffering for themselves.

Incidentally, we may gather from v. 2 that Paul was particularly sensitive to suffering. The shameful treatment meted out to Silas and himself in Philippi had clearly left its mark. Paul's public scourging, especially, had been a sheer outrage, and in the light of the autobiographical passage in 2 Cor. 11:13 ff. we may be sure that such experiences, for him, amounted to an ordeal of sheer agony and ignominy. And Paul quoted this as evidence that he had not come to Thessalonica out of selfish, empty desire. He bore upon his body the scars of recent maltreatment, and his eyes were open to the strong likelihood of its being repeated. How could he have ventured forth so boldly, to preach the gospel to the Thessalonians so fearlessly, had he not been specially strengthened by God and sent by Him?

2. *Their ministry had been delusory* (3a). This charge was not so much that Paul had wilfully deceived his hearers but that he himself had been deluded. Moffatt has captured the sense of this phrase, "For the appeal we make does not spring from any delusion." Putting it bluntly, Paul was being accused of madness rather than badness.

No Christian should be surprised at such a charge, for, very often, conversion has been counted as delusion. When Sarah Bentley, whom Dr. Sangster described as one of the lovely early evangelicals of Yorkshire, was converted, her former friends said, "Sally's gone daft." She had been a barmaid in the George Inn at York, and in her reminiscences she has told how, after her conversion, "They treated me like a mad woman who mustn't be left alone." Jesus himself tasted the same bitter cup, for when He began calling His disciples, His own kinsmen *went out to lay hold on him: for they said, He is beside himself* (Mark 3:21).

But God's "madmen" are the sanest on this planet, hence Paul was not slow in contending for his soundness of mind. "We speak as men . . . entrusted with the Gospel" (4, NIV), the implication being that such a divine trust was its own best witness to his sanity.

3. *Their ministry had involved immorality* (3b). Most commentators support the use of *uncleanness* in the KJV. To some such a charge implying sexual immorality is so atrocious as to appear ridiculous, yet when it is remembered that a common feature of pagan worship was religious prostitution, it can be seen that the missionaries

were by no means invulnerable, even at this point. William Neil observes that such licentious practices were looked upon as sacramental fornication, and that this was justified on the pretext that union with the servant of a god was tantamount to union with the deity itself. It was perhaps against this background that those Jews who sought to vilify the apostle had made a suggestive reference to the many women among his converts (Acts 17:4). But, as we have seen, Paul's defence rested squarely upon God's approval. He and his colleagues could not possibly have been entrusted with the gospel of God had they not been attested by God himself. Hence Paul could say, "We speak as men approved by God to be entrusted with the gospel" (4, NIV).

4. *Their ministry had employed trickery* (3c-4). In this case Paul was certainly being accused of having actively and intentionally deceived his hearers. The word *guile* (Gk., *dolos*) means a bait or a trap, thus implying that the unsuspecting converts had been caught by insidious, unscrupulous means. While again it may seem unthinkable to us that such a charge could be made to "stick," we must take into account an age in which religious charlatanry was rife. "'Holy men' of all creeds and countries, popular philosophers, magicians, astrologers, crack-pots and cranks; the sincere and the spurious, the righteous and the rogue, swindlers and saints, jostled and clamoured for the attention of the credulous and the sceptical."

Quite obviously Paul had no wish to be numbered with such transgressors. Accordingly, as in the previous case, he insisted that he had enjoyed approval from the highest Source. Against the charge of having been deluded he claimed to have been entrusted with the message of the all-wise God; against the charge of immorality he claimed that his character had been attested by the all-seeing God; now, against the charge of trickery, he declares that his motives had been tested by the all-knowing God—"We are not trying to please men, but God, who tests our hearts"

(4b, NIV). So he confutes the charge that he had occupied the role of the "popular preacher" who cunningly accommodates his message to the whims and wishes of his hearers merely to multiply converts.

Nevertheless, it is well to remember that, in Paul's estimation, the use of *guile* in preaching was by no means invariably reprehensible. It is interesting to note that Paul used the identical word, *dolos,* later, in 2 Cor. 12:16; and on that occasion, far from repudiating the charge of craftiness, he actually boasted that he had been guilty! And it was a greater than he who so daringly chose a creature, more *subtle than any beast of the field,* as a pattern for the preacher (Matt. 10:16).

Needless to say, there is a world of difference between the sinister craft of the trickster and the holy guile of the apostle. The former he unsparingly condemned, yet he himself was a master in employing the subtleties of love and the ingenuities of zeal in catching men for his Lord. By such means did he study to save the weak and ignorant that he might "entrap them into glorious freedom." Here is a paradox, the resolving of which is an essential discipline of the preacher who, as the herald of God, is called to be at once a warner and a winner of souls.

5. *Their ministry had employed flattery* (5a). This particular charge, with the two following, are closely interrelated, since all have to do with the preachers' alleged self-seeking. For example, the word "flattery" (Gk., *kolakias*) could be better translated "cajolery"; for, as Morris points out, the word refers to "the use of acceptable speech with the purpose of lulling another into a sense of security, so that he may obtain his own ends."[11] In this respect the present charge is closely linked with the former; for while the purpose of the trickster is to gain followers, the aim of the flatterer is to gain personal advantage, to "cash in" on one's ministry. It is difficult to conceive of any betrayal of preaching quite so despicable as this.

The nub of Paul's defence is seen in v. 2 with its reference to the fact that the missionaries had "declared the gospel of God . . . frankly and fearlessly" (Phillips). In the light of this the charge falls to the ground. Any man can persuade his hearers to accept what they want to hear, but it takes a man of sincere conviction and proved integrity to gain a favourable response to a demanding message uncompromisingly proclaimed.

6. *Their ministry had been a cloak for cupidity* (5*b*). Literally, as Hendriksen has put it, their ministry had been "a pretext to cover up their greed."[12] The word translated *covetousness* (Gk., *pleonexia*) signifies the very essence of greed itself, and this may mean greed for glory as well as gold. That this connection may have been in the minds of Paul's accusers is suggested in his denial in the next verse, *nor of men sought we glory,* but there seems little doubt that the apostle's main concern was to repudiate the charge that he and his fellow workers had used their preaching to fleece rather than to feed their sheep. Paul's reaction to such a contemptible accusation can be gauged from his solemn appeal for God to bear witness to his innocency.

7. *Their ministry had reflected self-glory* (6). Once again a word has been used the meaning of which is somewhat ambiguous—*baros* in the Greek. Translated as *burden* in the KJV, it has been interpreted as indicating a financial burden such as the Thessalonians would have had to bear had the missionaries claimed their keep. Moffatt's version illustrates the alternative use of the word—"as apostles of Christ we had the power of claiming to be men of weight," implying that, had they wished, they could have wielded the heavy hand of authority. In a sense both interpretations coincide, since any claim to hospitality would have been grounded on apostolic authority; but instead of piling burdens of any kind upon their converts, the missionaries had lavished spiritual care and nourishment upon them.

Charges Answered Positively

1 Thess. 2:7-12

> 7 But we were gentle among you, even as a nurse cherisheth her children:
> 8 So being affectionately desirous of you, we were willing to have imparted unto you, not the gospel of God only, but also our own souls, because ye were dear unto us.
> 9 For ye remember, brethren, our labour and travail: for labouring night and day, because we would not be chargeable unto any of you, we preached unto you the gospel of God.
> 10 Ye are witnesses, and God also, how holily and justly and unblameably we behaved ourselves among you that believe:
> 11 As ye know how we exhorted and comforted and charged every one of you, as a father doth his children,
> 12 That ye would walk worthy of God, who hath called you unto his kingdom and glory.

In these verses Paul has instanced three characteristics of the Thessalonian ministry. These add up to a convincing vindication of the missionaries' character and motivation.

1. *The gentleness of true motherliness* (7-8). Instead of playing the heavy father, they had acted like nursing mothers, as the ERV would indicate. G. Campbell Morgan quotes this rendering, "as when a nurse cherisheth her own children" (7*b*), and points out that the picture suggested is that of the trained, intelligent skill of the nurse merging with the natural warmth of mother love. But the full meaning of this verse is complicated because of a variant reading of the word translated *gentle* (Gk., *ēpioi*). This has come about through a theory held by some scholars that the word should be *nēpioi,* meaning "babes," and there is reason to believe that this latter word does enjoy rather better textual authority. However, those who take the alternative view argue that *nēpioi* makes awkward sense. This may be so, but the fact that in this very chapter Paul has likened the preachers to "mother-nurses" in v. 7, to "fathers" in v. 11, and to "orphans" in v. 17 (*being taken from you* here means, literally, "being orphaned"), would suggest that the writer had no qualms about mixing his metaphors!

Incidentally, some have added weight to their rejection of *nēpioi* by observing that, since the Greek manuscripts leave no spaces between words, a careless scribe could quite easily have tacked on the *ēpioi* the final *n* from the preceding word. But, once again, the essential meaning is not greatly affected by the variant readings. Even if the correct rendering should be *we were babes among you,* this could imply that Paul had talked to the Thessalonians in baby language, and this is a familiar skill of gentle motherhood. It is sometimes a required skill of the preacher whose language tends to soar far above the comprehension of newborn children of God. One can have some sympathy with the man who was discussing his minister with a friend. Said he, "The Lord commanded Peter, 'Feed my sheep.' He must have said to our pastor, 'Feed my giraffes'!"

With v. 8 Paul has climaxed his expression of tender solicitude for his spiritual children. An Italian proverb says, "The teacher is like the candle which gives light to others by consuming itself." The apostle has echoed the sentiment in words so beautifully rendered in the NIV, "We loved you so much that we were delighted to share with you not only the gospel of God but our lives as well." That is the epitome of true motherliness.

2. *The considerateness of true brotherliness* (9-10). Paul was acutely sensitive to the possibility of being charged with exploitation (see e.g., Acts 20:30-35), and here he shows the depth of his determination to avoid it by reminding the Thessalonians that the missionaries had worked themselves to the point of utter exhaustion rather than be chargeable to them. He summoned both God and the church to testify that the double function of evangelism and self-supporting toil had been fulfilled in all holiness and righteousness and blamelessness (10). Far from having come as bloodsuckers, they had come as true blood-brothers. Nevertheless, this immensely demanding exercise did not invalidate the principle of ministerial support. In fact, from Paul's comments about the "toiling

and moiling" in Thessalonica, one gains the impression that it would have been impracticable, if not impossible, to treat this as a set pattern. Taking a wider view of the apostle's concept of the so-called full-time ministry, one learns that—

a. Paul had been reared in the rabbinical tradition that "he that teacheth not his son a trade doth the same as if he taught him to be a thief" (see Acts 18:3). Yet when the occasion demanded, he reserved the right to forbear working with his hands (see 1 Cor. 9:6). The real question with him was what course of action, in a given situation, would be most effective in promoting the work of the Kingdom. Such a flexible principle was of particular importance in pioneering the work of God, and there are many modern instances of this on both home and foreign fields.

b. It was soon recognized that a developing church required a leadership free from secular and unduly heavy administrative responsibilities (Acts 6:1-4), and it would appear that, as he began to anticipate the close of the historic apostolic era, Paul attached increasing importance to a ministry devoted to *labour in the word and doctrine* (see 1 Tim. 6:17-18).

3. *The forthrightness of true fatherliness* (11-12). Much has been said regarding the note of tenderness in the apostolic ministry, but comfort had not implied compromise; tenderness had not precluded sternness. The missionaries' grand objective had been to raise up those who would *walk worthy of God* (12). This adds weight to the earlier denial that Paul had come as a smooth-tongued orator bent only on pleasing men and multiplying converts. V. 11 introduces an approach inseparable from a truly fatherly ministry—"we dealt with you one by one, as a father deals with his children (NEB). A paternal ministry is necessarily a personal one, exhorting the hesitant, encouraging the fainthearted, charging the wavering; and this simply cannot be accomplished en masse. No wonder these hand-raised Thessalonians became model believers.

The Response to the Apostolic Message
1 Thessalonians 2:13-16

The worth of a message derives initially from the character of the one who originates it, and ultimately from the results in the lives of those who receive it. This is the gist of the writer's argument in these verses.

1 Thess. 2:13-16

> 13 For this cause also thank we God without ceasing, because, when ye received the word of God which ye heard of us, ye received it not as the word of men, but as it is in truth, the word of God, which effectually worketh also in you that believe.
> 14 For ye, brethren, became followers of the churches of God which in Judaea are in Christ Jesus: for ye also have suffered like things of your own countrymen, even as they have of the Jews:
> 15 Who both killed the Lord Jesus, and their own prophets, and have persecuted us; and they please not God, and are contrary to all men:
> 16 Forbidding us to speak to the Gentiles that they might be saved, to fill up their sins alway: for the wrath is come upon them to the uttermost.

1. *The reception that the message was given* (13). There are two words translated *received* in this one verse. The first, *paralambanō*, is a technical word implying a general, external reception. The second word, *dechomai,* is commonly used to describe the welcoming of a guest, and its use in this place shows that, in the fullest sense, these Thessalonian believers had taken the message to their hearts.

2. *The recognition that the message was God-given* (13). This recognition had conditioned the reception. We see this negatively illustrated in Acts 17:18-21 where the Athenians had completely misjudged and underestimated the Word of God. But in the case of the Thessalonians recognition plus reception had equalled regeneration. They had proved that the Word of God is the Word that works,

as we saw in 1:5; it had come to them with power; and as Bertrand Russell said, "Power is the production of intended effects." Those effects were specified in 1:9-10.

3. *The opposition that the message received* (14-16). In vv. 15 and 16 Paul unsparingly denounced the actions of the unbelieving members of his own nation in Thessalonica. It is interesting to compare such an indictment with modern arguments in favour of mitigating the guilt of the Jews in crucifying Christ. This reference to the opposition of the unbelieving Jews underlines several points:

a. The opposition followed a familiar pattern (15-16a). Namely, the destruction of the messenger. One of the recurring sins of the unbelieving Jew has been his determination to eliminate those who bore the saving Word; and had Paul not fled, they might well have succeeded in accomplishing this in Thessalonica. But Paul had been no "eager martyr," nor should his flight be considered a cowardly act. He had simply followed Jesus' plain injunction to His disciples in Matt. 10:23.

b. The opposition produced diverse results (14, 16b). One of these was *persecution* (14). This was also according to pattern, for the Christian Church in Judea had suffered similarly. In this respect it is interesting to note that Paul again used the word translated *followers* (see 1:6). The Thessalonians had begun by imitating the missionaries; and now, under tremendous pressure, they had imitated the courage and fortitude of the Judean believers, thereby confirming their model status. For most of us persecution of this kind is unknown, though we may be sure that should the Church of today be called upon to share the Thessalonian experience, there would be no lack of sterling souls to endure it. However, the words of a modern observer are deserving of note. He suggests that the real question facing many Christians today is not so much whether they have the courage to face persecution, but whether they are worth persecuting, whether they are vital enough, dangerous enough, or even distinctive enough to be opposed.

Another result was *retribution* (16*b*). Here is a result of opposition to the gospel which brings disastrous consequences upon the opposers; for even where the Word of God is opposed, it cannot be ignored. In his *The Need to Preach,* A. L. Griffiths, commenting on Isaiah 28, reminds us that "God speaks twice to men, both times very plainly and simply. If they refuse to hear His words they must listen to His voice in events."[13] Herein lies the dreadful force of Paul's words, "All this time they have been making up the full measure of their guilt, and now retribution has overtaken them for good and all" (NEB), though the phrase translated "for good and all" does not imply that the cup of judgment is finally full. Moore is surely right in his comment to the effect that while God's *vengeance* now rests upon the Jewish people, in the sense that *the wrath is come,* the *woes* are yet to follow.

The Expression of Apostolic Concern
1 Thessalonians 2:17—3:13

The Reason for Paul's Absence

1 Thess. 2:17-20

> 17 But we, brethren, being taken from you for a short time in presence, not in heart, endeavoured the more abundantly to see your face with great desire.
> 18 Wherefore we would have come unto you, even I Paul, once and again; but Satan hindered us.
> 19 For what is our hope, or joy, or crown of rejoicing? Are not even ye in the presence of our Lord Jesus Christ at his coming?
> 20 For ye are our glory and joy.

Even in a letter so imbued with the spirit of tender concern the glow of affection reflected in these verses is unusually intense, as Paul explains his inability to return to Thessalonica. His slanderers would fain have had his readers believe that he had been a fickle friend. Had he not left them in the lurch when danger threatened? And where was he now? Probably living off others as gullible as they themselves had been. But Paul assures them that—

1. *His absence was not intentional* (17). As already observed, the phrase translated *being taken from you* means, literally, "being orphaned." But this could refer to a childless parent as well as to a parentless child, consequently some have rendered the phrase "we were bereft of you" (see Moffatt and RSV), though the NIV has used the still more forceful expression, "we were torn away from you." Far from having run away from the Thessalonians, Paul had been wrenched away from them. Nor had the missionaries passively accepted the severance. It had not been a case of "out of sight, out of mind," for they had repeatedly endeavoured to see their converts face-to-face, and with a fervour of longing only faintly expressed in the English. For instance, the culminating word in this verse, *epithumia,* translated here as *great desire,* has almost startling connotations; for its literal meaning is "lust," almost always used in a bad sense in the New Testament.

2. *The hindrances had been truly diabolical* (18). Paul had not always laid the blame for such hindrances at Satan's door (see Acts 17:6-7), but here he openly acknowledges the ability of the enemy to thwart the plans of God's servant. The word translated *hindered* has military connections, being used, especially in later Greek, to describe the breaching of enemy lines. What the precise details of Satan's manoeuvre had been we do not know, but apparently he had succeeded more than once. Nevertheless, the Thessalonians could at least take some comfort from the fact that nothing less than such satanic strategy had prevented their father in God from reaching them. And we all may receive encouragement from the fact that this letter is itself an assurance that Satan's wiles, however temporarily successful, are held rigidly within bounds by the only Almighty One, whose final purposes none can frustrate (see 1 Cor. 2:8).

3. *The reward had been exceptional* (19-20). This was already true, even in the present impasse, for the *ye* in v. 20 is emphatic, implying that Paul's readers were his peculiar *glory and joy* (21). But in the *parousia* (19)—incidentally, this is the first known occurrence of this word in Christian literature—the Thessalonians would constitute Paul's laurel crown (Gk., *stephanos*). In that day the words of Richard Crashaw, written in honour of Theresa, will apply to a far greater degree to Paul:

> *Thou shalt look round about to see*
> *Thousands of crown'd souls thronged, to be*
> *Themselves thy crown.*

1 THESSALONIANS 3

The Reasons for Timothy's Presence

1 Thess. 3:1-5

1 Wherefore when we could no longer forbear, we thought it good to be left at Athens alone;
2 And sent Timotheus, our brother, and minister of God, and our fellowlabourer in the gospel of Christ, to establish you, and to comfort you concerning your faith:
3 That no man should be moved by these afflictions: for yourselves know that we are appointed thereunto.
4 For verily, when we were with you, we told you before that we should suffer tribulation; even as it came to pass, and ye know.
5 For this cause, when I could no longer forbear, I sent to know your faith, lest by some means the tempter have tempted you, and our labour be in vain.

The chapter division at this point tends to obscure the fact that, while Paul, in the light of Timothy's report, is now looking towards a brighter scene, he still fears that there may be lingering shadows in the minds of his readers. To disperse any remaining doubts as to his genuine care for them, he gives his reasons for having sent Timothy.

1. *To give evidence of sacrificial love* (1-2). That Timothy was no mere apprentice preacher is apparent from v. 2 where Paul describes him as a *brother, and minister of*

God, and our fellow labourer or, as in the NIV, "God's fellow-worker." Indeed, Paul's estimate of Timothy's worth is seen in his choice of the word translated *left . . . alone*, in v. 1. The Greek is *kataleipō*, a word used in Mark 12:19 to describe the condition of a woman left in widowhood. Perhaps the Athens situation had deepened the apostle's sense of dereliction, for there the presence and support of his young lieutenant would have been invaluable. But, for the Thessalonians' sake, he had faced the cynical Athenians alone (the *we* in v. 1 is almost certainly to be understood in an editorial sense).

2. *To give assistance in spiritual need* (2-5).

a. They had need to be established (3:2). Morris suggests that the verb translated *to establish* might well have been "one of the technical words in the Pastoralia of the Early Church."[14] Later in this chapter we discover what constitutes "establishing grace" (see vv. 10-13).

b. They had need to be encouraged (2). It is significant that the verb *parakaleō* is no longer translated as *comfort* in the more recent versions. Samuel Chadwick wrote: "The translation [comfort] entirely misses the mark, and is responsible for untold mischief in both doctrine and experience . . . It has associated religion with soothing consolations rather than with conflict. The need is not comfort but power."[15] Paul, for all his tender solicitude, was no pampering parent. With typical realism he reminds his readers that they have been "destined" (NIV) to affliction and tribulation (3*b*-4).

c. They had need to remain unmoved (3*a*, 5). Again a descriptive word is employed to indicate the danger confronting the converts. Moore, commenting on the verb *moved* (Gk., *sainesthai*), says, "Properly it means the wagging of a dog's tail, and (presumably because dogs do this generally to ingratiate themselves!) it comes to mean 'to fawn upon' and so 'to beguile' and 'to deceive'."[16] This would reflect the tactics of the Jewish antagonists who, with their smooth talk, had constantly sown suspicion in the minds of the believers (2:1-12).

3. *To gain reassurance as to their spiritual endurance* (5). There can be no doubt as to the genuineness of Paul's fear that, under duress, the Thessalonians could conceivably have lost their faith. This verse does not in any sense imply a hypothetical concern about such a possibility, but one so real and urgent that he could bear the anxiety no longer and felt compelled to seek reassurance as to his converts' spiritual welfare. Yet Hendriksen, after a labored argument, has written that "in no sense whatever is it true that 3:5 teaches that God's truly chosen ones can, after all, perish everlastingly."[17] Paul would have thanked no one for assuming that his agonizing uneasiness expressed in this verse was virtually "much ado about nothing."

The Nature of Timothy's Report

1 Thess. 3:6-9

> 6 But now when Timotheus came from you unto us, and brought us good tidings of your faith and charity, and that ye have good remembrance of us always, desiring greatly to see us, as we also to see you:
> 7 Therefore, brethren, we were comforted over you in all our affliction and distress by your faith:
> 8 For now we live, if ye stand fast in the Lord.
> 9 For what thanks can we render to God again for you, for all the joy wherewith we joy for your sakes before our God;

1. *A report of good news* (6). A literal translation of *Timotheus . . . brought us good tidings* could be "Timothy . . . evangelized us," for Paul has used the word ordinarily reserved in the New Testament for "spreading the gospel" (Gk., *euaggelizomai*). This shows how deeply the apostle had been affected by the report. It had been to him a "gospel" indeed, and with saving results, as we see in succeeding verses.

2. *Good news of faith and charity* (6). The news of the Thessalonians' perseverance had dispelled the uneasiness expressed in v. 5. Their trust had not wavered, their beliefs had remained orthodox, and their behavior had been

impeccable. Moreover the flame of their love still burned fervently.

3. *Good news of kindly memories* (6). As we have already seen, while Paul set no great premium upon the opinions of men, he made no profession of being totally insensitive to it. In this verse, and the following, one is aware of his very human pleasure at being held in *good remembrance.* But aside from sentiment, such a warm relationship between pastor and people ensures that mutual love and respect apart from which no fruit can be brought to perfection. What is more, such a congenial climate of soul does much to provide the kind of atmosphere within which faithful rebuke, and even stern reproof, can best be administered.

4. *Good news of spiritual stability* (7-9). The knowledge that the Thessalonians had stood firm against every onslaught had given the apostle a new lease of life. Again the *ye* (8) is emphatic and from this we may infer that Paul saw the Thessalonian church as a European prototype. The success of his labours in this city would certainly act as a stimulus to press on with the evangelizing of a new continent. Barclay looks beyond even the continental horizon when he observes that "the coming of Christianity to Thessalonica was a crucial day in the making of Christianity into a world religion."[18] Small wonder that Paul's cup of joy ran over! (9).

Paul's Response and His Prayer

1 Thess. 3:10-13

> 10 Night and day praying exceedingly that we might see your face, and might perfect that which is lacking in your faith?
> 11 Now God himself and our Father, and our Lord Jesus Christ, direct our way unto you.
> 12 And the Lord make you to increase and abound in love one toward another, and toward all men, even as we do toward you:
> 13 To the end he may stablish your hearts unblameable in holiness before God, even our Father, at the coming of our Lord Jesus Christ with all his saints.

"Love is blind," says the proverb; but that is not strictly true, for the lover sees excellencies in the beloved that may be hidden from the eyes of the loveless. But the lover is not always blind to deficiencies either, though while others may see these as occasions to blame, he sees them as a call to pray. So it is that, at this point, Paul's praise gives way to prayer. Apparently Timothy's report had not brought unqualified commendation, but it is also worth noting that as a prelude to dealing with his readers' shortcomings the apostle thanks God once more for their overcomings.

While it is doubtful if Paul would have consciously used prayer as an occasion for teaching theology, his invocation in v. 11 is of exceptional theological significance. Commenting on the fact that the verb *direct* is in the singular, Morris writes, "There could hardly be a more impressive way of indicating the lordship of Christ and His oneness with the Father."[19]

The content of Paul's prayer in vv. 10-13 contains three basic petitions:

1. *That faith might be perfected* (10). Paul was not disparaging the present faith of his readers. He had already paid tribute to this in glowing terms (1:3; 3:5-6). But as Denney said, "In one sense faith is a very simple thing, the setting of the heart right with God in Christ Jesus. In another it is very comprehensive. It has to lay hold on the whole revelation which God has made in His Son, and it has to pass into action through love in every department of life."[20] Thus is faith perfected. This is the goal that beckons every Christian. Let him ignore it and he risks becoming one of the objects of Sangster's satire: "There is little about them (such goal-less Christians) to suggest resolute pilgrims. . . . Their gait is so waddling that, as someone has said, they seem more like penguins than pilgrims."[21]

2. *That love might be increased* (12). Again, Paul is not questioning the genuine love of his converts, but he is pas-

sionately longing to see it flaming and glowing in what Chrysostom called "unchecked madness." He desires that it might embrace *all men,* even, supposedly, their persecutors. The greatest single need of the Church is a visitation of such prodigal love, and when one sees so much religion that is "faultily faultless, icily regular, splendidly null," one can appreciate the lament of the poet—

> *On fire that glows with heat intense,*
> *Men turn the hose of commonsense,*
> *And out it goes—at small expense.*

3. *That holiness might be enjoyed* (13). Such holiness is divinely communicated. *The Lord make you to increase and abound in love . . . to the end he may stablish your hearts unblameable in holiness.* It is He who effects the work, imparting to the believer His own very nature of holy love through the agency of the Holy Spirit (Rom. 5:5). Such love is the "Spirit's instrument for the expulsion of that which is impure and incompatible from the heart."[22]

Such holiness is to predate the coming of Christ. Neil has pointed out that "the word used for 'holiness' here *(hagiosune)* does not mean 'sanctification' *(hagiasmos)*—the process of becoming holy—but the state of holiness itself, 'sanctity.'"[23] The Second Coming has, of itself, no sanctifying efficacy except insofar as it is the occasion when redemption achieves its ultimate, encompassing even the physical (Rom. 8:23).

Instructions to Those Who Live in Christ

1 Thessalonians 4:1-12

1 THESSALONIANS 4

Given by Divine Authority

1 Thess. 4:1-2

> 1 Furthermore then we beseech you, brethren, and exhort you by the
> Lord Jesus, that as ye have received of us how ye ought to walk and to
> please God, so ye would abound more and more.
> 2 For ye know what commandments we gave you by the Lord Jesus.

Unlike some of his less modest successors, Paul laid no
claim to apostolic infallibility. In fact there were times
when he made a quite specific point of disclaiming special inspiration (cf. 1 Cor. 7:10, 12, 25-26). Thus when he
did assert apostolic authority, it carried maximum weight.
So in v. 2: "You know what instructions we gave you by the
authority of the Lord Jesus" (NIV). In this same verse the
word translated *commandments* (Gk., *paraggelia*), a word
rarely found in Christian writings, denotes an order given
by a superior officer to be passed on by word of mouth
down the line (see Acts 16:23-24). This suggests two things
—the instructions must be *accurately conveyed* and they
must be *scrupulously obeyed*. As regards the latter the
apostle hints that there was some room for improvement
in the Thessalonian church.

Given in the Interests of Sexual Purity

1 Thess. 4:3-8

> 3 For this is the will of God, even your sanctification, that ye should
> abstain from fornication:

4 That every one of you should know how to possess his vessel in sanctification and honour;

5 Not in the lust of concupiscence, even as the Gentiles which know not God:

6 That no man go beyond and defraud his brother in any matter: because that the Lord is the avenger of all such, as we also have forewarned you and testified.

7 For God hath not called us unto uncleanness, but unto holiness.

8 He therefore that despiseth, despiseth not man, but God, who hath also given unto us his holy Spirit.

There is no doubt that v. 3 has more than sexual purity in view, yet Paul must have had good reason for setting sanctification within this context. So has the modern preacher, especially since it has become fashionable in certain theological circles to pour scorn on the very idea of moral laws which "come down direct from heaven, and are eternally valid for human conduct."[24] As we have seen, Paul certainly claimed that the instructions he was giving had come to him direct from the highest Source. He did not assume that the Thessalonian believers, model Christians though they were, had progressed beyond the need of being taught how to safeguard their morality. Surely no contemporary preacher, aiming to minister within the moral miasma of today's world, can afford to sidestep such a responsibility. And there is every reason why the pastor should preach this text to his people, as it stands, if only because of its prophylactic value.

But how are we to apply Paul's teaching? Are we to understand that *vessel,* in v. 4, refers to a man's wife, or to his own body? Much may be said on both sides. For instance, in 1 Pet. 3:17 the writer speaks of the wife as the "weaker vessel." If this was in Paul's mind, it would mean that he was advising his readers to treat their wives with due respect and not merely as sexual objects. On the other hand, Paul himself wrote, in 2 Cor. 4:7, of the body as an "earthen vessel." It seems more likely that this was his thought here. At any rate, in this passage the apostle has prescribed four reasons why Christians cannot entertain sexual laxity.

1. *Sexual promiscuity wrongs one's fellowman* (6a). "You

cannot break this rule without in some way cheating your fellow men" (Phillips). That the adulterer defrauds a husband of his wife, as well as defrauding his own wife, is easy to see. But a man who engages in illicit sex before marriage is still guilty of fraud, for "the impure person cannot bring to his marriage that virginity which is the other's due."[25]

2. *Sexual promiscuity incurs divine vengeance* (6b). That God's judgment on such behavior operates within the bounds of this life is clear from Rom. 1:18, 24, 26, 28, but the main thrust of this warning is eschatological.

3. *Sexual promiscuity is a rejection of the divine call* (7). That call is not to impurity but to sanctity. Nor is this call an external one only, for when Rudolf Otto declared that holiness is the "hidden predisposition of the spirit,"[26] he rightly implied that, inherited depravity notwithstanding, deep with man's fallen nature are the shattered remains of a longing to be pure. This is why Samuel Chadwick could say that the more of a sinner a man is, the less of a man he is; hence sexual promiscuity is the prostitution of man's true humanity.

4. *Sexual promiscuity is the rejection of the Spirit by whom the call is made* (8). He is God's *holy* Spirit whose gracious purpose it is to sanctify those in whom He dwells. Phillips' rendering powerfully conveys that sense of peril presently facing those who do despite to Him: "The calling of God is not to impurity but to the most thorough purity, and anyone who makes light of the matter is not making light of a man's ruling but of God's command. It is not for nothing that the Spirit God gives is called the HOLY Spirit" (7-8).

Given in the Interest of God's Family

1 Thess. 4:9-10

> 9 But as touching brotherly love ye need not that I write unto you: for ye yourselves are taught of God to love one another.
> 10 And indeed ye do it toward all the brethren which are in all Macedonia: but we beseech you, brethren, that ye increase more and more;

In v. 9 two different words are translated "love." The first, *philadelphia* (brotherly love), when used in classical Greek, denoted the love which unites the children of one father, but in the New Testament it invariably means the love which binds together the members of the family of God. One might think of this as being exclusive, yet it is, in fact, powerfully attractive. James Denney has written, "The early Christian Church were little companies of people where love was at a high temperature. . . . Men were drawn to them irresistibly by the desire to share this life of love."[27] This helps to explain the growth of the church in Macedonia.

Paul indicates that such a love is of God, for it springs from a quality of love which is wholly divine—*Ye yourselves are taught of God to love [agapao] one another.* As Calvin said, "Love had been engraved on their hearts so that there was no need to write about it on paper."[28] Yet such divine activity does not relieve the Christian of responsibility. He cannot achieve such love but he must improve what he has received. The apostle now goes on to describe how this was to be done within the Thessalonian church.

Given in the Interests of Christian Industry

1 Thess. 4:11-12

> 11 And that ye study to be quiet, and to do your own business, and to work with your own hands, as we commanded you;
> 12 That ye may walk honestly toward them that are without, and that ye may have lack of nothing.

According to some, certain members of the church had become so obsessed with the imminence of Christ's return that they had ceased working. In any case they had earned the reputation of being "busybodies," and, on the pretext of being brotherly, they were not only invading their brethren's privacy but subsisting on their brethren's charity. Paul proceeds to deal with this situation by insisting that everyone make his own contribution towards the good of the community by his own industry. This underlines several matters of practical concern.

1. The Christian should be a model of diligent industry. The "gospel of hard work" not only keeps one out of meddling mischief but, as Barclay has said, "when we Christians prove that our Christianity makes us better workmen, truer friends, kinder men and women, then and only then are we really preaching."[29]

2. The Christian should cultivate a spirit of humble independence. The phrase translated *that ye may have lack of nothing* may also be rendered "that you will not be dependent on anybody" (NIV). No one stressed more than Paul the intimate interdependence of Christians. His analogy of the Church as a body amply illustrates this. But his word here, and in 2:9, underlines the difference between being a member of the Church and a parasite upon it.

Encouragement to Both the Living and the Dead in Christ

1 Thessalonians 4:13-18

The Provision for Those Asleep in Christ

1 Thess. 4:13-14

> 13 But I would not have you to be ignorant, brethren, concerning them which are asleep, that ye sorrow not, even as others which have no hope.
> 14 For if we believe that Jesus died and rose again, even so them also which sleep in Jesus will God bring with him.

Paul repeatedly recognized God's desire that His people, as far as possible, should understand His purposes (see also Rom. 1:13; 11:25; 1 Cor. 10:1; 12:1; 2 Cor. 1:8). It is certainly possible to place too great an emphasis upon an intellectual apprehension of Christian truth, but there is an even greater danger in adopting an anti-intellectual position. Herein lies a problem in certain areas of neo-Pentecostalism. Stott has referred to "one of the movement's leaders [who] said recently, apropos of the Catholic Pentecostals, that what matters in the end is 'not doctrine but experience.' This is tantamount to putting our subjective experience above the revealed truth of God."[30] It is significant that Jesus himself, in His parable of the sower, stressed the importance of understanding (Matt. 13:19). Hence, in our preaching we must reason with a man's mind as well as plead with his heart if we are to move his will and then establish him in the will of God.

Never was it more important to convey enlightenment than in this local situation where relatively young believers were beset by a problem which provoked deep disturbances, emotional and intellectual. What was the status of their beloved, believing dead who had passed away since the missionaries had left Thessalonica? Would these be at some disadvantage when Christ returned? Had they perhaps forfeited their place in this great event?

In giving his answer, Paul has drawn a sharp contrast between the Christian and the pagan attitudes towards death. For the non-Christian death is the end of all hope (Eph. 2:12). For the believer death is "sleep"; and, while this euphemism definitely does not signify an intermediate state of unconsciousness ("soul sleep"), it does show that, for the Christian, the whole concept of death has been transformed. But in v. 14, Paul's careful use of the words *died* and *sleep* suggests the price Christ paid to rob death of its sting. "He died that death which is the wages of sin; and because He endured the full horror implied in that death He has transformed death for His followers into sleep."[31]

The Priority of Those Asleep in Christ

1 Thess. 4:15-18

> 15 For this we say unto you by the word of the Lord, that we which are alive and remain unto the coming of the Lord shall not prevent them which are asleep.
> 16 For the Lord himself shall descend from heaven with a shout, with the voice of the archangel, and with the trump of God: and the dead in Christ shall rise first:
> 17 Then we which are alive and remain shall be caught up together with them in the clouds to meet the Lord in the air: and so shall we ever be with the Lord.
> 18 Wherefore comfort one another with these words.

In order to give the greatest possible emphasis as to the place reserved in the *parousia* for those who have died in Christ, Paul has used a double negative of great force rarely found in the New Testament. He then proceeds to outline the sequence of events. According to Neil, "It would be quite wrong to regard the primary purpose of [this] passage as a detailed, factual description of what the apostle expected to happen. We would do well not to press this imaginative sketch into a literal prophecy."[32] The need to exercise wise restraint in expounding matters prophetical is obvious for, as Reinhold Niebuhr has so wittily said, "It is unwise for Christians to claim any knowledge of either the furniture of heaven or the temperature of hell."[33] In this case, however, Alford's comment in his *Greek New Testament* is conclusive: "The apostle's declarations here are made in the practical tone of strict matter of fact, and are given as literal details to console men's minds under an existing difficulty. Never was a place where the analogy of symbolical apocalyptic language was less applicable. Either these details must be received by us as a matter of practical expectation, or we must set aside the apostle as one divinely empowered to teach the Church."[34] Paul has mentioned four points in particular.

1. *The descent of Christ* (16). In the light of contemporary cosmology some have rejected the imagery in this verse. Yet the fact remains that clear scriptural assurance is given that Christ's descent would be in the manner of His ascent (Acts 1:11).

2. *The heralding of His return* (16).

   a. A shout. The word *keleusma* signifies a shout of command such as was given in battle. There is about it a note of authority and urgency, engendering great excitement and expectation.

   b. The voice of the archangel. Since *archaggelou* is without the article, one can only conjecture that the reference is to Michael; but since he is the only archangel named in the New Testament, this is a reasonable assumption.

c. *The trump of God.* The trumpet is twice mentioned in 1 Cor. 15:52. Paul clearly regarded it as having a special place in the events of the *parousia*. Phillips has caught something of the awesomeness and grandeur of this scene in his translation: "One word of command, one shout from the archangel, one blast from the trumpet of God and the Lord himself will come down from Heaven!"

3. *The resurrection of the believing dead* (16). This accords perfectly with 1 Corinthians 15; though, having in mind the particular need of the Thessalonians, Paul again makes the point that the believing dead will be the first to answer the summons of the returning Christ.

4. *The rapture* (17). As Morris points out, the verb translated "caught up" combines the ideas of force and suddenness, denoting the irresistible power of God. It is also used of Philip in Acts 8:39, and in Rev. 12:5.

5. *The reunion* (17-18). Since this takes place *in the air,* which is usually recognized as the abode of all manner of evil powers (Eph. 2:2), this suggests the measure of the completeness of the Lord's supremacy. So Augustine's exhortation is, "Let sorrow perish where there is so much consolation."

Since a number of commentators have expressed the view that when Paul wrote the words *we which are alive and remain unto the coming of the Lord,* he obviously expected that he and his readers would live to see Christ's return, it would be well to briefly examine the position. While we may have reservations regarding C. H. Dodd's theory of "realized eschatology," he has made an apt reference to the fact that it was not an *early* Advent that the primitive Church proclaimed, but an *immediate* Advent. Skevington Wood takes up this comment and writes, "The early Christian preachers were wise enough not to predict an early Advent, for they had been expressly advised by our Lord not to be curious about times and seasons. But they undoubtedly announced an immediate Advent in the sense that it was the next event on the prophetic programme."[35]

Exhortations to Those Who Live in Expectation of the Day

1 Thessalonians 5:1-22

1 THESSALONIANS 5

Live Consistently as Children of the Day

1 Thess. 5:1-11

> 1 But of the times and the seasons, brethren, ye have no need that I write unto you.
> 2 For yourselves know perfectly that the day of the Lord so cometh as a thief in the night.
> 3 For when they shall say, Peace and safety; then sudden destruction cometh upon them, as travail upon a woman with child; and they shall not escape.
> 4 But ye, brethren, are not in darkness, that that day should overtake you as a thief.
> 5 Ye are all the children of light, and the children of the day: we are not of the night, nor of darkness.
> 6 Therefore let us not sleep, as do others; but let us watch and be sober.
> 7 For they that sleep sleep in the night; and they that be drunken are drunken in the night.
> 8 But let us, who are of the day, be sober, putting on the breastplate of faith and love; and for an helmet, the hope of salvation.
> 9 For God hath not appointed us to wrath, but to obtain salvation by our Lord Jesus Christ,
> 10 Who died for us, that, whether we wake or sleep, we should live together with him.
> 11 Wherefore comfort yourselves together, and edify one another, even as also ye do.

Having disposed of one difficulty relating to the *parousia*, Paul now proceeds to deal with a second. This concerns not the dead but the living. In approaching it, the apostle reminds his readers that they are not without knowledge of the *times and the seasons* ("times and dates"

—NIV). *Times* (Gk., *chronoi*) has to do with the duration of time, while *seasons* (Gk., *kairoi*) refers to the quality of time.

1. *The day of the Lord comes stealthily* (2). This phrase, *the day of the Lord,* from as far back as Amos who was probably the first to use it, carried the three-fold idea of judgment, the blessing of the righteous, and the restoration and renewal of all things. In the New Testament the element of judgment has a personal rather than a national reference, and this vivid image of the day stealing up on the unprepared, like a thief in the night, probably owed its origin to our Lord's own sayings (Matt. 24:42-43; Luke 2: 39; etc.).

2. *The day of the Lord comes suddenly* (3). "While they are talking of peace and security, all at once calamity is upon them" (NEB). Such is the consequence of the sinner's folly who fails to reckon not only with the stealth, but the speed with which time moves. Ralph Hodgson asks,

> *Time, you old Gypsyman,*
> *Will you not stay?*
> *Put up your caravan*
> *Just for one day?*

No. Before the question is asked, time has fled.

3. *The children of the day are not ignorant* (4-5). They are *children of light.* This means more than children who dwell in light, it means children in whom light dwells, those whose very nature is light. Similarly, they are *children of the day.* In other words, by nature and by virtue of their inheritance they belong to the New Age. Yet it would appear that in spite of all they knew, and all they were, they were failing to realize as they should that they must be ready for that day.

4. *The children of the day must be alert* (6-7). It is possible to have knowledge and lack the wisdom to use it aright. It is possible to have an inheritance and fail to claim it. It is

possible to have a name and fail to live up to it. "Therefore," Paul says, in effect, "become what you are" *(watch and be sober)*. "Watch," a term frequently on the lips of Jesus, implies both mental and spiritual alertness. "Be sober" denotes that serious and responsible behavior which drunkenness forfeits.

5. *The children of the day must be armed* (8). This marks a transition of thought somewhat difficult to follow but, as Lightfoot comments, "The mention of vigilance suggested the idea of a sentry armed and on duty."

6. *The children of the day are appointed to salvation* (9-11). *God hath not appointed us to wrath,* but we dare not be complacent on that account. Heinrich Vogel's words are timely: "Whoever thinks he can smile at God's wrath will never praise Him eternally for His grace."[36]

Paul's reference to the fact that salvation has been provided graciously through the death of Christ is most revealing, for since it is made in passing, as it were, this confirms that the doctrine of Christ's vicarious sacrifice was already well understood by his converts. Because they are saved, Paul could continue, "Whether we are 'awake' or 'asleep' we share his life" (10*b*, Phillips). This could be construed as a further exhortation to be alert, though it is more probable that "awake" and "asleep" here are used as euphemisms for life and death respectively. Thus the apostle is giving his readers a further word of assurance in prospect of Christ's return. Concluding his personal exhortations, he admonishes the Thessalonians to regard encouragement and edification as a mutual ministry (11), especially against the background of the coming day (see Heb. 10:25).

Live Congregationally as Children of the Day

1 Thess. 5:12-22

> 12 And we beseech you, brethren, to know them which labour among you, and are over you in the Lord, and admonish you;
> 13 And to esteem them very highly in love for their work's sake. And be at peace among yourselves.

14 Now we exhort you, brethren, warn them that are unruly, comfort the feebleminded, support the weak, be patient toward all men.
15 See that none render evil for evil unto any man; but ever follow that which is good, both among yourselves, and to all men.
16 Rejoice evermore.
17 Pray without ceasing.
18 In every thing give thanks: for this is the will of God in Christ Jesus concerning you.
19 Quench not the Spirit.
20 Despise not prophesyings.
21 Prove all things; hold fast that which is good.
22 Abstain from all appearance of evil.

From v. 12 we are introduced to detail of considerable importance to any fellowship of believers seeking to live in the Advent light. Paul points out important characteristics of the members of this fellowship.

1. *Respect for the leadership* (12-13). Paul and Barnabas had ordained elders in all the Asian churches (Acts 14: 23), and it is reasonable to suppose that this action established a precedent. There seems evidence to support the view that the missionaries, in spite of having been under such pressure in the Thessalonian campaign, had taken time to care for this responsibility. Acts 17:6 specifically mentions *Jason and certain brethren,* and these were obviously recognized by the civic authorities as standing in a special relationship to the local church. In any case, the reference to the three-fold function of labor, oversight, and discipline in v. 12 strongly suggests the exercise of an official leadership.

Nevertheless, it is significant that Paul made his plea for due respect to be accorded to the leaders, not by virtue of their office or personal eminence, but on the grounds that they were *in the Lord,* and *for their work's sake. Be at peace among yourselves* (13) offers a hint that there was probably some strain between leaders and led, and some would suggest that this may have been due to a lack of tact in the exercise of authority. This may well have been so, for neither ecclesiastical office nor spiritual qualifications, or both, imply leadership infallibility. But happy indeed is that church where leaders are men who "work hard"

(NIV), who recognize that they are indeed leaders *in the Lord,* and where assessment of them is engendered not by carnal preference or prejudice, but in accordance with the law of divine love.

2. *Responsibility within the fellowship* (14-15). Since Paul again addresses the brethren (see 12) at this point, it would appear that recognition of an official leadership did not relieve the general membership of the need to cooperate in what might be called a mutual pastoral ministry. Within the modern church one of the most fruitful expressions of such a ministry was found in the early Methodist class-meeting. It is conceivable that a good deal of membership wastage could still be avoided where, under overall pastoral supervision, the sheep function as shepherds, with discretion and true sympathy. In this connection five points are noted.

a. Warn the unruly (14). In classical Greek the word translated "unruly" was used of the "idler"; hence Moffatt's version, "Keep a check upon loafers."

This had special application to those in Thessalonica already mentioned, whose notion of being busy was to be "busybodies." The best way to deal with such ill-employed is to see that they are well employed.

b. Comfort the feebleminded (14). While *feebleminded* suggests mental rather than volitional weakness and does not therefore give the sense that Paul intended, the KJV translation does warrant a comment. For it is a fact that most churches do have within their fellowship some whose minds would not be considered normal. Concerning these a recent author has written, "A church is often an asylum for those who are mentally retarded and who find no companionship in the world outside. If the average church does not have more than its fair quota of mental cases, it is not doing its job."[37] However, the NIV has caught the more accurate sense of the phrase in "encourage the timid."

Here is an admonition that might have particular

relevance to a holiness fellowship where, quite rightly, much is made of the need for a "holy boldness." Yet sometimes short shrift has been given to those who fail to manifest this quality in the more obvious ways, and without detracting in any way from the sufficiency of sanctifying grace, it is worth remembering that "since God requires nothing impossible, unnecessary, or unreasonable of His child, the divine command, 'Be ye holy,' is compatible with the human nature possessed by the man to whom the command is given."[38]

c. *Support the weak* (14). Paul has much to say about this responsibility of the strong towards the weak (1 Cor. 8:7-13; Rom. 14:1-6), but his choice of word here implies more than mere support. It is used in the sense of "clinging to," as in Matt. 6:24 and Titus 1:9, so William Neil beautifully renders the phrase, "Put your arm around the weak." The thought is to refuse to let him go. That this may often need to be a long-term treatment is suggested in the next exhortation.

d. *Be patient toward all men* (14). There is nothing passive about such patience, rather does it imply an active perseverance. Such long-suffering is of the very nature of God (Rom. 2:4; 9:22), and it reminds one of Dick Sheppard's constant aim to have a "God-sight of all his fellows."

e. *See that none render evil for evil; but ever follow that which is good* (15). This also applies to all men. As regards the second phrase, Neil again comments, "This does not mean simply performing little acts of kindness, as opposed to little acts of retaliation, but means making Christian charity the mainspring of all activity."[39] As demanding as this admonition is, when the love of God floods the heart, filling it to full capacity and then overflowing to friend and foe alike, such behavior becomes "supernaturally natural."

3. *Response to the will of God* (16-18). James Denney called these three commands "the standing orders of the

Christian Church." John Wesley saw them as the three-fold evidence of perfect love: "By perfection I mean perfect love, or the loving God with all our heart, so as to rejoice evermore, to pray without ceasing, and in everything to give thanks."[40]

a. Rejoice evermore (16). New Testament Christianity was permeated with the spirit of holy joy. Jesus was a Man of Joy as surely as He was the Man of Sorrows. And if joy and sorrow seem strange bedfellows, Paul saw nothing incongruous in such a partnership. Tertullian spoke of the "hilarity of the saints," and Henry Drummond frequently described Christian fellowship as "the Gaiety Club." This does not mean that Christian joy is a mere emotional, nor even a natural effervescence, for its manifestation will not always be uniform. Samuel Chadwick said that while oil and water are both symbols of the Holy Spirit, water bubbles when it boils but oil isn't boiling till it has stopped bubbling.

b. Pray without ceasing (17). Paul's life was not one of monastic seclusion, rhyming by rote his prayers and devotions. Like Wesley he was "out of breath pursuing souls." But, in prayer, he practised what he preached, as his frequent petitionary and intercessory ejaculations testify. No Christian need be too busy to engage in perpetual prayer. A Scots mother who had brought up a large family in a room and kitchen was asked how she managed to maintain her prayer life. She replied, "Betimes Ah just throw ma apron ower ma heid, then it's no' difficult to talk tae God." This is no substitute for the exercise of public prayer, but "they best pray together who often pray alone."

c. In everything give thanks (18). Sangster once said that the mass of people can be divided into two classes: those who take things for granted, and those who take things with gratitude. The Christian takes nothing for granted and everything with gratitude. This is an exercise to which none but the Christian can aspire. Halford

Luccock writes somewhere of a printer's error in a programme of Handel's *Messiah*. It showed one item as "The Lord God Omnipotent Resigneth"! There is such a dearth of thankfulness in the world because so few believe that the Lord God omnipotent *reigns,* but let a man stand on that bedrock of faith and he will not find it difficult to thank God for whatever comes (see Rom. 8:28).

4. *Response to the Spirit of God* (19-21).

a. Quench not the Spirit (19). "Do not put out the Spirit's fire" (NIV). Of James Denney it was said, "When preaching the Gospel he was often at white heat." Richard Baxter's biographer declared that he would set the world on fire while another was striking a match, and someone said of William Booth that "he was always ninety in the shade." Yet the same general warned his officers that "the tendency of fire is to go out." It can be quenched simply by neglect, and holy fire is needed not only as a source of power but as a safeguard of purity. J. H. Jowett so aptly said, "As the fire dies out, the enemy comes in. Just as soon as radiation ceases, the invasion begins." It was because Paul believed that the soul's safety lies in its heat that he wrote this warning, and there is reason to believe that, in Thessalonica, the danger of heat loss was connected with the next exhortation.

b. Despise not prophesyings (20). It has been suggested by some that while in Corinth Paul was obliged to curb the undiscerning pursuit of the gifts of the Spirit, in the relatively conservative Thessalonian church he had to do the very opposite. Hence his word, "Do not treat prophecies with contempt" (NIV). As to the function of the New Testament prophet Paul declared it to include edification, exhortation, and comfort (1 Cor. 14:3), in other words a forthtelling ministry. Acts 11:27 ff. and 21:10 ff. reveal that, on occasion, the prophet of New Testament times was also a foreteller. At this point Moore's comment on the Thessalonian situation is of interest: "[We may conjecture] that there had been prophetic outbursts in connection with second advent expectations. At all times in history the two have tended to go together." So far as the church in Thessalonica was concerned, 2 Thess. 2:2 tends to confirm this (see especially NIV). From this verse we may deduce that some erratic prophetic utterances had led to confusion, dismay, and to lack of confidence in the exercise of the gift. In the light of this the apostle's advice would seem to have implied that no ministry should be judged on the basis of its worst advocate.

c. *Prove all things; hold fast to that which is good* (21). While warning his readers not to disdain prophetic revelations, Paul did not advocate uncritical acceptance of all that purported to come from God. "Test everything" (NIV), apply spiritual criteria, and, as Neil states, there will be results which will accrue to "the well-being of the Church, the furtherance of the Gospel, and the supreme law of love."[41] As the day draws on, it is imperative that God's people seek and exercise the Spirit's own gift of discernment, so that John's command might be obeyed, "Do not trust any and every spirit, my friends; test the spirits, to see whether they are from God, for among those who have gone out into the world there are many prophets falsely inspired" (1 John 4:1, NEB).

d. *Abstain from all appearance of evil* (22). Finally, Paul reminds his readers that if one is to exercise a continuing discernment, not only must one hold fast to that which "rings true" (the word translated "good" was sometimes used of testing coins), but one must "steer clear of evil in any form" (Phillips). No one can see straight whose ways are crooked. So Wesley cried,

> O grant that nothing in my soul
>   May dwell, but Thy pure love alone!
> O may Thy love possess me whole,
>   My joy, my treasure, and my crown;
> Strange fires far from my heart remove;
>   My every act, word, thought, be love!

Final Prayer, Charges, and Benediction
1 Thessalonians 5:23-28

A Prayer to God
1 Thess. 5:23-24

> 23 And the very God of peace sanctify you wholly; and I pray God your whole spirit and soul and body be preserved blameless unto the coming of our Lord Jesus Christ.
> 24 Faithful is he that calleth you, who also will do it.

1. *A prayer to the God of peace* (23). In this prayer the very name by which Paul addresses God, "the God of peace himself" (RSV), gives the clue to his deep concern for the Thessalonians. In v. 13 he has already admonished them to be at peace, but the word "peace," as it is used here, implies much more than an absence of tension. It speaks of positive soundness and rightness—that condition apart from which his readers could never have lived as he had exhorted them.

2. *A prayer to the God who sanctifies wholly* (23). Reinhold Niebuhr writes, "The question is whether the grace of Christ is primarily a power of righteousness which so heals the sinful heart that henceforth it is able to fulfil the law of love; or whether it is primarily the assurance of divine mercy for a persistent sinfulness which man never overcomes completely."[42] This question has vexed generations of Christians, but it never entered the apostle's mind. He saw the need for positive soundness and rightness in the lives of his readers, he prayed that God might grant it, and he had no shred of doubt as to the answer (24). Nor was his prayer couched in vague terms. He knew precisely what he was praying for.

   a. He prayed for those who were undoubtedly Christian. As Paul Rees remarks, their "birth certificate" had been written out in the first chapter of the Epistle, and none could doubt its authenticity.

b. He prayed for their entire sanctification. That regeneration does mark the beginning of personal sanctification has never been more convincingly demonstrated than in Thessalonica, yet that such sanctification is no more than initial is made abundantly clear in this prayer on the Thessalonians' behalf. The verb "sanctify" *(hagiazō)* conveys the thought of external and internal purification as well as separation and dedication, while the adverb "wholly" *(holoteleis),* found only here in the New Testament, combines the ideas of wholeness and completeness. Hence the NIV translates, "May God himself, the God of peace, sanctify you through and through."

c. He prayed for their instant sanctification. Richard Howard has observed, "It is of particular significance that, after using the present tense, which depicts progressive action, five times in verses 19 through 22, Paul carefully uses the aorist tense in verse 23. This decisive change of tenses would seem to identify God's sanctifying work as a crisis act."[43]

d. He prayed for the preservation of their sanctification. (1) For the preservation of the entire man, "spirit, soul, and body." Though the apostle is surely speaking rhetorically rather than theologically—and certainly not psychologically! His concern is to show that when a man is entirely sanctified, the entire man, in all his parts, is at peace, in himself, and with his God. (2) For preservation in blamelessness—not faultlessness. The NEB is misleading in its translation "without fault." Paul's prayer is fully in harmony with that of Jude 24, where faultlessness is seen as a feature of that final sanctification which awaits the "presence of his glory." (3) For preservation dynamically, not statically. The correct rendering is "kept blameless at the coming" (NIV) rather than "unto" (KJV). Nevertheless, this does not give warrant to those who teach that entire sanctification, as Paul understood it, must await the Second Advent. "The *parousia* is seen as the time when . . . the Christian will be seen for what he is."[44] Nor should we imagine that Paul's prayer implies the preservation of a static holiness. One is reminded of the foreign student who had picked up a smattering of English. Eager to impress the friends with whom he had lived while studying, he later wrote in a letter of thanks, "The Lord bless and pickle you"! But preservation as Paul saw it had a very different connotation. He saw it not as a maintenance of the spiritual status quo, but as an experience permitting, and demanding, increasing development in holiness.

3. *A promise of divine performance* (24). The literal rendering here is "he will do," that is, sanctify and keep. However, Neil wisely adds a caution, "This is not a statement upon which we can base the view that once a Christian receives the call of God and the gift of His Spirit, he is beyond all further concern or obligation; that he has God's grace and can never fall from it; that his eternal salvation is assured. Paul has just told his readers that, chosen and children of the Light though they be, they must be wakeful and sober, and arm themselves with the panoply of God (vv. 7-8). He assumes, therefore, that the two-sidedness of the New Covenant is understood. . . . Notwithstanding, he urges them to go forward undaunted in hope: God who has brought them into His Kingdom will strengthen them and enable the Apostle's prayer to be fulfilled."[45]

Charges to the People of God

1 Thess. 5:25-27

> 25 Brethren, pray for us.
> 26 Greet all the brethren with an holy kiss.
> 27 I charge you by the Lord that this epistle be read unto all the holy brethren.

1. *A request for prayer* (25). Thus did the greatest saint of all advertise his dependence upon the prayers of the weakest.

2. *The bequest of peace* (26). It is reputed that by the middle of the second century the kiss of peace had become a regular feature of the Eucharist. It was essentially an Oriental practice and, largely due to abuse, was eventually abandoned by the churches of the West. Its modern counterpart may be the loving greetings appended to letters between friends, though Phillips gives his own modern construction, "Give a handshake all round among the brotherhood."

3. *The charge to read* (27). Several reasons have been adduced for the giving of this order. Some have suggested that, in view of the situation mentioned in 2 Thess. 2:2, there may have been some of the more influential members of the church, not well disposed towards Paul, who did not wish his authentic word to be read. Such a situation suggests a tension more serious than was likely, for the whole tone of this letter bespeaks a much happier state of affairs. Probably the charge grew out of Paul's concern that all the brethren, even the weakest and the least literate, should be given the benefit of his guidance and the assurance of his love. And it is most probable that this practice of publicly reading Paul's Epistles contributed largely to their being early accepted as Scripture.

A Benediction upon the People of God

1 Thess. 5:28

28 The grace of our Lord Jesus Christ be with you. Amen.

While the length and form of his benedictions varied, Paul invariably included the word "grace." This is not surprising since the word was peculiarly his.

The Second Epistle
to the
THESSALONIANS

Topical Outline of Second Thessalonians

Greetings to a Tried but Triumphant Church (1:1-4)
    Introduction and Salutation (1:1-2)
    Perseverance in Tribulation (1:3-4)

God's Sovereign Purpose Through Tribulation (1:5-12)
    God's Present Purpose for Those Who Endure Tribulation
        (1:5)
    God's Solemn Purpose for Those Who Inflict Tribulation
        (1:6-9)
    God's Supreme Purpose for Those Who Endure Tribulation
        (1:10)
    Paul's Ceaseless Prayer That This Purpose Will Be Realized
        (1:11-12)

God's Advent Program and Its Associated Mysteries
(2:1-15)
    The Immediate Problem (2:1-3)
    The Mystery of Lawlessness (2:4-10)
    The Mystery of Unbelief (2:11-12)
    The Mystery of Faith (2:13-15)
    The Concluding Prayer (2:16-17)

Paul's Directions to Develop Spiritual Discipline (3:1-15)
    Paul's Plea for Prayer in Face of External Pressures (3:1-5)
    Paul's Pattern of Practice in Face of Internal Problems
        (3:6-15)
    Final Petition, Salutation, and Benediction (3:16-18)

Greetings to a Tried but Triumphant Church
2 Thessalonians 1:1-4

2 THESSALONIANS 1

Introduction and Salutation

2 Thess. 1:1-2

> 1 Paul, and Silvanus, and Timotheus, unto the church of the Thessalonians in God our Father and the Lord Jesus Christ:
> 2 Grace unto you, and peace, from God our Father and the Lord Jesus Christ.

The differences between this address and that in the first letter are textually slight but they add significantly to statements previously made. For instance, the close association of Father and Son is further emphasized. Here they are together treated as a single source of grace and peace. Then, instead of "God the Father," we read *God our Father,* so that the sense of fellowship in and with God is given greater depth and warmth.

Perseverance in Tribulation

2 Thess. 1:3-4

> 3 We are bound to thank God always for you, brethren, as it is meet, because that your faith groweth exceedingly, and the charity of every one of you all toward each other aboundeth;
> 4 So that we ourselves glory in you in the churches of God for your patience and faith in all your persecutions and tribulations that ye endure:

1. *A case of answered prayer.* The NEB reads: "Your faith increases mightly, and the love you have, each for all and all for each." This was a classic answer to the apostle's prayer in 1 Thess. 3:10, 12, and it was all the more satisfying because he could add, "Your faith remains so steadfast

under all your persecutions, and all the troubles you endure" (4, NEB).

2. *A cause for abundant praise.* It goes without saying that in praise, as in all things, God must have the preeminence. But Paul never withheld merited praise from his converts and, in spite of the wording of the KJV, his praise was not grudging. *We are bound to give thanks to God always for you* is better rendered by Phillips, "I thank God for you not only in common fairness but as a moral obligation!" Nor was his praise fulsome. Some scholars have suggested that the Thessalonians had suspected Paul of overpraising them in his First Epistle, and that he was now assuring them that his approbation had been well deserved. Others feel that the apostle's fervent thanksgiving, carried to the point where he said, "We actually boast about you in the churches of God" (Phillips), was for the benefit of those who had previously protested their unfittedness to stand up to the demands of faith (see 1 Thess. 5:14). This could well have been Paul's purpose, for none knew better than he the value of the grace of encouragement. Tennyson once commented on the genius of the young Rudyard Kipling. Years later Kipling said about Tennyson's recommendation, "When the private in the ranks is praised by the general . . . he fights the better next day."

But the apostle gave more than encouragement, he gave enlightenment too, for he went on to shed some light upon the philosophy of tribulation.

God's Sovereign Purpose Through Tribulation
2 Thessalonians 1:5-12

God's Present Purpose for Those Who Endure Tribulation

2 Thess. 1:5

> 5 Which is a manifest token of the righteous judgment of God, that ye
> may be counted worthy of the kingdom of God, for which ye also suffer:

1. *To fit His people for His kingdom.* This verse reflects Paul's concern to square the divine purpose with the persecution and tribulation through which his readers were even then passing. Already, in v. 4, he had shown that out of the fire had emerged a quality of faith and endurance that had become a wonder to their brethren. Now he is about to show that,

> *The steps of faith*
> *Falling on the seeming void,*
> *Find the Rock beneath.*

That Rock is the certainty that God is working to a plan, that plan is to fit His people for His kingdom, that Kingdom is made up of men and women who have come through the fire, so that while the sufferings of the Thessalonians might be extreme, they are not unique (Acts 14:22).

It seems that this is a lesson that the child of the Kingdom must relearn in every generation, and ours is no exception. For Christianity is not a superior hallucinatory drug that guarantees a "good trip." It promises tribulation, as any honest reading of the New Testament will prove. On the other hand, the Christian is not morbidly preoccupied with pain, deliberately plucking the thorn and leaving the rose. Yet any Christian whose experience is invariably easy has some reason for being uneasy.

However, Paul has more to say about God's purpose for His persecuted children.

2. *To furnish evidence of His justice,* or, as Moffatt translated, to give "proof positive of God's equity." For what God demands He first provides. The remarkable fortitude exhibited by the Thessalonians was not of their doing. Here let us look at the phrase *that ye may be counted worthy of the kingdom of God.* Leon Morris points out that,

> The verb *kataxioō* means not "to make worthy," or "to be worthy," but "to declare worthy" or "to count worthy," reminding us strongly of that other great Pauline word *dikaioō,* "to justify," in the sense of "to declare" or "count as just." By his choice of this word the apostle is excluding human merit even in a section where he is drawing attention to a noteworthy piece of endurance, and is emphasizing that attainment to the kingdom is not the result of human endeavour at all, but of the grace of God."[1]

Perhaps Morris is somewhat underestimating the place of human response to the grace of God, but he does well to remind us that "it is God which worketh in us both to will and to do of his good pleasure" (Phil. 2:13). The gift of enduring faith which God had bestowed on the Thessalonians, in answer to Paul's prayer, had been outstanding. But it was a gift, a gift to be improved, but a gift nonetheless.

Helmut Thielicke was speaking to a young man of exceptional talent, "You are a gifted young man. You must use your ability to the highest degree." The young man showed signs of embarrassment and was in the process of protesting that he did not deserve the compliment when the preacher went on, "There's no need to get embarrassed. If you are gifted your gifts were given. You didn't manufacture them."

God's Solemn Purpose for Those Who Inflict Tribulation

2 Thess. 1:6-9

> 6 Seeing it is a righteous thing with God to recompense tribulation to them that trouble you;
> 7 And to you who are troubled rest with us, when the Lord Jesus shall be revealed from heaven with his mighty angels,
> 8 In flaming fire taking vengeance on them that know not God, and that obey not the gospel of our Lord Jesus Christ:
> 9 Who shall be punished with everlasting destruction from the presence of the Lord, and from the glory of his power;

In this section Paul develops his thought on the "proof of God's equity," but now within the eschatological context. Having discussed the righteous judgment of God in the present experience of the believer in fitting him for His kingdom and giving needed grace for every trial, he proceeds to show that, just as the righteous are being ripened for the day of final glory, so are the unrighteous being prepared for the day of final wrath.

1. *God will administer judgment in the form of recompense* (6). Those who dispute the authorship of this Epistle claim that this verse is such a forthright expression of the *lex talionis,* as in Lev. 24:20, that Paul could not possibly have written it. But the thought in this verse is not of arbitrary justice, nor of a specific punishment made to fit the crime, but of that retribution for sin that is inherent in the nature of a moral universe. James Denney once said that punishment is the other half of sin. A man reaps what he sows. Whatever is evil has already within itself the seeds of its own destruction. To this truth this verse gives emphatic expression, "grounding it, not in general philosophical opinions, but in the righteous nature of God."[2]

2. *God will administer judgment at the time of the revelation* (7-8a). Significantly, the word here describing the Lord's return is *apokalupsis,* meaning an "uncovering or unfolding." His coming will be supremely a revelation of himself, but in the light of His presence what truth, solemn as well as glorious, will be uncovered! Three preposi-

tions tell us how our Lord will be revealed in such an apocalypse.

a. The Lord Jesus will be revealed *from* heaven, not in heaven. Since to Him belongs the attribute of omnipresence "He is everywhere spiritually present. But in His humanity—which He assumed never to lay down—He is located in heaven at God's right hand. It is 'from thence' that He shall come again to judge both the quick and the dead."[3] It will, in truth, be "this same Jesus" that shall be revealed, for as He went up at the Ascension, so shall He come down at the Advent.

b. He will be revealed *with* His mighty angels. This is in line with His own promise (Matt. 13:41-42; 24:31; 25:31), and these references indicate that the presence of the angelic hosts will not be merely for the enhancement of His glory, but in order to show obedience to His will.

c. He will be revealed *in* flaming fire, for the reference in v. 8 belongs properly to v. 7. This, too, is in keeping with the biblical records of the theophanies. In alluding to this scene, Adeney declares that "it signifies a splendid terror, a dangerous majesty."[4] For our God *is* a consuming fire.

3. *God's vengeance includes all the unrighteous* (8*b*). Not only those who have actually afflicted the righteous (v. 6), but the unrighteous without exception. In this verse Paul refers to two groups of people.

a. Those that know not God. Though this must be seen as culpable ignorance—"Then will he do justice upon those who refuse to acknowledge God" (NEB). This echoes the apostle's thought in Rom. 1:18-23, for "it is not that they are ignorant of Him: it is that they ignore Him. It is not that God never gives them a chance: it is that they never give God a chance."[5] But while this group has sinned against the light of nature, the second group has sinned against the light of revelation.

b. They obey not the gospel. They have heard the saving message. We are not told that they could not understand it; they just would not obey it. They grasped the implications all too well and were unwilling to meet the demands. Samuel Johnson was once asked whether he was ever troubled by the passages of Scripture that are so hard to understand. His trenchant reply has often been quoted: "What worries me is the number of passages I *do* understand." Those who know but do not obey what they know have good reason to worry for, as Christ himself said, "This is the condemnation, that light is come into the world, and men loved darkness rather than light, because their deeds were evil" (John 3:19).

4. *God's vengeance excludes all the unrighteous* (9). Destruction in this instance is not annihilation, but exclusion. "This is not the absence of being but of well-being." It is the loss of all that makes life worth living. Coupled with the adjective "eternal," it is diametrically opposite to eternal life. As James Denney once said, "If there is any truth in Scripture at all, this is true—that those who stubbornly refuse to submit to the Gospel, and to love and obey Jesus Christ, incur at the Last Advent an infinite and irreparable loss. They pass into a night on which no morning dawns."[6] The essence of such eternal destruction is that sinners will be severed from the face of the Lord forever. What a solemn purpose is this! Well may men pray, with Wesley—

> *Thou Judge of quick and dead,*
> *Before whose bar severe,*
> *With holy joy, or guilty dread,*
> *We all shall soon appear:*
> *Our cautioned souls prepare*
> *For that tremendous day,*
> *And fill us now with watchful care,*
> *And stir us up to pray.*

God's Supreme Purpose for Those Who Endure Tribulation

2 Thess. 1:10

> 10 When he shall come to be glorified in his saints, and to be admired in all them that believe (because our testimony among you was believed) in that day.

1. *That Christ may be glorified in His people* (10). While some will be excluded from the Lord's presence, others are to be transformed into the likeness of His presence. In a reassuring personal word to the Thessalonian believers Paul writes, "This includes you, because you believed our testimony to you" (10*b*, NIV). Paul seems to have reserved this word translated "glorified" (Gk., *endoxazō*) to describe this unprecedented event, for he uses it only here and in v. 12.

A mother was teaching her little girl the catechism, and in answer to the question "What is man's chief end?" the child replied, correctly, "Man's chief end is to glorify God and enjoy Him forever."

On the spur of the moment the mother then asked, "And what do you think God's chief end is?"

With the oft startling insight of childhood the little girl answered, "I suppose God's chief end is to glorify man and to enjoy him forever." This is very near the truth, for not only will each of the redeemed rejoice, seeing the reflection of Christ's joy in each other, but Christ will rejoice in their joy.

2. *That Christ may be admired in His people.* This is where the emphasis must lie, for the thought is that the saints will be a kind of mirror in which the glory of Christ will be reflected. The object of all heaven's admiration will be not the saints but their Lord. This is the wondrous vision that A. J. Gossip had in mind in a never-to-be-forgotten sermon preached to his Glasgow congregation. Said he, "When the saints go marching in, the angels will look at one another in sheer amazement and exclaim, 'How very like Jesus these people are!'" Jesus founded no family

in the biological sense, yet in the light of such a verse as this how meaningful do the words of Isaiah become, "He shall see his seed. . . . He shall see of the travail of his soul, and shall be satisfied."

Paul's Ceaseless Prayer That This Purpose Will Be Realized

2 Thess. 1:11-12

> 11 Wherefore also we pray always for you, that our God would count you worthy of this calling, and fulfil all the good pleasure of his goodness, and the work of faith with power:
> 12 That the name of our Lord Jesus Christ may be glorified in you, and ye in him, according to the grace of our God and the Lord Jesus Christ.

1. *That our God would count you worthy of this calling.* While Paul was careful to point out that both God's call and the fitness to respond to it were all of grace, he recognized no merely superficial fitness. The false dichotomy between "standing" and "state" is not to be found in his theological scheme. Admittedly, as Moore has observed, "a similar verb to that in 1:5 is used meaning, usually, 'to count' worthy rather than 'to render' worthy, although in fact the stress here may well fall on the latter idea. The thought is probably 'that God may account you worthy by making you worthy.'"[7] This must necessarily be so, in the light of such scriptures as Rom. 8:1-4 and 1 John 3:1-3.

2. *That our God would . . . fulfil all the good pleasure of his goodness, and the work of faith with power.* Or as the NIV has it, "That by his power he may fulfil every good purpose of yours and every act prompted by your faith." Paul's concern is that "every good impulse may be translated into action and not left as a pious intention, and that the acts of charity that their faith would suggest to them should not remain still-born."[8] Thus Paul lays stress where it must always be laid in the Christian faith, namely, on *action.* Halford Luccock tells that Averell Harriman, when asked how his French was, replied, "My French is excellent, all except the verbs." That is the way with most

languages: the nouns and adjectives are relatively easy. The verbs give the bother! Someone said recently that many intellectuals today are accepting Christianity as an interpretation of life, but they are not yet prepared to accept it as a way of life. Until they do their intellect alone will be of little use. Jesus' order was "do" and "know." If every act prompted by faith was fulfilled, how faith would grow apace!

3. *That the name of our Lord Jesus Christ may be glorified in you.* As always in this sense "name" stands for the whole personality of the one in view, so that to glorify the name of Jesus is to exalt Him in one's life. Paul's prayer at this point brings very much to mind our Lord's own prayer in John 17:21 ff.

As this chapter closes, solemn as much of its content is, it is clear that God's ultimate purpose of blessing must prevail. The universe is not a closed circle of human and material forces. Christ has ways of breaking in so that, regardless of all the appearances to the contrary, the climax of God's purpose will be reached, and at the name of Jesus every knee shall bow, and every tongue confess that Jesus Christ is Lord, to the glory of God the Father (Phil. 2:10-11). Nevertheless, again Neil's words come as a salutary reminder that "there is nothing automatic about a man's salvation. He may be called and yet be lost by betraying his calling."[9] Hence Paul's ceaseless prayer to that One who is "able to keep [us] from falling, and to present [us] faultless before the presence of his glory with exceeding joy" (Jude 24).

God's Advent Program and
Its Associated Mysteries
2 Thessalonians 2:1-15

The Immediate Problem

2 Thess. 2:1-3

> 1 Now we beseech you, brethren, by the coming of our Lord Jesus Christ, and by our gathering together unto him,
> 2 That ye be not soon shaken in mind, or be troubled, neither by spirit, nor by word, nor by letter as from us, as that the day of Christ is at hand.
> 3 Let no man deceive you by any means: for that day shall not come, except there come a falling away first, and that man of sin be revealed, the son of perdition;

In this chapter Paul deals with the root problem in the Thessalonian Church. The believers, already undergoing sore trials, were now being beset by erroneous teaching relating to the Lord's return. The initial mental shock of this (the verb translated "shaken" suggests a ship torn from its moorings and tossed by wind and storm) had led to such alarm and distress that Paul had been constrained to write this second letter.

1. *The nature of the error* (2). "The day of the Lord has already come" (NIV). Since this phrase, "day of the Lord," conveys a complex idea and includes many events within its scope, any detailed understanding of which is colored by one's millennial and eschatological preferences, it is not possible to treat it comprehensively here. But the implication of the erroneous rumors seems clear, namely, that if the Day of the Lord had arrived, then the coming of the Lord must be impending. This prospect had evidently distressed those who felt unprepared, it had con-

firmed the idle in their indolence, and had cast the entire church into a ferment of unhealthy excitement.

2. *The source of the error* (2). Paul has mentioned three possibilities. *(a)* "By some prophecy" (NIV). Moore thinks that some utterance, inspired by the Holy Spirit, had been misunderstood, though it might have been a pretended prophecy. *(b) By word,* an expression that could refer to any form of verbal communication. Since it is probable that the phrase *as from us* could apply to prophecy, word, or letter, we may assume that Paul was disclaiming responsibility for any of these media. *(c) By letter.* We cannot be sure whether this was spurious or a genuine Epistle falsely interpreted.

3. *The correction of the error* (3). "That day cannot come before the final rebellion against God" (NEB). There are various opinions as to the precise nature of this rebellion. The use of *apostasia* certainly indicates that the Church is involved (Matt. 24:4-5, 10-13; 1 Tim. 4:1), but that it will include the wider world seems plain from such scriptures as Psalm 2 and Luke 18:8*b*. Morris comments "It is as though Satan were throwing all his forces into one last despairing effort" (see Rev. 12:12).

The Mystery of Lawlessness

2 Thess. 2:4-10

> 4 Who opposeth and exalteth himself above all that is called God, or that is worshipped; so that he as God sitteth in the temple of God, shewing himself that he is God.
> 5 Remember ye not, that, when I was yet with you, I told you these things?
> 6 And now ye know what withholdeth that he might be revealed in his time.
> 7 For the mystery of iniquity doth already work: only he who now letteth will let, until he be taken out of the way.
> 8 And then shall that Wicked be revealed, whom the Lord shall consume with the spirit of his mouth, and shall destroy with the brightness of his coming:
> 9 Even him, whose coming is after the working of Satan with all power and signs and lying wonders,
> 10 And with all deceivableness of unrighteousness in them that perish; because they received not the love of the truth, that they might be saved.

1. *The identity of the man of lawlessness.* This title is slightly better attested than *man of sin* as in KJV. Unfortunately, since in this chapter Paul has drawn upon information previously given to his readers (5) but quite unavailable to us, we are faced with some baffling problems in seeking to elucidate important details of his teaching. This is the case as we attempt to establish the identity of this man of lawlessness.

 a. This title does not refer to Satan. Since we are told that it is through the power of Satan that this man makes his appearance (9), it is manifestly incorrect to refer to him as "the devil incarnate."

 b. This title does not imply an abstract principle. There certainly is a principle of lawlessness already at work (7), but this principle is to be embodied in a person (8).

 c. This person is to be revealed. Indeed he is to be the subject of a *parousia.* Doubtless there have been those who, imbued with the spirit of this man of lawlessness (or Antichrist, as John has called him), have anticipated him to a greater or lesser degree. But it is just as wrong to confuse this person with his precursors as it is to confuse him with the principle of lawlessness presently operating. John has observed these essential distinctions (see 1 John 2:18; 4:3).

2. *The activity of the man of lawlessness.* Here he comes into somewhat clearer focus.

 a. He opposes all that is called God (4). Thus he shows himself to be a loyal agent of Satan, one of whose titles is "the adversary."

 b. He exalts himself above all that is called God (4). Not only does he oppose all that men hold sacred, but he masquerades as divine. This is the ultimate evil.

 c. He sits as God in the temple of God (4). Some have attempted to interpret this picture historically. For example Antiochus Epiphanes, in 168 B.C., set up a heathen altar within the Temple and sacrificed swine upon it. In A.D. 40, Caligula caused riots in Jerusalem by attempting to have his statue set up in the Temple. But the event described here far exceeds these or any such incidents, for here Antichrist actually presents himself as God incarnate. Other commentators have understood this event spiritually, interpreting the temple as the body and taking it as a further indication of the widespread abandonment of the acknowledgment of God. To accept the prophecy literally would necessitate the rebuilding of the Temple; yet, as unlikely as this may seem, there are persistent rumors of this possibility.

d. *He performs counterfeit miracles at his coming* (9). As already mentioned, he is the subject of a *parousia,* but the words which describe his miracles, *power, signs,* and *wonders,* are all used in connection with the miracles which Christ wrought. As might be expected of Antichrist, he seeks to parallel the works of the one true Lord.

3. *The activity of the mystery of lawlessness* (7). Here *mystery* is used in its true New Testament sense. This denotes a secret undiscoverable by human reason. It must be made known by God to men through His Spirit. It is therefore spiritual in its perception, and it is eschatological in its outcome. This would account for the otherwise inexplicable blindness which seems to have afflicted men in general today. Even up to the highest echelons in government the natural man is often utterly, and sometimes confessedly, frustrated in the face of latter-day lawlessness. He sees it as a universal phenomenon but is unable to explain it and powerless to deal with it.

Perhaps most astonishing of all is the fact that lawless elements no longer need to operate clandestinely. Through political, social, and cultural channels they blatantly pursue their anarchical aims; yet when it comes to coping with these overt threats, the powers that be seem so often to be the victims of an uncanny paralysis. Nevertheless, Paul reminds us, mercifully, of a restriction which continues to be imposed upon such sinister forces.

4. *The restraint upon both the man and the mystery of lawlessness* (6-7). There has been much speculation as to whom, or what, is meant by the phrases "you know what is holding him back" and "the one who now holds it back" (6-7, NIV). Several suggestions have been offered but the following seem most feasible.

a. *The principle of law and government.* A difficulty arises here inasmuch as in v. 6 the restraining power is neuter, while in v. 7 it is masculine. However, law is a principle that has often been personified, and Paul certainly saw civil government as an agency of rule ordained by God.

b. *The gospel era.* In this interpretation that which restrains is seen as the gospel message, while the one who restrains is the gospel messenger. By such means the warning note is sounded, opportunity is given to repent and believe, and thus is provision made for the maintenance of a spiritual curb upon the forces of lawlessness.

Here is where we might well wish to have been partakers of that intelligence that Paul had given to the Thessalonians. However, what we do know from this chapter is that the precise time when restraint upon lawlessness will be removed and the man of lawlessness will be revealed is determined, not by him, but by God (v. 6).

5. *The destruction of the man of lawlessness* (8). "Once the restraining power is removed (7c), the opportunity for preaching, for repentance, and faith will cease and the End arrive . . . It is only the provision of grace for preaching which stands in the way of the final unmasking of God's adversaries."[10] But that unmasking will be the occasion of Antichrist's destruction. That destruction will be effected by the power and brightness of a revelation glorious beyond comprehension. "For the Lord even to show Himself will be sufficient to destroy the enemy."[11]

6. *The deceitfulness of the man of lawlessness* (9-10). Mention has already been made of the present blindness of men due to the effects of the "mystery of lawlessness," but

this is as nothing in comparison with the woeful condition of those who are hoodwinked by the man of lawlessness. Reference to his revelation and its attendant wonders (v. 9) leads Paul to a description of the utter delusion of the disciples of Antichrist. "Paul thinks of Antichrist's attendant hosts, the ones who are perishing, being dazzled by his appearing just as the 'saints' will 'marvel at' the appearance of Christ."[12] The cause of this irreparable blindness is not ignorance or misunderstanding of the truth, but a refusal to love it. This phrase, *love of the truth,* is used nowhere else in the New Testament, though a similar expression is found in 1:8. The truth which saves is that which is clasped to the heart in the full purpose of the obedience of faith.

The Mystery of Unbelief

2 Thess. 2:11-12

> 11 And for this cause God shall send them strong delusion, that they should believe a lie:
> 12 That they all might be damned who believed not the truth, but had pleasure in unrighteousness.

According to vv. 13-17, believers are drawn of God to faith in Christ, while vv. 7-10 intimate that others are attracted by Satan into allegiance to Antichrist. But in vv. 11-12, Paul shows that God is the Author of *both* processes. As Neil has said, "Antichrist is the servant of the Devil, the incarnation of evil—but both he and his master Satan are under the hand of God."[13] Consequently, in the ultimate sense, it is God and not Satan who *shall send them strong delusion, that they should believe a lie.* This is startling truth but the only alternative is dualism, a doctrine which, for the Christian, is completely untenable since it denies the Sovereignty of God. Nevertheless, the Sovereignty of God must not be taken to mean that He acts either arbitrarily or capriciously. He works through the moral law. But the moral law is neither impersonal nor self-existent; it operates because it is the will of God.

That will declares that when a man pursues an open-eyed, deliberate rejection of the gospel, unless he repents and believes, he will reach the point where he loses the ability to discern between the true and the false. In this sense the Bible describes God putting a lying spirit into the mouths of prophets (1 Kings 22:22; Ezek. 14:9), and hardening the heart of Pharaoh (Exod. 4:21).

We may summarise this dread process as follows: *(a)* refusal to love the truth (10*b*); *(b)* inability to discern the truth (11*a*); *(c)* acceptance of the lie (11*b*); *(d)* approval of unrighteousness (12*b*), and *(e)* inevitable condemnation (12*a*).

The Mystery of Faith

2 Thess. 2:13-15

> 13 But we are bound to give thanks alway to God for you, brethren beloved of the Lord, because God hath from the beginning chosen you to salvation through sanctification of the Spirit and belief of the truth:
> 14 Whereunto he called you by our gospel, to the obtaining of the glory of our Lord Jesus Christ.
> 15 Therefore, brethren, stand fast, and hold the traditions which ye have been taught, whether by word, or our epistle.

With obvious relief Paul turns to what has been called "the other half of the mystery" of God's purpose for mankind. He lifts his eyes from the grim prospects of the wicked to the happy state of those who have committed their lives to God. In doing so, in a few words (vv. 13-14), he has given what James Denney called "a system of theology in miniature." However, "Paul's aim . . . is practical. His concern is not with speculative philosophy on free will and predestination, nor with the metaphysical aspects of election, but it betrays a real pastoral desire to comfort his flock in their perplexity, by re-assuring them that, as God's people, they have nothing to fear."[14] That reassurance rests upon three factors.

1. *God's eternal purpose to save His people* (13). A variety of words are used in the New Testament to express the idea of election. This verb translated "chosen" (Gk., *heilato*) is rarely used by Paul and conveys the thought of "preferred." It is probably used in the present context to

carry forward the idea of contrast between the chosen and the rejected. Paul declares that such a choice was *from the beginning* (see Eph. 1:4), and that its purpose is salvation. Thus election is not unto faith, as such. This salvation is wrought through the purifying work of the Spirit, so preparing the believer for the appearing of Christ, and *through belief in the truth.* So "Paul has no place in his theology for an inscrutable despot who 'sends ane to heaven an' ten to hell a' for his glory.' God's choice of men is not deterministic—however much some interpretations of Paul suggest that it is; it is by the interplay of Spirit upon spirit . . . the operation is mutual. God is the author, but man must make his response."[15]

2. *God's present provision for the implementing of His purpose* (14). Paul teaches that God's eternal purpose is effected by an event in time—*he called you by our gospel.* This call has in view nothing less than *the obtaining of the glory of our Lord Jesus Christ.* The order here is similar to that in Rom. 8:30. Once again it is of interest to note how Paul, apparently incidentally, has included, within verses 13 and 14, all the elements of Trinitarian doctrine; God as loving Father, Christ as Lord, and the Holy Spirit as Sanctifier.

3. *The present responsibility of the people of God* (15). From the use of the word *traditions* it is evident that, thus early in the life of the Church, there existed, at least germinally, a recognized body of Christian truth. The word itself belongs to that vocabulary of the Early Church which had to do with the transmission of the gospel message. It was adopted from Jewish custom and usage in which the law was seen as having been delivered by God to Moses, who in turn delivered it to Joshua, and so on. Examples of this concept in Paul are seen in 1 Cor. 11:2, 23; 15:3. See also Jude 3. Thus Paul is emphasizing that the content of his ministry to the Thessalonians, both oral and written, was not of his invention. He had not "discovered" such truth but had simply delivered it. As an apostle it was his

task not to originate but to communicate the truth. His reference to *our epistle* probably refers to 1 Thessalonians, and *by word* would include his entire ministry of preaching, teaching, and exhortation. In such truth the converts are to *stand fast,* refusing to be carried away by the errors being propounded (2:1-3).

The inescapable conclusion within this verse is that "neither sanctification nor faith are altogether the work of man, but neither are they altogether the work of God excusing man from active, serious, and persistent co-operation. Therefore Paul can turn directly, as he does here, from the account of God's fore-ordination . . . to exhortation to the converts to stand firm."[16]

The Concluding Prayer

2 Thess. 2:16-17

> 16 Now our Lord Jesus Christ himself, and God, even our Father, which hath loved us, and hath given us everlasting consolation and good hope through grace,
> 17 Comfort your hearts, and stablish you in every good word and work.

As a still further evidence of the apostle's conviction of the equality of Father and Son, we note that Christ is here given prior mention. To Paul the two Persons were one. The emphasis upon *good hope* bears witness to the overwhelming superiority of the Christian's faith, for hope of any kind found little place in the pagan religions of that day. It is no less rare in this day of widespread irreligion. The words of James Russell Lowell echo the hopelessness and futility of millions as he writes of

> *Life's emblem deep,*
> *A confused noise between two silences,*
> *Finding at last in dust precarious peace.*

We "whose souls are lighted" would do well to ensure that what ought to be a shared hope does not degenerate into a selfish one. Comfort and encouragement are given that we may be established *in every good word and work.*

Paul's Directions to
Develop Spiritual Discipline

2 Thessalonians 3:1-16

2 THESSALONIANS 3

Paul's Plea for Prayer in Face of External Pressures

2 Thess. 3:1-5

> 1 Finally, brethren, pray for us, that the word of the Lord may have free course, and be glorified, even as it is with you:
> 2 And that we may be delivered from unreasonable and wicked men: for all men have not faith.
> 3 But the Lord is faithful, who shall stablish you, and keep you from evil.
> 4 And we have confidence in the Lord touching you, that ye both do and will do the things which we command you.
> 5 And the Lord direct your hearts into the love of God, and into the patient waiting for Christ.

At v. 6 Paul will give expression to some of the most forthright pronouncements in the Thessalonian correspondence. True to character he prefers the indirect approach and prefaces his stern admonitions with an earnest plea for prayer, adding his confidence that his readers will respond now as they had done in the past (4).

1. *His plea for the gospel's advancement* (1). The wording of his prayer that "the word of the Lord may speed on and triumph" (RSV) resembles his phrase in 1 Thess. 2:13 in which he speaks of the Word's "effectual working." It is as if the gospel were almost an independent spiritual force. Wesley expresses the same idea in his great missionary hymn,

> *Now the word doth swiftly run,*
> *Now it wins its widening way;*
> *More and more it spreads and grows*

Ever mighty to prevail;
Sin's strongholds it now o'erthrows,
Shakes the trembling gates of hell.

Unfortunately, there was little enough evidence of this at the time of writing. Indeed, one detects a touch of nostalgia as he recalls the speedy advance of the Word in Thessalonica—"just as it was with you" (NIV). Yet such was the spirit of this redoubtable soldier of the Cross that, as we know, after persevering in Corinth for 18 months, he saw the gospel break through into victory. How essential is the grace of persistence.

In his journal, John Wesley describes how he preached for the last time in Epworth churchyard, "to a vast multitude gathered from all parts." Then he adds, "Let none think his labour of love is lost because the fruit does not immediately appear. Near forty years did my father labour here, but he saw little fruit of all his labour. I took some pains among this people too, and my strength also seemed spent in vain; but now the fruit appears." Yet Paul saw that the grace of persistence must be exercised in prayer as well as in preaching.

2. *His plea for the preacher's deliverance* (2). Paul had no illusions about the strength, and spleen, of his adversaries, "these perverse and evil men" (NASB). Almost certainly they were his traditional Jewish enemies (Acts 18:12-17). Yet while in such personal peril his first concern was not for the safety of the missionaries but for the advance of their message. A handbook on camping was published some years ago bearing the intriguing title, *Roughing It Smoothly*. Its opening gambit went something like this: "There is no reason why the present-day camper should have to put up with the hardships and discomforts of yesterday. This book is a plea for camping in comfort." We should treat with much reserve and no little scepticism any modern handbook on evangelism that promises a much easier discipline than Paul and his colleagues endured.

3. *His plea for his readers' endurance* (5). It is difficult to determine Paul's precise meaning here. Did he pray that his readers might know the patient waiting *for* Christ, as in the KJV? Or did he have in mind the steadfastness *of* Christ? Either could be true, for the genitive is difficult to interpret. However, the second alternative seems the more likely, especially taking into account the need for the Thessalonians to deal patiently, yet strictly, with problem people in the church.

Paul's Pattern of Practice in Face of Internal Problems

2 Thess. 3:6-15

> 6 Now we command you, brethren, in the name of our Lord Jesus Christ, that ye withdraw yourselves from every brother that walketh disorderly, and not after the tradition which he received of us.
> 7 For yourselves know how ye ought to follow us: for we behaved not ourselves disorderly among you;
> 8 Neither did we eat any man's bread for nought; but wrought with labour and travail night and day, that we might not be chargeable to any of you:
> 9 Not because we have not power, but to make ourselves an ensample unto you to follow us.
> 10 For even when we were with you, this we commanded you, that if any would not work, neither should he eat.
> 11 For we hear that there are some which walk among you disorderly, working not at all, but are busybodies.
> 12 Now them that are such we command and exhort by our Lord Jesus Christ, that with quietness they work, and eat their own bread.
> 13 But ye, brethren, be not weary in well doing.
> 14 And if any man obey not our word by this epistle, note that man, and have no company with him, that he may be ashamed.
> 15 Yet count him not as an enemy, but admonish him as a brother.

Already in his First Epistle Paul had spoken directly to the potential troublemakers (1 Thess. 4:11) and had besought the more responsible members to caution them (1 Thess. 5:14). Since the word translated in vv. 6 and 11 as *disorderly* is the same as that translated "unruly" (Gk., *ataktōs*) in 1 Thess. 5:14, we may gather that the trouble already caused by these idlers and busybodies had not only persisted but had increased. No wonder that, before beginning to discuss discipline, Paul pauses to pray that his readers might be kept firmly in the path of God's love and Christ's patience. He now presents some basic commands.

1. *The continuation of spiritual discipline* (6). A. L. Moore sees in this pattern of discipline commanded by Paul a reflection of those principles already laid down by Christ in Matt. 18:15-17. For instance, in Matt. 18:15, Jesus had said, "If thy brother shall trespass against thee, go and tell him his fault between thee and him alone." As far as circumstances permitted, Paul seems to have followed this initial stage. Further, Jesus had said, "But if he will not hear thee, then take with thee one or two more, that in the mouths of two or three witnesses, every word may be established." Again, since Paul had involved the "brethren," as in 1 Thess. 5:14, his action would approximate to this second stage. Now, in his command to the Thessalonians to act as a church (6), Paul seems to have pursued the third disciplinary stage (see Matt. 18:17). It should be noted, however, that excommunication is not in view. The disorderly person is still to be looked upon as a *brother* (6).

2. *The application of personal example* (7-13). "Don't do as I do, do as I tell you" was not a Pauline maxim. "For you yourselves know how you ought to imitate us; we were not idle when we were with you, we did not eat any one's bread without paying, but with toil and labor we worked night and day, that we might not burden any of you" (7-8, RSV). And Paul adds that, in refusing to accept support during the Thessalonian campaign, they had relinquished what was theirs by right; this they had done with the express purpose of reinforcing their example (9). Moreover, the "tradition" which his readers had received from him (6) had included the commandment: "If a man will not work, he shall not eat" (NIV).

From this distance in time it could appear as if Paul's concern was somewhat overdrawn, but if certain points are noted, some of which have a perpetual significance, it will be seen that idleness has several facets.

a. Theological implications. That work was in God's purpose for men from the beginning is clear from such scriptures as Ps. 104:19-24, and that it is meant to constitute an integral part of the divine purpose is implied in the fourth commandment. As the perfect Man Christ himself was a worker (Mark 6:3). Consequently, from its inception, Christianity has condemned idleness (see also Eph. 4:28).

b. Social implications. Sir Frederick Catherwood, the well-known British industrialist, has said, "Social security, the payment of money to those who are ill, impoverished and out of work, has been called in question by its abuse. The apostle Paul's blunt principle was, 'If anyone will not work, let him not eat.' If he *cannot* work, that is not his fault. But social security now protects those who *will* not work, and every authority knows that their number is now uncomfortably high."[17] It has been said that in v. 10 Paul has virtually established a law of social economics. Contravention of this law has more to do with Britain's current economic problems than many care to admit. Most especially, however, those who are Christ's must loathe the very idea of unnecessarily becoming a burden to others. Rather will they seek for opportunities, unless providentially hindered, to share what they have with those in genuine need.

c. Moral contingencies. A Persian proverb states that while "Satan tempts all men, the idle man tempts Satan." This is just as true when idleness is indulged in the name of religion. While not specifically stated, there is reason to believe that, under the cloak of the imminent expectation of Christ's return and, possibly, with a sense of superior piety, there were those who had laid aside their employment and whose only business now was minding other people's business (v. 11). It still sometimes happens in church life that those who do least have most to say!

d. Local responsibility. First, not to encourage idleness. Kenneth Grayston thinks that this rule meant that those who refused to earn their living should not qualify for church support.[18] In any event, Paul is maintaining that it is no part of brotherly love to allow a man to exploit the concern and generosity of his fellows. Secondly, to refuse to be discouraged by the idleness of others. In vv. 12 and 13 Paul leads on to a positive exhortation, solemnly uttered in *our Lord Jesus Christ,* urging such people to "settle down and earn the bread they eat. And as for you, brothers, never tire of doing what is right" (NIV). Finally, to do something to relieve idleness. By an extension of Paul's words one might say that a local church should seek, whenever possible, to assist its unemployed members to find work.

3. *The ultimate aim of spiritual discipline* (14-15). Paul reckons realistically with the possibility that the discipline so far ordered may not have the desired result. He therefore adds this further and, presumably, final measure (cf. Matt. 18:17). While the exercise of familiar intercourse was to be restrained (14), the offender was not to be counted as an enemy but still regarded as one of themselves. Even this extreme action was to be viewed, not so much as the purging of the flock, but as a means of recovering a stray sheep. Salutary as this entire disciplinary process was—indeed because it was—Paul was seeking scrupulously to avert a situation where unwonted zeal might be to the detriment of brotherly love. The quality of spirituality has been variously defined but, as Paul shows in his Galatian letter (6:1), one essential sign of a truly spiritual church is its ability to restore an erring brother.

Final Petition, Salutation, and Benediction
2 Thess. 3:16-18

> 16 Now the Lord of peace himself give you peace always by all means. The Lord be with you all.
> 17 The salutation of Paul with mine own hand, which is the token in every epistle: so I write.
> 18 The grace of our Lord Jesus Christ be with you all. Amen.

Such a petition (16) is a fitting conclusion to the Thessalonian correspondence, for in both letters peace has been given a prominent place. Here the reference is peculiarly apt, for Paul pleads that peace may be the portion of his beloved readers "at all times and in every way" (NIV), though he sees such peace not so much as an experience but as a Presence. In concluding his brief petition with *The Lord be with you all,* the apostle has revealed that between the peace and the Presence there is an inseparable connection. The gift stands with the Giver; they cannot be separated.

As Paul so frequently does, towards the end of his letter, he takes the pen from the hand of his amanuensis and adds his personal postscript. In this instance, in view of 2:2, the token has particular significance. And so, as in his First Epistle, he commends his readers to the grace of his Lord and Master, but with a notable addition. Here, "with the truth expounded, and with praise and rebuke intermingled," and with characteristic tenderness, he includes *all,* even the disorderly, in his farewell benediction.

Introduction to
The Pastoral Epistles

Designation and Character

The Epistles to Timothy and Titus are so closely linked in style, theology, and historical association, that it seems advisable to view them as a single group. Like the short Epistle to Philemon, but unlike the remainder of the Pauline correspondence, they are written to persons. This alone gives them a distinctive character, but it is as Pastoral Epistles that they fall into a category peculiarly their own. This designation, which did not pass into current use until the early eighteenth century, may be somewhat misleading, for it could suggest that here we have all the makings of a manual on the cure of souls. This is not the case. Yet the title is not inappropriate. For one thing the letters show how an ongoing leadership was appointed during the most critical transitional period in the Church's history, but they also provide a mine of information and direction to Church leaders in every era. Furthermore, they present us with a graphic picture of a Church which was, to use Barclay's phrase, "a little island of Christianity in a wide sea of paganism."

Yet it is precisely their distinctiveness which, in comparatively recent times, has led many critics to question their authorship. In the estimation of these scholars the letters are so very different that it is impossible to imagine Paul having written them. It should be said that even such critics recognize that the Pastorals are of considerable value, and that they are of inestimable worth as historical documents, but this does little to alter the fact that, for many, to raise serious doubts as to the authorship of the Epistles is tantamount to questioning their authenticity. The matter of authorship is therefore of primary importance. Space does not permit anything like an exhaustive examination of all the problems involved, but we shall touch upon some of these now and seek to deal with textual matters arising in the course of the exposition.

Authorship

Those who have found it impossible to accept Pauline authorship have usually based their case on the alleged insolubility of certain problems.

1. *The Historical Problem*

On the grounds that these Epistles show Paul engaged in activities which cannot be fitted into the Acts record (e.g., 1 Tim. 1:3; 2 Tim. 1:17; 4:13; Titus 1:5; 3:12), it has been assumed that the letters are the work of a later author. Certainly pseudonymity, the practice of publishing one's own writings under the name of some notable deceased personage, was common in New Testament times, but as regards the historical problem two points should be noted. *First,* none who hold the theory of pseudonymity would deny that in these letters are to be found a number of authentic Pauline "fragments," but as to the identity of these it is impossible to find anything approaching unanimity. *Secondly,* there is reason to believe that Paul had been released from his Roman imprisonment and consequently had every opportunity to pursue the activities already mentioned, prior to his being reimprisoned. While traditional evidences of this are relatively late (e.g., The Epistle of Clement about A.D. 90 and the Ecclesiastical History of Eusebius about A.D. 325), these are not to be lightly dismissed.

But internal evidence is by no means lacking. For instance, after writing from prison in Rome to the Philippians, to say that he was sending Timothy to them, Paul went on to say, "But I trust in the Lord that I also myself shall come shortly" (Phil. 2:24). When he wrote to Philemon, sending back Onesimus the runaway slave, the apostle said, "But withal prepare me also a lodging; for I trust that through your prayers I will be given unto you" (Philem. 22). It could be added that, judging from Acts 28:30-31, the apostle's first Roman imprisonment was very different from the second, when he wrote 2 Timothy. In the former instance he spent two whole years in his own hired house and, since nothing is said beyond this, it is at least as great a possibility as not, that he was released. But, as 2 Timothy indicates, when he wrote this Epistle, Paul was a lonely, well-nigh deserted prisoner. Indeed, when Onesiphorus sought to visit him, he experienced great difficulty in locating him (2 Tim. 1:17). Even later, after he had established some contact with the brethren in Rome, he was still far from enjoying that full intercourse which is suggested in the earlier Prison Epistles. Finally, while according to Philippians he was looking forward to release and a resumption of his ministry, in 2 Timothy the situation is radically and pathetically different.

2. *The Ecclesiastical Problem*

Two assumptions have been made under this heading which, if confirmed, would certainly prove that the Pastorals could not have belonged to the Apostolic Age. First is the insistence that the supposedly elaborate and highly developed scheme of church organization revealed in these Epistles is inconsistent with that obtaining within the primitive Church. But one must bear in mind that it was the apostle's policy, early on, to ordain elders in every church (Acts 14:23), and his earliest letters reveal a high doctrine of the Church and its ministry. Understandably, these later letters bear witness to some development, but both Church and ministry are recognizably the same. Secondly, it is urged that the prevailing heresies discussed and denounced in the Pastorals point strongly to the Gnosticism of the second century. However, in view of the fact that modern scholarship increasingly recognizes that Gnosticism had much earlier roots, this assumption falls to the ground.

3. *The Doctrinal Problem*

E. F. Scott has spoken for many who reject Pauline authorship when he writes, "The theological position is not that of Paul. . . . We cannot but feel that the mind at work in these epistles is different, in the whole bent and outlook, from that of Paul."[1] Barclay has echoed this position: "The stress is on *orthodoxy*. Instead of being a close personal relationship to Jesus Christ, as it was in the thrilling and throbbing days of the early Church, faith has become the acceptance of an orthodox creed."[2] But surely these comments fail to take into account a factor of fundamental importance in the period under consideration. Donald Guthrie has asked the question, "Is it conceivable that Paul had no interest in conservation? Sabatier's oft-quoted statement supplies the answer. 'Paul was an apostle before he was a theologian. To him the need of conservation was more urgent than that of innovation.'"[3]

4. *The Linguistic Problem*

There is no doubt that this problem has provided a great deal of grist for the mill of the critic. J. N. D. Kelly has written, "Most students . . . have noticed the correct and formal diction of the Pastorals. They show little or none of the dialectical tension, and few if any of the signs of pent-up thought breaking the very framework of language, which normally distinguish the Apostle; the writer seems content for the most part with assertion and exhortation."[4] But while this argument may be weighty, it cannot be considered decisive. R. F. Horton aptly comments, "It does not follow, because a man has 'literary peculiarity and greatness,' that he will display these qualities in all his private letters. There are letters of Mr. Ruskin which show none of the style which makes *Modern Painters* immortal; sometimes he puts off the cothurnus and speaks like an ordinary man. Tennyson, though he wrote a few letters which might live side by side with his poems, was on the whole quite undistinguished in his epistolary style."[5] In all, it is the consensus of much modern scholarship that none of the foregoing problems give reason to abandon the traditional view that Paul was the undoubted author of the Pastoral Epistles. In asserting this, it should be said that the Pauline authorship was never in doubt until the 19th century. Donald Guthrie has observed that "objections to authenticity must therefore be regarded as modern innovations contrary to the strong evidence from the early Church."[6]

Date of Writing

Owing to the difficulty of establishing a precise chronology of Paul's life, it is not possible to assign exact dates to these Epistles, though there is very good reason to believe that the margin of uncertainty is narrow. According to the most widely accepted dating scheme Paul arrived in Rome during the spring of A.D. 59, and this would give the spring of A.D. 61 as the date of his release. Another possible scheme suggests these dates as A.D. 61 and A.D. 63 respectively. It is probable that Paul's re-arrest occurred in the wake of the violent persecution and consequent anti-Christian legislation under Nero, following the Great Fire of Rome in July, A.D. 64.

Being a Roman citizen, the apostle would be sent to the capital city for trial and subsequently imprisoned there. This would mean that his second arrest and resultant martyrdom would have occurred between the second half of A.D. 64 and A.D. 67, possibly nearer the latter date. We may thus assume that, since the traditional sequence of the letters is the most likely, 1 Timothy and Titus would be written around A.D. 63 and A.D. 64 respectively, and 2 Timothy between A.D. 66 and A.D. 67.

Destination and Purpose

We know from the text that Timothy was a relatively young man, a child of many prayers, the son of a heathen father and a converted Jewish mother, and that he enjoyed a pious upbringing (2 Tim. 1:5). He did not enjoy robust health (1 Tim. 5:23) and was of a timorous disposition; as Patrick Fairbairn remarked, he was "disposed to lean rather than to lead" (see 1 Cor. 16:10-11). Yet, after having been circumcised by Paul as a concession to Jewish preference, he became the apostle's constant companion and trusted deputy, acquitting himself most creditably in missions of some delicacy and extreme importance (e.g., see 1 Thess. 3:2 and 1 Cor. 4:17).

Titus we know less well. For some reason his name does not appear in Acts, though W. A. Ramsay accounts for this by suggesting that, as he was a relative of Luke, the latter may have omitted his name from the record out of a sense of family modesty. Yet his historical reality is confirmed by references in 2 Corinthians and Galatians, and from the latter Epistle we learn that he was a Greek, and that in his case Paul did not yield to Jewish pressure to have him circumcised (Gal. 2:1-4). It would seem that he was somewhat older than Timothy and that he did not stand in such a close relationship with Paul. However, he was a no less efficient lieutenant who also justified the apostle's confidence in his ability to handle difficult situations (2 Cor. 7:6-16; 8:6; 12:17 ff.).

According to details within the Epistles themselves both men served in the nature of apostolic delegates, Timothy being temporarily in charge of the church in Ephesus, and Titus similarly in Crete. In his letter to Titus Paul implies that he had shared a recent mission with him in Crete. While it would appear that his ministry there was to be of fairly short duration, since Paul was anticipating joining him in Nicopolis, Titus was nevertheless assigned the tasks of setting up a regular ministry in every town on the island, as well as putting down false teaching in the church.

To Timothy Paul gave similar directions, though much of the apostle's correspondence in this case was occupied with directing admonitions to remain steadfast. The aging apostle longs to see the young man, and in his second letter pleads with him to come before winter sets in, bringing food for mind and soul and warm clothing against the biting chill of a Roman dungeon. Of the Second Epistle Bishop Moule confessed that he had difficulty in reading it "without finding something like a mist gathering in the eyes."

The First Epistle to
TIMOTHY

Topical Outline of First Timothy

Paul and Timothy (1:1-20)
> A Significant Salutation (1:1-2)
> A Reminder of a Former Charge (1:3-7)
> A Right Appraisal of the Law (1:8-11)
> A Typical Testimony to the Grace of God (1:12-17)
> A Reaffirmation of the Former Charge (1:18-20)

Congregational Worship and Order (2:1—4:15)
> The Worship of the Church (2:1-15)
> The Officers of the Church (3:1-13)
> The Character of the Church (3:14-16)
> The Threat to the Church (4:1-16)

Pastoral Administration and Behavior (5:1—6:2a)
> Relationships Within the Church Family (5:1-2)
> Responsibilities Within Church Families (5:3-16)
> Responsibilities Regarding Elders (5:17-25)
> Relations Between Slaves and Masters (6:1-2a)

A Final Miscellany (6:2b-21)
> Untruth and Its Consequences (6:2b-10)
> Faith and Its Challenges (6:11-12)
> Final Charges (6:13-19)
> A Closing Exhortation (6:20-21)

Paul and Timothy

1 Timothy 1:1-20

1 TIMOTHY 1

A Significant Salutation

1 Tim. 1:1-2

> 1 Paul, an apostle of Jesus Christ by the commandment of God our Saviour, and Lord Jesus Christ, which is our hope;
> 2 Unto Timothy, my own son in the faith: Grace, mercy, and peace, from God our Father and Jesus Christ our Lord.

One recent commentator has complained that the contents of this letter are "so haphazard and miscellaneous that no neat scheme will fit it."[1] Yet, while personal letters are not usually written with an eye to facilitating analysis, there is evidence of design in this salutation. As always with Paul, the common epistolary form is preserved, but within these opening verses one can discern details which anticipate certain of the matters with which the writer will later deal.

1. *The apostleship of the writer* (1). The fact that Paul should have begun such a personal letter to one who knew him so well with a reminder of his apostolic status suggests that it was intended also for public reading. And his unprecedented use of the phrase *an apostle of Jesus Christ by the commandment of God our Saviour* may well betray the fact that not everyone in the church accepted the genuineness of his apostleship, for while he usually based his apostolic standing upon the *will* of God, he here presents himself as having been "commissioned by royal command." (The word *epitagē* combines the ideas of royal authority and solemn responsibility. See J. N. D. Kelly.)

How essential is such a commission for any ambassador of Christ. It will not be so exalted as that which Paul enjoyed, but it must be divinely authenticated. Whenever Murray M'Cheyne passed the church door of "a certain self-appointed herald," he "raised his hand with vehemence as he spoke of the people left to perish under such an incumbent."

2. *The Saviorhood of God* (1). This reminder of God as Savior effectively guards against the almost pagan concept of propitiation presented by some who see Christ's death as the price exacted by a vengeful deity. One is not surprised that, after listening to a sermon in the course of which such an impression had been given, a child burst out to his parents, "I love Jesus, but I hate God!" But *God our Saviour* reveals how absolute was God's involvement at Calvary, so that Paul could say that "God was in Christ, reconciling the world unto himself" (2 Cor. 5:19), and he could preach about "the church of God, which he bought with his own blood" (Acts 20:28, NIV).

3. *The certainty in Christ; The Lord Jesus Christ, which is our hope* (1). Nowhere else among the Pauline salutations do we find such a description of Christ. Its inclusion here may reflect the aging apostle's keen expectation of his soon being ushered into the immediate presence of his blessed Lord, for *Christ Jesus our hope* (NEB) has distinct eschatological overtones, presenting Christ as both our present and our future Hope (see Col. 1:27; Rom. 8:18-24).

What a contrast to the prevailing pessimism of our day, conveyed in the words of T. S. Eliot,

> *This is the way the world ends,*
> *This is the way the world ends,*
> *Not with a bang but a whimper.*

And Paul's word for *hope* (Gk., *elpis*) speaks of much more than a wistful longing. Here is no plaintive hoping against hope but an absolute certainty.

4. *The relationship to the reader.* In addressing Timothy as "his trueborn son in the faith" (NEB), Paul is not only expressing the warmth of his affection, he is also underlining the genuineness of his young colleague's faith. It is not possible to say with certainty if Paul meant *in the faith* to refer to Timothy's loyalty to the truth, or to his faithfulness in the Lord (see 1 Cor. 4:17), though perhaps it is most likely that the reference is to the fact that through his faith he had been "begotten through the gospel" (see 1 Cor. 4:15). While it is customary to think of a "timorous Timothy," we can be sure from this word that, far from being a moral weakling, he was a credit both to his Heavenly Father and to his spiritual sire. However, it is interesting that only here and in 2 Tim. 1:2 has Paul inserted *mercy* in his opening salutation. This may be a pointer to Paul's continuing concern that God might strengthen him in his confrontation with the enemies of the truth.

A Reminder of a Former Charge

1 Tim. 1:3-7

> 3 As I besought thee to abide still at Ephesus, when I went into Macedonia, that thou mightest charge some that they teach no other doctrine,
> 4 Neither give heed to fables and endless genealogies, which minister questions, rather than godly edifying which is in faith: so do.
> 5 Now the end of the commandment is charity out of a pure heart, and of a good conscience, and of faith unfeigned:
> 6 From which some having swerved have turned aside unto vain jangling;
> 7 Desiring to be teachers of the law; understanding neither what they say, nor whereof they affirm.

This incident of Timothy's sojourn with Paul in Ephesus, broken by the latter's departure into Macedonia (3), cannot be placed either in Acts or the other Epistles. But those who would appeal to this as a reason for doubting the traditional authorship of this letter (see Introduction) should mark a typical Paulinism in the original of verse 3. For the apostle is so eager to remind Timothy of his former charge that he forgets to finish the sentence beginning *As I besought thee.* To help the reader, the translators of the KJV have inserted the words *so do* in verse 4, but Paul does not actually take up the thread of his sentence again until 1:18. "This eager breathlessness of a writer who is too absorbed in the matter to remember the grammar is a mark of Paul's style."[2] The matter in question includes some specific reminders to Timothy:

1. *To prevent the spread of heresy* (3-4). Paul's earlier fears that unorthodox teachers would infiltrate the Ephesian church had, unfortunately, not been unfounded (Acts 20:29-30). Now the strength of the apostle's feelings may be gauged by his use of the word *charge,* a military term meaning "to give strict orders," hence "You were to command certain persons" (3, NEB). Some scholars have seen in this a further indication of non-Pauline authorship. They have protested that such a hard-line attitude toward heterodoxy could not be attributed to one who frankly confessed his inability to fully comprehend divine truth (Rom. 11:33). Admittedly, none could question Paul's intellectual modesty. He would certainly have stood with the one who acknowledged that the longer the shoreline of knowledge, the vaster the ocean of mystery. But when a theological student declared that the Christian concept of truth must always have a mystery at its heart, a wiser than he retorted, "No. The Christian concept of truth has always had a mystery at its circumference, but at its heart is the face of Jesus Christ." That was Paul's own conviction (2 Tim. 1:12). Nevertheless, he was not so naive as to imagine that one can enjoy a clear vision of Christ without holding the true doctrine of Christ, hence his forthright pronouncement, here and elsewhere (see 2 Cor. 11:3-4; Gal. 1:6-12).

In spite of the contrary view of certain critics, there is nothing in verse 4, or elsewhere in the Pastorals, to suggest that the heresies in question were part of the full-blown Gnostic system of the second century, rather do Paul's words imply "a clutter of endless lists and names." In this connection J. N. D. Kelly has given a revealing summary in which he points out, first: the Gnostic system of aeons were never, so far as we know, called genealogies; secondly: had he had them in mind, we should have expected the writer to go more fully into their content instead of being satisfied with a passing, imprecise allusion; thirdly: we should also have expected a much sharper, more far-reaching criticism than that they had encouraged idle speculation and contentiousness; finally: the fables are expressly labelled "Jewish."[3]

Incidentally, while the Bultmannian scholars would persuade us that the New Testament writers were creating myths, Paul was bent on exploding them. He was the original demythologizer!

2. *To promote the cause of charity* (5-7). "The aim of our charge is love" (RSV). "The ultimate aim of the Christian ministry, after all . . . is love" (Phillips). Love is the goal Paul wants his spiritual son to keep constantly in view, for only thus will he be able to counteract the spirit of contentiousness being fomented by the false teachers. But the apostle discloses that this divine fruit springs from a threefold root, a pure heart, a good conscience, and a sincere faith. This at once identifies it as something special. There is nothing sensual about this love, no hint of "the coarse muck of careless passion." There is nothing cheaply sentimental about it. One unkind critic has remarked about "the Church's ability to say nothing beautifully," and this has sometimes been all too obvious when she has uttered her homilies on "love." But this love is the very nature of God shed abroad by His Spirit in the heart (Rom. 5:5). It springs from—

a. A pure heart, a heart undivided in its allegiance. This is one meaning of *pure*. As Dr. Barclay has pointed out, this word was used of "an army which has been sifted and purified of all cowardly and undisciplined soldiers until there is nothing left but first-class fighting men."[4]

b. A good conscience, a conscience uncompromising in its obedience, for only thus am I conscience-free, and only as I am conscience-free can my words awaken and liberate the consciences of others. Emerson once said of Seneca that "he said the loveliest things if only he'd had the right to say them."

c. *A sincere faith,* a faith unblemished by pretence. One reason why some have failed to enter into the blessing of perfect love is that they have not realized that "faith is something more than belief in spite of the lack of evidence, it is obedience in scorn of consequence." Any lesser faith is liable to be shot through with shame.

3. *The futility of heresy* (6-7). Paul seems less concerned about the falsity of heresy than about its futility. Perhaps no one has better described the sheer vanity of the false doctrine being peddled in Ephesus than William Barclay. Here is a resume of what he has to say about the Ephesian heretic: *(a)* He was driven by a desire for novelty. To him religion was a fashion, hence old truths were despised merely because they were old. *(b)* He exalted the mind at the expense of the heart. To him religion was speculation and not experience. *(c)* He dealt in argument instead of action. To him religion was an exercise in mental acrobatics. *(d)* He was moved by arrogance rather than by humility. He was eager to teach but loth to learn. *(e)* He was guilty of dogmatism without knowledge. He sought to blind with science, falsely so-called.[5]

This last heretical pretence had to do with the law (7), so that Paul finds it necessary to deal with this subject.

A Right Appraisal of the Law

1 Tim. 1:8-11

> 8 But we know that the law is good, if a man use it lawfully;
> 9 Knowing this, that the law is not made for a righteous man, but for the lawless and disobedient, for the ungodly and for sinners, for unholy and profane, for murderers of fathers and murderers of mothers, for manslayers,
> 10 For whoremongers, for them that defile themselves with mankind, for menstealers, for liars, for perjured persons, and if there be any other thing that is contrary to sound doctrine;
> 11 According to the glorious gospel of the blessed God, which was committed to my trust.

While Timothy was exhorted to take summary action against those who were making a travesty of law, he was not to "throw out the baby with the bathwater." The very fact that the concept of law had been so corrupted by the self-styled teachers was sufficient to prompt Paul to spring to the defence of the law, properly so-called and justly applied.

1. *The restraint of law upon the wicked* (8-10). While Paul's was essentially the gospel of grace, he would permit no denigration of the law (8; see also Rom. 7:12, 14). According to his teaching, *(a) The ministry of law precedes salvation by grace,* for without the law there is no knowledge of sin (Rom. 7:7). As the old Puritan said, "The crimson thread of the Gospel is attached to the sharp needle of the law." *(b) The ministry of law renders grace indispensable.* It shuts up men to faith and leads men to Christ (Gal. 3:22-24). *(c) The purpose of grace is the fulfilment of the law.* See Rom. 8:3-4 and Titus 2:11. Compare Gal. 2:17-18. *(d) The power of grace makes the law redundant.* See Gal. 5:13-14, 18. The Ten Words of the Decalogue are fulfilled in the one word, LOVE. Hence Paul can write that the law is not made for the righteous man.

However, this is vastly different from the notion expressed by such as John Robinson who considers that contemporary man, having "come of age" morally, no longer has need of a moral law which "comes direct from heaven."[6] A mere glance at verses 9-10, especially in a modern version, will provide a grim reminder of how deplorably lacking in any real progress is our "morally adult" generation. In this verse 9 Paul goes on to say that the law is made for *the lawless and disobedient,* and the Christian still believes that such restraint needs to be imposed. To some the list of sins catalogued in verses 9-10 may seem to be unnecessarily shocking, but not to those with eyes to see and read. As Sir Frederick Catherwood puts it, "We live in what is known as a permissive society, but we are now finding that permissiveness is indivisible. We cannot have permissiveness in sex and expect that we will not also have permissiveness in violence, or in tax avoidance, or in corruption and bribery in high places. People today want permissiveness in the bedroom, but not in the board room. . . . If we promote permissiveness where we want it, we will find permissiveness where we do not want it."[7]

2. *The relation of law to the gospel* (10-11). Donald Guthrie says, "Paul has been speaking of law not according to his own opinion but *according to* the Gospel."[8] That gospel, far from giving the believer liberty to break the law, gives him liberty in keeping it. J. N. D. Anderson has justly observed that "Christ . . . offers a salvation unequivocally based on grace, not morality, which is wide open to the most debased of men, and need only be accepted by the empty hand of faith; but he also calls his disciples to the highest standard of ethical living—and makes available to them a supernatural grace which, alone, can enable them to respond."[9]

A Typical Testimony to the Grace of God

1 Tim. 1:12-17

> 12 And I thank Christ Jesus our Lord, who hath enabled me, for that he counted me faithful, putting me into the ministry;
> 13 Who was before a blasphemer, and a persecutor, and injurious: but I obtained mercy, because I did it ignorantly in unbelief.
> 14 And the grace of our Lord was exceeding abundant with faith and love which is in Christ Jesus.
> 15 This is a faithful saying, and worthy of all acceptation, that Christ Jesus came into the world to save sinners; of whom I am chief.
> 16 Howbeit for this cause I obtained mercy, that in me first Jesus Christ might shew forth all longsuffering, for a pattern to them which should hereafter believe on him to life everlasting.
> 17 Now unto the King eternal, immortal, invisible, the only wise God, be honour and glory for ever and ever. Amen.

Paul would have been greatly puzzled by the attitude of those who, frowning upon the preacher if he makes reference in the course of his sermon to his own personal experience, consider this to be a breach of pulpit etiquette. In the apostle's heart the springs of "wonder, love, and praise" lay so near the surface that the mere mention of the gospel of glory was enough to precipitate this outburst of testimony. However, spontaneous as it was, it is a model of its kind.

1. *It emphasizes the grace of God* (12-14). It speaks of that grace not only as unmerited favor towards the undeserving but enabling power towards the impotent (12). Glover once said that he didn't give tuppence for the man who went into the pulpit just to tell him what his duty was, but he would give all he had to anyone who told him from whence the power came to do it. In typical fashion Paul shows that "where sin abounded, grace did much more abound" (13-14). Commenting on verses 12 to 14, Hendriksen has said, "Grace is ever the *root,* faith and love are the *trunk,* and good works are the *fruit* of the tree of salvation."[10] But E. F. Brown has seen this phrase, *with faith and love which is in Christ Jesus,* from a different angle.

Barclay writes, "[He] suggests that the meaning is this—that the work of the grace of Christ in Paul's heart was helped and supported by the faith and love he found in the members of the Christian Church; that the effect of the grace of Christ was aided by the sympathy . . . understanding and kindness he received from men like Ananias, who opened his eyes and who called him brother (Acts 9:10-19), and like Barnabas, who stood by him when the rest of the Church regarded him with bleak suspicion (Acts 9:26-28)."[11] How very often in testimony we are given such glimpses of the human channels through whom the grace of God has flowed.

2. *It exercises the ministry of memory* (13). Memory has power to burn as well as to bless, and we may gather from this verse something of the degree to which Paul's soul had been scorched by the recollection of his sins. The words *blasphemer . . . persecutor . . . injurious* form an ascending scale of sins, and the last word is far stronger than the translation implies, for *hubristēs* denotes a violent, insolent person. Yet upon such an one mercy had been bestowed so that, by the grace of God, burning was transmuted into blessing. And it is essential that faith

should so prove the power of grace, for it is possible to allow memory's burnings to lead to unhealthy consequences. E. F. Scott has misunderstood Paul when he considers that his "self-abasement is morbid and unreal."[12] But the one who described memory as a "crazy witch who stores her sticks and stones and throws her jewels out of the window" knew what he was writing about. One has listened to testimonies which have included references to preconversion experiences that should never have been uttered in public and which would be far better committed fully and forever to the One who has promised to remember them no more. Nevertheless, if memory be given her *perfect* way in testimony, it can prove not only a blessing to the testifier but a source of encouragement to the listener. Moreover, it can serve as a safeguard against the sin which the saint had in mind when he prayed, "Lord, keep forever green in my heart the memory of Thy Calvary, lest I should sin against Thee by taking Thy grace for granted."

3. *It is based upon a sound theology* (15). A convincing testimony must be more than truthful biographically, it must also be truthful theologically. This does not mean that one needs to be a theologian in order to be a true witness, but Paul's testimony serves as a model because it was built upon Christ, upon the Person He was, the way in which He came, and the work that He did. As most commentators point out, verse 15 is the first of five "trustworthy sayings," all of which are found in the Pastorals (see also 1 Tim. 3:1; 4:8-9; 2 Tim. 2:11-13; Titus 3:4-8). These are theological "capsules" fashioned out of the truth of the time so that second-generation Christians might receive inspired truth in succinct and accurate form. Paul's selection of this particular "capsule" is most fitting; and it is most unfortunate that, in commenting upon it, some should have done despite to the Christ to whom it refers by suggesting that His salvation had left Paul virtually unsaved.

Daniel Steele wrote, "Our readers may be surprised to

learn that Paul the aged, in the fulness of his faith and love and professed holiness (1 Thess. 2:10), was, at the time he was writing this epistle, actually out-sinning all the sinners on the earth. This is the interpretation of some who search the Scriptures with the microscope to find proofs that sin must continue in the heart and crop out in the daily life of the best Christian so long as he is in the body."[13] J. N. D. Kelly has struck the right note as he comments on this verse, "Paul . . . regards himself . . . rather as having the status of sinner-redeemed, dedicated to an ever deeper penitence and service."[14] In this connection the place of penitence in the life of the believer should not be overlooked, for "an attitude of penitence is appropriate to anyone who has been redeemed from sin. One remembers in gratitude his deliverance and looks upon present limitations and faults with regret, praying both to be forgiven any possible trespass and to be given grace to become a finer, better child of God."[15]

4. *It provides for continuity* (16-17). Of the word *pattern* (Gk., *hupotupōsis*), Scott has said, "Before attempting his final work, an artist or author prepares a sketch in which he tries to indicate his main idea. So Christ, the great artist of noble lives, had used Paul for His experiment; by His mercy to this wicked man He showed what might be made of unpromising material."[16]

Personal testimony is obligatory if, from one generation to another, men are to witness the grace and power of God in redeemed human lives. However humble it may sound, when a person protests, "I don't believe in spoken testimony, I just let my life speak," he is betraying spiritual pride at its worst. Paul, great apostle though he was, did not consider his deeds so perfect and explicit that he did not need to witness by word. The truth is that the gospel has never been effectively spread by keeping silence, and "Let the redeemed of the Lord say so" was never more relevant than now, with unbelief so eloquent and arrogant.

So, this pattern testimony is climaxed by a typical Pauline doxology (17).

The Reaffirmation of the Former Charge

1 Tim. 1:18-20

> 18 This charge I commit unto thee, son Timothy, according to the prophecies which went before on thee, that thou by them mightest war a good warfare;
> 19 Holding faith, and a good conscience; which some having put away concerning faith have made shipwreck:
> 20 Of whom is Hymenaeus and Alexander; whom I have delivered unto Satan, that they may learn not to blaspheme.

After his long digression Paul takes up again the matter of the charge.

1. *The origin of the charge* (18). Paul acknowledges that, as Timothy's superior officer, he had only communicated a charge which had originated at a higher level, *according to the prophecies which went before on thee.* Opinion is divided as to the incident of which Paul was thinking. The NEB has "that prophetical utterance which first pointed you out to me," and there would appear to be some scriptural warrant for this interpretation in Acts 13:1-3, where such a procedure was followed leading up Barnabas and Paul being sent forth. However, since there is no record of similar action connected with Paul's choice of Timothy, and especially in the light of 4:14 and 2 Tim. 1:6, it would seem better to assume that the phrase refers to his ordination.

2. *The essential equipment: Faith and a good conscience* (19a). These items of spiritual equipment are particularly fitted to the needs of Timothy in his present situation (see also 1:5 and 3:9), and they are certainly fitted each to the other, for there must always be the closest connection between religion and morality. "More often than we know, religious error has its roots in moral rather than intellectual causes."[17] The verb *put away* implies a violent, deliberate spurning of conscience and accounts for the fact that the Ephesian errorists had gone hopelessly astray.

3. *The inevitable alternative* (19b-20). If anything, this switch in metaphor adds to the force of Paul's warning, for

Walter Lock has aptly remarked that the Christian teacher must be a good sailor as well as a good soldier! Maybe we are meant to deduce that if faith is the vessel, conscience must be the rudder; but however we may apply the analogy, the lesson is plain—let conscience be spurned and faith is doomed. So proved Hymenaeus and Alexander. While the former is again mentioned in 2 Tim. 2:17, we cannot be certain as to the identity of Alexander. Nor can we be sure as to the precise nature of the discipline imposed upon these misguided men. Comparison with Paul's use of a similar formula in 1 Cor. 5:5 would suggest that the purpose was remedial rather than merely punitive, but it is obvious that the process was severe in the extreme. Nonetheless, if church history is anything to go by, the decline and now virtual disappearance of discipline has done nothing to help her influence. Too often the Church has been so ready to be made all things to everybody that she has failed to mean anything to anybody.

Congregational Worship and Order
1 Timothy 2:1—4:16

1 TIMOTHY 2

The Worship of the Church

1 Tim. 2:1-15

> 1 I exhort therefore, that, first of all, supplications, prayers, intercessions, and giving of thanks, be made for all men;
> 2 For kings, and for all that are in authority; that we may lead a quiet and peaceable life in all godliness and honesty.
> 3 For this is good and acceptable in the sight of God our Saviour;
> 4 Who will have all men to be saved, and to come unto the knowledge of the truth.
> 5 For there is one God, and one mediator between God and men, the man Christ Jesus;
> 6 Who gave himself a ransom for all, to be testified in due time.
> 7 Whereunto I am ordained a preacher, and an apostle, (I speak the truth in Christ, and lie not;) a teacher of the Gentiles in faith and verity.
> 8 I will therefore that men pray every where, lifting up holy hands, without wrath and doubting.

> 9 In like manner also, that women adorn themselves in modest apparel, with shamefacedness and sobriety; not with broided hair, or gold, or pearls, or costly array.
> 10 But (which becometh women professing godliness) with good works.
> 11 Let the woman learn in silence with all subjection.
> 12 But I suffer not a woman to teach, nor to usurp authority over the man, but to be in silence.
> 13 For Adam was first formed, then Eve.
> 14 And Adam was not deceived, but the woman being deceived was in the transgression.
> 15 Notwithstanding she shall be saved in childbearing, if they continue in faith and charity and holiness with sobriety.

It is not until later that Paul states explicitly the main purpose of this letter, "I am writing you these instructions so that, if I am delayed, you will know how people ought to conduct themselves in God's household, which is the church of the living God" (3:14-15, NIV). But with the first verse of this chapter we see the Epistle beginning to take on its true pastoral character. Its personal significance is never lost sight of, but it now assumes a relevance to the needs of generations of Christians yet unborn. "Throughout the history of the Church these Epistles have been used to instruct the ministers of Christ in their duties and demeanour, and have been invaluable in providing a pattern of practical behaviour."[18]

1. *The primacy of prayer* (1). Far too frequently, in determining congregational priorities today, prayer is treated as the "Cinderella of the ministries." This was demonstrated many years ago when Dr. Andrew Murray, himself one of the great intercessors of the century, was addressing a large gathering of Christians. He asked how many of those present spent half an hour a day in prayer. Only one hand was raised. He halved the period and about half of the company responded. When he reduced the period to five minutes, every hand was raised, but after the meeting was over one man sought out Dr. Murray and confessed that he wasn't sure if he spent even five minutes a day in prayer. There is no reason to believe that the situation has improved in the past 50 years. Significantly, Paul placed prayer first, and in the very variety of terms he

used to describe it we are given an indication of the value he attached to it. While to some extent the terms overlap, their order reveals a gradation of thought. *Supplications* refer to asking in the most elementary sense, for

> *Prayer is the simplest form of speech*
> *That infant lips can try.*

However, within this primary word there inheres the spirit of urgency and persistency. *Prayers* is the more familiar term and relates our asking to God exclusively, while *intercessions* adds the thought of petitioning a superior. *Giving of thanks* is a feature too often lacking in prayer. When a little boy was asked if he prayed every night, he answered, "No, sir, not every night. Some nights I don't want anything!" But here thanksgiving is shown to be, not additional to, but an essential of prayer.

2. *The province of prayer* (2). One of Paul's main concerns was to draw Timothy's attention to the universal outreach of prayer. It must embrace all men, with particular reference to those in high places, this latter emphasis probably arising from the believers' dilemma as to praying for rulers openly hostile to Christianity. This problem still persists, and in very aggravated forms in certain countries; yet, in the main, the Church has followed the New Testament in encouraging prayer for the civil power. However, some churches have helped to finance terrorist organizations opposed to regimes who practise racial discrimination, and Dietrich Bonhoeffer's execution in the closing days of the Second World War was the result of his part in a plot on Hitler's life.[19] This Christian pastor sincerely believed that Hitler was so evil, and "so deeply stained with innocent blood, that he had no option but to participate in a plot to destroy him."

While Bonhoeffer's case aroused considerable sympathy, there can be no doubt as to the position the New Testament takes, not only in the light of these verses, but according to Rom. 13:3 and 1 Pet. 2:13-17. As Simpson has said, "The supplication of faithful intercessors for the commonweal lays invisible restraint on the powers of darkness and their tools and brings reinforcement to honest rulers from the Governor among the nations (Ps. 22:28)."[20] But surely the world situation today lays an almost irresistible constraint upon every Christian to obey the apostle's admonition. Well may the poet write,

> Prayer is no longer a theme for eloquence,
> or a way of life for a few to choose
> whose hearts can desire it.
> It is the sternest ncessity.[21]

3. *The propriety of prayer* (2b-3). "Such prayer is right" (3a, NEB). And it is right for two reasons: *(a)* "that we may live peaceful and quiet lives in all godliness and holiness (2b, NIV). This accent upon a life of settled piety may sound strange coming from one who had endured much more than his share of storm and riot in the course of preaching the gospel, until we note his second reason *(b)* for demanding that such intercessions be made, "This is good and pleases God our Saviour who wants all men to be saved and to come to a knowledge of the truth" (3, NIV). The apostle's concern was not so much because he wished that he and his readers might enjoy freedom to practise their religion without disturbance, but because he knew full well that, in the ordinary course, missionary advance and consolidation depend considerably upon continuity of civil rule and at least a measure of political stability.

4. *The provisions of the atonement* (4-8)

a. The universality of God's saving purpose (4-6a). While this passage is parenthetical, it is in no sense a digression, for it is the theological consequence of Paul's universal emphasis (see *all* in vv. 1, 4, 6). As Donald Guthrie has stated, "Intercession for all men could be justified only on the ground of God's willingness to save all (cf Jeremias)."[22] Notwithstanding, many and varied have been the arguments employed to restrict the application of this universal purpose. In order to escape the force of the *all,* Calvin and his followers have interpreted the word as referring to "men of all kinds." "This is the way in which a theory colours a truth,"[23] rightly observes R. F. Horton, though with equal justification he continues, "an equally striking example, however, of the same fact is found in the dogmatic use which universalists make of this text. The will of God does not override the will of man."[24]

b. ˙ *The unity of God's person* (5). *There is one God.* With the conjunction *for* Paul links this verse with the preceding, thus making the unity of God a basis of his argument for the universality of the gospel. He pursues a similar line of reasoning in Rom. 3:29-30, where he declares that there are neither two Gods nor two means of salvation. God is the God of all, and He has purposed, by one means, to save all. *There is one mediator between God and man, the man Christ Jesus.* This excluded, on the one hand, traditional Jewish ideas as to the mediatorship of Moses (Gal. 3:19), or of angels (Heb. 2:6ff.); and on the other hand it denied any plurality of mediatorship. This might have been implicit even in the incipient Gnosticism of the period. "The unity of God is asserted to show that there is only one God of all men. . . . The unity of the mediator is asserted to show that there can be no other way to God (Jn. 14:6), but also that there is a way for all."[25]

c. The punctuality of God's purpose (6b-7). "So providing, at the fitting time, proof of the divine purpose" (6b, NEB). Though the wording of the original is obscure, it appears to echo the thought of Paul in Rom. 5:6 and Gal. 4:4. "What Paul is saying is that, by dying for all mankind in accordance with the divine plan, Christ has borne overwhelmingly convincing witness to God's desire for the salvation of all men."[26] In view of these foregoing proofs of God's universal purpose of salvation, Paul has emphatically reaffirmed his authority as a "herald and an apostle" (7, NIV). His commission to proclaim the gospel to all men was in marked contrast to the exclusivist doctrines of the false teachers. Nevertheless, he concludes this section by reminding his readers of the need for

d. The purity of the pray-er (8). In the work of evangelization, as preaching and prayer must go together, so must prayer and purity. "As other religions demanded a ritual purity as the condition of approach to God, so Christianity required a moral purity. . . . The hands must be pure, and the heart likewise, *from anger and dissension* (Moffatt)."[27]

5. *The piety and place of Christian womanhood* (9-15). While the teaching in this section may appear incongruous to some in the light of contemporary attitudes, account should be taken of the historical framework within which the apostle's directions were given. Barclay's enlightening comments are well worth reading on this point. Having said this, those who imagine that the sponsors of extreme "women's liberation" have the monopoly of wisdom would do well to ponder Hanson's comment that "the modern conventions which govern women's place in society have still to be proved superior to the old ones. We have not yet had time to see the full effects of the change."[28]

In any event, a scripturally balanced view of Paul's words presents truth that we can ill afford to neglect. In this respect the phrase in verse 9, *In like manner also,* can hardly be taken to mean that the ensuing directions as to women's dress and demeanor were to apply only to public worship. It is far more likely that Paul was legislating for behavior in general, including conduct in God's house. The directions themselves apply mainly to two matters. First, to women's adornment and, secondly, to her place in relation to man. The statement subsidiary to this latter (15) contains an obscure reference linking salvation and motherhood.

a. Concerning female adornment (9-10). There is nothing in Paul's words, here or elsewhere, to excuse slovenliness in dress, or to suggest that, as in some other religions, women by their dress should seek to obliterate evidences of their God-given grace and beauty. But the apostle does insist that Christian women must not dress so as to unchastely accentuate, much less exploit, their physical charms. They are to "dress modestly, with decency and propriety" (9, NIV). Moreover, female extravagance in dress and ornamentation is deplored, especially the elaborate and expensive braiding and embellishment of the hair which, in New Testament times, was far in excess of anything commonly known today. However, pride of dress can assume many and subtle forms. This was witnessed in the manufacture and wearing of the superb and costly Quaker lace which was worn as part of the "modest" dress of some women of that sect a century or so ago. The writer was astute enough to appreciate that while clothes do not make the man, or woman, they do give a fair indication of the character of the wearers. So it was that he laid such emphasis upon what some have reckoned to be of relative unimportance, if not an unwonted male intrusion into a purely feminine sphere.

b. Concerning sexual adjustments (11-15). These verses quite evidently reflect local coloring. In the church at Corinth also there were signs that woman's newfound freedom in Christ had run to excess, and this would be particularly objectionable in Greek society in which the female sex occupied a very low place. What is more, as Guthrie observes, "The entire subjection . . . mentioned by Paul relates primarily to public worship as it was then enacted, and reserve must be exercised in deducing universal principles from particular cases."[29]

That Paul had already modified the rigid Jewish attitudes towards the place of women in public worship is evident from 1 Cor. 11:5, and he warmly and repeatedly acknowledged his indebtedness to women as his fellow laborers in the gospel. Yet he refused to allow the woman to "lord it" over the man (1 Cor. 11:3; Eph. 5:22-25), and verse 13 is the expression of his biblical warrant, leading to the comment that "God created everything 'after his kind,' and men and women with different functions and attributes. There is a functional balance which must not be upset. The tendency to equate women and men in every way upsets that balance. Men and women are equal before God, but they have functional differences in the family order and in the social order. To confuse them by treating the differences as though they did not exist is to throw a wholly unnecessary strain on the individuals, the family and society."[30] Paul would have totally abhorred the "unisex image" so prevalent today.

In tracing biblical authority back to creation, the apostle is again pursuing a line already taken (1 Cor. 11:9). As regards his application in verse 14, *The Expositor's Greek Testament* has made this ingenious comment: "Eve's reasoning faculty was overcome by the allegation of jealousy felt by God, an allegation plausible to a nature swayed by emotion rather than by reflection."[31] This observation may not find favor with the modern Eve, but it seems to be a fair assessment of Paul's view.

In a more general sense Paul's teaching in this section is clear, namely, that he treated Adam and Eve as historical figures. In referring to Eve's having been deceived, he by no means qualified Adam's guilt (see Rom. 5:12 ff.) and, according to Gal. 3:28 and elsewhere, he confirmed the Christian status of women.

Commentators have proposed a number of alternative exegeses in the case of verse 15, but E. M. Blaiklock's preference seems the most tenable and truest to the context: "The simpler explanation is better—the thought that woman's noblest and finest fulfillment is motherhood and all that it implies. In the carrying out of this function she escapes much of the stress of temptation, the drag of society, and its corruption, and the wear and damaging burden of public life."[32]

The Officers of the Church

1 Tim. 3:1-13

1 This is a true saying, If a man desire the office of a bishop, he desireth a good work.

2 A bishop then must be blameless, the husband of one wife, vigilant, sober, of good behaviour, given to hospitality, apt to teach;

3 Not given to wine, no striker, not greedy of filthy lucre; but patient, not a brawler, not covetous;

4 One that ruleth well his own house, having his children in subjection with all gravity;

5 (For if a man know not how to rule his own house, how shall he take care of the church of God?)

6 Not a novice, lest being lifted up with pride he fall into the condemnation of the devil.

7 Moreover he must have a good report of them which are without; lest he fall into reproach and the snare of the devil.

8 Likewise must the deacons be grave, not doubletongued, not given to much wine, not greedy of filthy lucre;

9 Holding the mystery of the faith in a pure conscience.

10 And let these also first be proved; then let them use the office of a deacon, being found blameless.

11 Even so must their wives be grave, not slanderers, sober, faithful in all things.

12 Let the deacons be the husbands of one wife, ruling their children and their own houses well.

13 For they that have used the office of a deacon well purchase to themselves a good degree, and great boldness in the faith which is in Christ Jesus.

1. *The office of overseer* (1-7). Translators and editors have gone to some lengths arguing whether *This is a true saying* qualifies as one of the "trustworthy sayings" in which important elements of the faith were to be handed down from one generation to another (cf. 1:15) and, if it is, whether it should be referred back to 2:15 or forward to the subject of this chapter. In regard to the first point there should be little reasonable doubt, for while both Moffatt and the NEB prefer "a popular saying," almost all the Greek and Latin manuscripts render the phrase as a "faithful, sure saying." As to its proper context, while neither 2:15 nor the verses immediately preceding contain maxims likely to have been current in the primitive Church, 3:1*b* bears the marks of a proverbial saying and it

certainly introduces a matter of great importance to the Church of the period.

One curious criticism of verse 1, as it stands in the KJV, is that it amounts to an incitement to carnal ambition! But this is surely to misunderstand the prevailing situation. Considering that the bishop, or overseer, was likely to be viewed as the ringleader of a proscribed sect, as well as the chairman of a prohibited gathering, his would be a most vulnerable position during times of persecution. Oversight of the Church in Timothy's day was hardly calculated to appeal to one whose chief motivation was an itch for office. Indeed, reading between the lines, one gains the impression that there was no surplus of candidates for this position.

a. The nature of the office (1). Some have seen in *the office of a bishop* an authentication of rule by a single bishop, but in the use of the singular, "All that is meant is 'the typical bishop'—just as we speak of 'the solder,' 'the physician.'"[33] Nor was the office "episcopal" in the popular, modern sense of that word. "The modern word *bishop* does not represent the Greek word *episkopos,* which properly means 'overseer.' . . . In the proverbial saying in this verse, the office referred to is quite general and might encompass any position, secular or ecclesiastical, where 'oversight' was necessary."[34]

One may well ask how the word "bishop" came to acquire its present meaning, and to answer this question calls for a brief survey of the evolution of the episcopal office. Without question, in the Church of this period the titles "bishop" and "elder" *(presbuteros)* were synonymous. In Titus 1:5-9 these words are used interchangeably, and a comparison of 1 Tim. 3:2-7 with Titus 1:6-9 shows that the qualifications of bishop and elder were virtually identical. As Barclay says, the word "elder" describes the *man,* as an older or respected member of the community; "bishop" describes the *function of the man* in his oversight and superintendence of the work of the Church.[35]

It is the functional aspect that suggests what lay behind the gradual ascendancy of the office of the bishop for, inevitably, a group of elders in a given area would require someone to preside at their meetings. Consequently, an elder who gave evidence of marked ability in this respect came to be called, in a particular sense, the *episkopos,* though, as Barclay further observes, "he was simply a leader among equals."[36] Originally, then, there was no thought of such an *episkopos* arrogating to himself hierarchical precedence and privilege, so that our passage does not have in view a "mitred, aproned, gaitered ecclesiastic," but those who would occupy the place of leadership within the local church and would exercise, more particularly, a pastoral responsibility.

b. The qualifications for the office (2-7). Since "to aspire to leadership is an honourable ambition," (NEB), he who would exercise it must be a man of personal excellence. "There are some things which a merciful God will forgive in a man which the Church can never forgive in its ministry."[37] This is said not to justify a double standard; it is simply laying the emphasis where Paul laid it, that is, upon the necessity for the Church to exercise scrupulous care in selecting none but men of unexceptionable moral and spiritual calibre to lead it.

Such blamelessness covers a multitude of virtues. Against the background of general sexual licence it is not surprising that an unblemished marital relationship should rank so highly, though it is difficult to determine what the precise requirement was. Literally, *the husband of one wife* means "the man of one woman." This could amount to a directive against adultery or polygamy, or it could simply stipulate that the overseer must be a married man. But as is indicated in a footnote in the NEB, it may also mean that a candidate for this office must have *married only once* and since, in New Testament times, to remain unmarried after the death of one's spouse was considered most commendable, this may well have been the meaning intended. In any case, the dominant idea was "monogamous fidelity." The second feature of blamelessness is not vigilance, as in the KJV, but "temperateness" (RSV and NIV), and the NIV has also well rendered the four following virtues as, "self-controlled, respectable, hospitable, able to teach."

To the modern reader it may seem strange that qualities such as those in verse 3 should need to have been listed until he remembers that those to whom this letter was written had recently come out of, and probably still had close contact with, a pagan environment. For instance, we know that some in the church in another Greek city, Corinth, had been guilty of drunkenness at the Lord's Table. For a fuller discussion on wine and the Christian see at 5:23.

The Christian leader was to be *no striker,* and here Blaiklock thinks that probably Paul had the treatment of slaves in mind. The meaning of the next stipulation is perfectly clear, *not greedy of filthy lucre;* for unless a man is free from covetousness, he can neither cope with possible financial stringency, nor can he be trusted with financial responsibility. Far from being a *brawler,* a contentious man, the overseer must be *patient.* Kelly translates the word "magnanimous" suggesting that spirit of gracious forbearance in which the pastor should deal with the most recalcitrant.

Moving from the person to the family, Paul requires that the home of the overseer be a model of domestic governance (4-5). This is understandable for no man can presume to lead the wider family of the church if his own home is in disarray. But the exercise of family discipline does not imply undue harshness on the part of the parent. *Having his children in subjection with all gravity* (4) means that filial submission was to be won rather than severely enforced. In such ways is the family at home to be a sort of microcosm of the family in church.

Now reverting to more personal matters, Paul demands that the overseer be a man of mature experience (6). Scott sees in this "an unguarded admission that the

Pastorals are considerably later than the time of Paul";[38] but this does not necessarily follow, for, as Guthrie has pointed out, in a church as large as Ephesus, with a constant flow of converts, a few years would suffice to provide many members of relative maturity. It is significant that this requirement is absent from a similar list of directions given through Titus to a church newly founded. Perhaps no stipulation was more called for. Too many instances could be quoted where new converts have been encouraged to accept positions of responsibility while still virtual infants in grace.

Horton, commenting on the phrase *lifted up with pride,* declares that the Greek word *tuphoō* means literally "to wrap up in smoke," and suggests that a new convert, thrust into a position of some eminence, would be likely to find himself "in a cloudland of conceit"[39] from whence he would be in danger of proving that "the higher they ride the harder they fall."

Finally, Paul insists that the candidate for spiritual leadership must be a man of general acceptance (7). While Jesus warned His followers to beware when all men spoke well of them, this should not be interpreted as a reason for the Christian leader adopting a cavalier attitude towards the opinion of those outside.

Paul frequently impressed upon his readers the importance of safeguarding their reputation among outsiders (see 1 Cor. 10:32; Phil. 2:15; Col. 4:5; 1 Thess. 4:12). This is particularly necessary where the pastor is concerned, for very often the world will judge the church in the light of his conduct. Hence "he must . . . have a good reputation with the non-Christian public, so that he may not be exposed to scandal and get caught in the devil's snare" (NEB).

2. *The office of deacon* (8-13).

a. The nature of the office. The origin of a formal order of deacons is somewhat obscure for, while the Seven, in Acts 6, were appointed to exercise diaconal functions, they are nowhere given the title of "deacons." In fact, in this same chapter, the Twelve are described as exercising the ministry *(diakonia)* of the Word. This is because, in the broad sense, any servant of Christ can rightly be called a "deacon," indeed Christ applied this title to himself, and in the lowliest sense (Luke 22:27).

Nevertheless, it seems fairly certain that the division of responsibilities between the Apostles and the Seven, already referred to, came to be looked upon as a precedent for the subsequent development of the diaconate (see Phil. 1:1.). When due allowance is made for the various denominational evolutions of this office, one basic fact remains, namely, that originally its significance did not reside in the institution of an order so much as in the delegation of administrative and charitable responsibilities to those who gave evidence of the requisite character, gifts, and abilities. This was so in the church at Ephesus.

b. The qualifications for the office (8-13). These were similar to those demanded of the elder, with one or two important differences. The deacon was not to be *double-tongued,* that is, saying one thing to one person and something different to another. Consistency in speech is of great importance to one whose ministry takes him from house to house. It was probably because the ministry of the deacon frequently involved him in house calling, so offering a strong temptation to a man with a weakness for wine and a greed for gain, that the sternest of warnings against these evils was given.

Most important among the special requirements of the diaconate was that mentioned in v. 9, *Holding the mystery of faith in a pure conscience.* This demanded that the deacons be men "not merely of practical acumen but also of spiritual conviction."[40] The NEB has given a good sense of the original, "They must be men who combine a clear conscience with a firm hold on the deep truths of our faith." Paul was concerned that when the deacon spoke of God, and the things of God, what he said should have its fair share of what Thomas Aquinas called "intelligible light."

The Church is still in great need of men who can express clearly and convincingly what they believe. Paul insisted also that the character of the deacon, no less than that of the overseer, should stand up to the closest scrutiny. It has been suggested that the apostle had a probationary period in mind; but if we are to take Acts 6:3 as any kind of guide, it is more likely that the proving of the candidate occurred prior to his appointment.

The words *even so,* in v. 11, show a close connection with the foregoing, and this has led to the conclusion that the office of deaconess is now in view. But this seems slender evidence upon which to build a case for the existence of a formal order of deaconesses in the primitive Church, and while there is every reason to accept that Phoebe held such a position in the church at Cenchrea (Rom. 16:1), this was probably a local appointment.

In all, it seems better to understand this verse as referring simply to the wives of the deacons. We know that the early Christians were meticulous in their observance of the proprieties, so that such work as visiting women in pagan households and attending to women candidates for baptism would fall naturally to the deacon's wife. Such work did become part of the function of the official deaconess at a later date.

The abiding lesson here is that the usefulness of the deacon, or of any servant of God, is immeasurably enhanced by the fullest cooperation of like-minded, discreet, and diligent wives. Thus will God's man be the better able to serve and "gain an excellent standing and great assurance in [his] faith in Christ Jesus" (18, NIV).

The Character of the Church

1 Tim. 3:14-16

> 14 These things write I unto thee, hoping to come unto thee shortly:
> 15 But if I tarry long, that thou mayest know how thou oughtest to behave thyself in the house of God, which is the church of the living God, the pillar and ground of the truth.

16 And without controversy great is the mystery of godliness: God
was manifest in the flesh, justified in the Spirit, seen of angels,
preached unto the Gentiles, believed on in the world, received up into
glory.

1. *The importance of Christian behaviour* (14-16). We now
reach what has been described as the culminating point,
not only in this Epistle, but in the Pastorals, for this section forms "the bridge between the first part, with its instructions about prayer and the ministry, and the practical
directions of the second part, [and] by highlighting the
true functions of a church it provides the theological basis
for the rules and regulations, as well as for the onslaught
on false teaching, which make up the body of the letter."[41]
The four words which Paul has used to describe certain
features of the Church suggest four of her greatest functions.

a. The household of God (15). The apostle will change
to an architectural metaphor later, but his prior emphasis
is upon the Church as a family, a fellowship of kindred
minds. There are Christians, rejoicing in their liberty as
the children of God, who would say, "We have our Bibles,
we have freedom of access to God through Christ, what
need have we of church or pastor?" Martin Luther once
wrote, "At home in my house there's no warmth or vigor in
me; but in the church, the household of God . . . a fire is
kindled in my heart." And it is within the spiritual glow of
the family of God that we are most likely to walk in the
light of God. But it is into this fellowship of the burning
heart that we must bring others, especially in these days of
ever-widening social cleavages.

As the household of God the Church has a redemptive-
ly cohesive function that no other organization on earth is
capable of fulfilling. "Almost all other societies bring together people of similar tastes and background. But the
Christian faith touches everyone—Matthew the tax-gath-
erer as well as Paul the Pharisee—and brings them all together. In the world the rich have one kind of club, the
poor another; the young want one kind of entertainment

and the old another; and different races notoriously band together in their different ghettos. The constitution of the Christian church tells it to cross all these barriers."[42]

b. The elect of God (15). *The church [ekklēsia] of the living God,* His called-out ones. Though this gives us no warrant for the unscriptural exclusivism satirized by Jonathan Swift—

> *We are God's chosen few;*
> *All others will be damned;*
> *There is no place in Heaven for you,*
> *We can't have Heaven crammed.*

As Paul has already taught, the Church's task is to proclaim salvation to all. "It is not that God has chosen some and rejected others; it is that not all men have accepted. The invitation and the call come to all; but to an invitation there must be an answer and to a call there must be a response."[43]

c. The pillar of truth (15). The chief thought in this analogy of the pillar is the Church's duty to display, rather than support, the truth of God. If the latter is pressed unduly, it lends credence to the claim of the church of Rome, that the church herself, as teacher of the truth, is greater than the truth she teaches. But it is the truth of God that is primary and must be held as supreme. As the statue is greater than the plinth, or pillar, upon which it stands, so is the divine revelation greater than the Church which declares it.

d. The foundation of the truth (15). This, properly understood, does not in any sense contradict or qualify the teaching, uniform throughout the New Testament, that the Church is grounded on the truth, and not vice versa. The thought here is that the truth of God is no mere poet's dream or castle in the air; it has a firm foundation in historic fact.

Philosophers have been prone to build their theories and systems on pure logic and abstract thinking, but this divine revelation is embodied in the Church, which is the "body of Christ." It is this which marks the Christian faith as unique in the world's religions. For example, in most religious books one finds an abundance of wise thoughts, observations, and moral lessons. These are found to perfection in the Bible, yet they are subordinate to a record of events, biographies, deeds, and achievements. This is why Luke has preserved the order in his prologue to Acts, "The former treatise have I made . . . of all that Jesus began both to *do* and teach" (Acts 1:1).

2. *The importance of Christian belief* (16). Scott has commented that "the writer is no mere ecclesiastic, more concerned with the mechanism of the Church than with its spiritual life. . . . In the life of the Church, as of the individual, body and soul must work together."[44] So Paul, having illustrated that the Church's task is to uphold the truth, naturally goes on to declare what that truth is.

As most scholars observe, in doing so he has quoted from a primitive Christian hymn, thus revealing how very early on the Church saw the wisdom of setting the truth to music. But here is a characteristic of the Christian faith which is far more fundamental, for, while other religions give priority to doctrine, Christianity is primarily the religion of a Person—He is *the mystery of godliness.*

Again, in using the word *mystery*, Paul has drawn a deliberate contrast with pagan usage; the *mystery of godliness* is set over against the "mysteries of ungodliness," some of which consisted of rites which were often unspeakably vile and sometimes cruel. Then, while the pagan mysteries were kept jealously hidden from the bulk of mankind, reserved rigidly for the privileged initiates, the mystery of godliness, though once hidden, is now revealed to all men, manifested in the flesh of the incarnate Christ.

a. The truly human Christ. God was manifested in the flesh. While, on strictly textual grounds, the newer versions have omitted the direct mention of *God,* there is no doubt that the reference is to Christ as God Incarnate.

Since this is merely a fragment of a hymn, it is certain that an earlier clause must have mentioned Him.

b. The sinless, risen Christ. It is difficult to decide whether, in this case, *Spirit* refers to Christ's human spirit or to the Holy Spirit. The probability is that the former is correct, though in either instance we are taught a vital truth about Christ. For (1) *In His earthly life He was vindicated by His human spirit.* Though manifested in the flesh He was justified in His own spirit. The challenge which He threw out to the Jews, "Which of you convinceth me of sin?" was one which He could confidently make to His own conscience. It had nothing against Him and could not accuse Him. And (2) *In His resurrection life He was vindicated by the Holy Spirit.* See Rom. 8:11, where there is little doubt that Paul refers to the Holy Spirit being the Agent of Christ's resurrection. When this verse is linked with Rom. 1:4, we see how abundantly Christ was "vindicated in the Spirit" (RSV).

c. Christ the Object of angelic wonder (16). James Hastings comments at this point, "The stainless sons of light, the high intelligences . . . had some new message borne in upon them by the Incarnation. If we think in the forms of the New Testament we may boldly say that the angels could not know the glory of being humbled, or the new power that would be gained by laying power aside. When the Son of God emptied Himself and became a servant, what a mystery there was! And when He returned as a Captain of Salvation, bringing with Him the first of a new world of ransomed men, how that mystery was justified."[45]

d. Christ the Subject of the universal gospel. *"Preached among the nations"* (NIV). "A Hebrew Christ had become a Christ for the nations."[46]

e. Christ the Savior of the world. When Christ ascended, He left 120 followers. Seventy years later, when the gospel had spread to the ends of the earth, men of every nation had accepted Him as Savior and Lord. Well may

Barclay exclaim, "Here in this simple phrase there is the whole wonder of the divine expansion of the Church, an expansion which on any human grounds was incredible."[47]

f. Christ the Man in the glory. Barclay continues, reminding us that the story of Jesus which began in heaven also ended in heaven. That is true—yet the ending was marvellously different from the beginning, in that Christ was received up into glory in human form. The hymn writer asks—

> *And didst Thou take to heaven*
> *A human brow?*

The Apostle John answers, "Yes," for in Rev. 1:13-18 he has described the ascended Lord in the lineaments of a glorified humanity.

1 TIMOTHY 4

The Threat to the Church

1 Tim. 4:1-16

1 Now the Spirit speaketh expressly, that in the latter times some shall depart from the faith, giving heed to seducing spirits, and doctrines of devils;

2 Speaking likes in hypocrisy; having their conscience seared with a hot iron;

3 Forbidding to marry, and commanding to abstain from meats, which God hath created to be received with thanksgiving of them which believe and know the truth.

4 For every creature of God is good, and nothing to be refused, if it be received with thanksgiving:

5 For it is sanctified by the word of God and prayer.

6 If thou put the brethren in remembrance of these things, thou shalt be a good minister of Jesus Christ, nourished up in the words of faith and of good doctrine, whereunto thou hast attained.

7 But refuse profane and old wives' fables, and exercise thyself rather unto godliness.

8 For bodily exercise profiteth little: but godliness is profitable unto all things, having promise of the life that now is, and of that which is to come.

9 This is a faithful saying and worthy of all acceptation.

10 For therefore we both labour and suffer reproach, because we trust in the living God, who is the Saviour of all men, specially of those that believe.

11 These things command and teach.
12 Let no man despise thy youth; but be thou an example of the believers, in word, in conversation, in charity, in spirit, in faith, in purity.
13 Till I come, give attendance to reading, to exhortation, to doctrine.
14 Neglect not the gift that is in thee, which was given thee by
prophecy, with the laying on of the hands of the presbytery.
15 Meditate upon these things; give thyself wholly to them; that thy
profiting may appear to all.
16 Take heed unto thyself, and unto the doctrine; continue in them:
for in doing this thou shalt both save thyself, and them that hear thee.

Wherever the wheat of truth is flourishing, the tares of untruth will rear their heads. But the servant of the Lord should not be caught unawares, for Jesus had said that "when he, the Spirit of truth, is come, he will guide you into all truth" (John 16:13). Already that Spirit had spoken, through Paul, of the impending encroachment of heresy (Acts 20:28-30); now that the threat had material-ized, the apostle could write, *the Spirit speaketh expressly,* that is, in specific terms.

1. *The peril of a false asceticism* (1-6). In the Ephesian church, as we have seen, heresy had taken the form of an incipient Gnosticism, a leading feature of which was a false asceticism. It was particularly dangerous for, while error which is unashamedly wicked is readily recognizable, this claimed a superior sanctity. Herein lay its peculiar peril, and this was why Paul denounced it as the work of *seduc-ing spirits* who taught the *doctrines of devils.* He declared that the human agents ("hypocritical liars," NIV) who were spreading such error had themselves become the victims of a rough kind of poetic justice, for they had forfeited their ability to discern the wrongness of their teaching, their consciences having been *seared with a hot iron.* This phrase may have a double meaning, for the word *kauteriazō* may signify a cauterizing of the conscience, rendering it impervious to feeling (Eph. 4:19). But this word was also used to describe the branding of a slave, and this image could well include the other, for to lose one's liberty to Satan is tantamount to surrendering the sensitivity of one's conscience.

This heretical asceticism involved the observance of two mandates:

a. The prohibition of marriage (3). As regards this, "It is noticeable that, while implicitly condemning it, Paul does not refute it by argument. The explanation probably is that he has already made his views on the naturalness and propriety of marriage abundantly clear in his treatment of the qualities required in officebearers."[48] While the apostle made no secret of his personal preference for the single state (1 Cor. 7:7), and in this same context even expressed his wish that others might emulate him, this was very far removed from according spiritual superiority to the celibate. In this case the advice given must be seen from a practical rather than a moral standpoint. It was not given by commandment (1 Cor. 7:25), and it applied to matters local and temporary (1 Cor. 7:26).

b. The prohibition of certain foods (3). Paul's views regarding ritual diet are also clearly stated in such passages as Rom. 14:1 ff. and 1 Cor. 10:25 ff., but here his reaction against the imposition of food restrictions in the name of religion is a vehement one. The reason for this is not far to seek, for in Ephesus he saw it to be a direct outcome of that dualism inherent even in the rudimentary Gnosticism prevailing at that time. Such dualism stemmed from the idea that matter was essentially evil, therefore God could not have created it. Consequently the human body and all its functions must be intrinsically evil.

Against the errorists' views the apostle writes, "Anything God has created is good, and nothing is to be tabooed —provided it is eaten with thanksgiving, for then it is consecrated by God's word, by the prayer uttered over it" (4-5, Moffatt). This version rightly draws attention, not only to the true doctrines of creation and providence, but also to the very early practice in the Church of saying grace before meals, a spiritual exercise the importance of which should not be minimised.

Lest v. 4 should be taken as providing an unwarranted

licence, the observations of E. M. Blaiklock are well worthy of note. Linking this verse with 1 Cor. 8:8-12, he comments, "The decisive question is: Viewing this thing in the light of health, social impact, my testimony, the 'weaker brother,' responsible stewardship, and my family—is it such that I can without incongruity, ask God's blessing on my consumption or use of it? Does it measure up to the two points in the verse, that is, 'made by God' and 'received with thanksgiving'?"

It is typical of the apostle that, in concluding his instructions to Timothy on how to deal with error, he moves into the positive approach. In doing so he uses the phrase *put the brethren in remembrance of these things.* E. F. Scott has here translated "lay it under them," and he adds this illuminating comment: "An expressive word is used which carries with it the idea of putting something beneath the feet. The precepts given in the first part of the chapter are to be like stepping-stones which will enable Timothy's hearers to pass securely over treacherous ground."[49] Such positive indoctrination is the sign of *a good minister of Jesus Christ* (6).

2. *The profit of a true athleticism* (7-10). After having written off the teachings of the errorists as "godless myths and old wives' tales" (7, NIV), far from disdaining discipline the apostle proceeds to lay down the lines of a healthy spiritual athleticism.

a. Physical fitness has some value (8a). This must be kept in its place. A young athletic type remarked to his studious friend, "I don't know how you keep going like you do. It takes me all my time to keep fit." "Keep fit? Fit for what?" The athlete had no answer. Yet physical fitness must be given its place. Since the body is the temple of the Holy Spirit, neglect of its proper well-being is as great a sin as pampering it or employing it for wrongful purposes. Normally, both mind and soul will function most effectively when the body is kept fit and healthy.

b. Spiritual fitness has supreme value (8b). Indeed it

would seem that Paul's reference to bodily exercise was little more than a device for giving emphasis to the vast superiority of godliness. In effect, he declares that the godly man has the best of both worlds.

c. Spiritual fitness demands exercise (9-10). And exercise of the most rigorous kind (10). Here again there has been some dispute as to whether this third "trustworthy saying," in v. 9 (cf. 1:15 and 3:1), applies to v. 8 or v. 10. Those who favor the former verse state that it reads more like a proverbial saying, while others assert that v. 10 possesses the greater theological worth and therefore merits the tag. Whichever preference is correct, Charles Simeon was well justified in using v. 10 in admonishing his Cambridge undergraduate audience, "My dear young friends, you can't go to heaven in an armchair."

A false asceticism is delusory and dangerous, but so is a casual and superficial evangelicalism. And what shall one say of that superficial emotionalism which sometimes passes for religion? Can it be denied that some suffer from a kind of inverted spirituality which thinks that nothing is of value in religion unless it be the outcome of a gust of emotion? This is not meant to derogate genuine emotion, for no true-born child of God could be satisfied with less than a "heartfelt religion." And God forbid that Christian experience should be denied those spontaneous visitations of the Spirit which are altogether too rare. But to Paul religion is "ribbed with steel." He can see no possibility of enjoying the promise of that fullness of life which now is, and is to come, apart from the toil and strife which go along with it.

d. Such exercise is inherent in saving faith (10). This is not a gospel of works, "for to this end we toil and strive, *because* we have our hope set on the living God" (10, RSV, italics mine). For, as Dietrich Bonhoeffer so pointedly said, there is no such thing as cheap grace. Free, yes, but not cheap. For those who accept the provisions of grace cannot reject the attendant responsibilities (see Titus 2:11-14). Here the responsibility is to *believe,* and such believing must involve toil and struggle (see also Acts 14: 22). It is important, therefore, to note the fundamental distinction Paul makes in v. 10*b*. For, while in emphasizing that God is the Savior of all men the apostle has countered the spurious exclusivism of the false teachers, he has not substituted an equally spurious universalism. God certainly is the potential Savior of all men, but He is the personal Savior only of those who believe, and such is the incalculable profit enjoyed by the spiritual athlete.

3. *The pattern of pastoral evangelism* (11-16).

a. *The ability to command others* (11-12*a*). Johnson said of William Pitt that he must needs defend himself against "the atrocious crime of being a young man," and the apostle had to reckon with the fact that his young colleague might find himself in a similar situation. Not that Timothy was young according to our understanding of the word but, as Barclay reminds us, Greek custom dictated that the word "youth" *(neotēs)* described anyone of military age, that was, up to 40 years old; and, particularly in New Testament times, men below that age were not ordinarily entrusted with positions of leadership.

So how could Timothy overcome his age handicap and assume an effective leadership? Reading between the lines, it would seem that, as a first step, in v. 11, Paul is seeking to inject some firmness into the younger man. In v. 6 he had used a relatively gentle term in reminding Timothy to put his people on their guard against the heretical teachers, but here we read, *these things command and teach,* and "command" is a strong verb with decided military overtones. Paul is virtually saying, "Young as you are, Timothy, you must speak with authority."

b. *The necessity of commending oneself* (12*b*-16), that is, to the confidence of those whom one is seeking to lead. For authority is not something external to a man. It does not derive from the length of his years or the rank which he boasts, nor does it depend upon the peremptoriness of his speech. Thus G. Campbell Morgan used to say that a man enamored of the dignity of his office, and seeking to impress other people with that dignity, is always despicable and is invariably despised. So it is that Paul writes, "Don't let people look down on you because you are young; see that they look up to you because you are an example" (12, Phillips). Hence Paul impresses upon Timothy the importance of several qualifications:

(1) *Moral example* (12*b*). Five points are mentioned: speech, behavior, love, fidelity, purity (NEB). As E. F. Scott says, "Although a young man, he was to excel in those very qualities in which youth is wont to be deficient—gravity, prudence, consideration for others, trustworthiness, mastery over the passions."[50]

(2) *Ministerial expertise* (13). "Until I come, devote yourself to the public reading of Scripture, to preaching and to teaching" (NIV). Here Paul reminds us that however good a man may be he cannot expect to command respect as a pastor unless he is able to fulfil his pastoral duties. In the ministry not even godliness is an acceptable substitute for gifts, and, as the writer indicates, the gifted man is required to develop his God-given abilities. "'But good preachers are born, not made.' So are good nurses, good writers, good artists. Technique and teaching will never impart the gift. But the 'born nurse' without knowledge of what she is doing will remain helpless; the gifted doctor without adequate training will be dangerous; the uninstructed writer will be incoherent, as the artist without skill to match his talent will remain frustrated and unintelligible. . . . [Without developing his own gifts] the most earnest preacher of the gospel hacks away with a blunt knife at the most delicate of operations."[51]

(3) *Spiritual equipment* (14). However, be a man ever so skilled in the arts of preaching and teaching, these do not of themselves guarantee fitness for the Christian ministry. In v. 14 Paul has used a word that is widely used today and is sometimes ill-used, the word *charisma*, translated "gift." Some have suggested that it has reference to

Timothy's call to preach, but this cannot be so since the verse tells us that it was received at his ordination, and one must assume that his call antedated this. There can be little doubt, however, that at his ordination the young man had received a special enduement of the Spirit which enabled him to preach and to teach, and that it is to this that the apostle here refers.

Nevertheless, this should not be taken as a precedent, for the primitive Church had to cope with needs peculiar to the period and, in his appointment as pastor of the Ephesian church, there was apparently need for Timothy to be given this special charismatic endowment. Today the preaching and teaching gift is rightly considered to be a *prior* evidence of a call to the ministry. But such a gift must still be received by anyone duly called to the ministry, for without it a man is ill equipped for the task (see Rom. 12:6-8).

In concluding this "Pattern of Pastoral Evangelism," Paul focuses Timothy's attention upon himself. First, as regards the foregoing teachings, the apostle writes, *give thyself wholly to them.* The NIV renders v. 15 as "Be diligent in these matters; give yourself wholly to them, so that everyone may see your progress." Secondly, *Take heed unto thyself, and unto the doctrine.* Phillips has paraphrased this as "Keep a critical eye both upon your own life and on the teaching you give," thus showing how intimately the teacher and the teaching are linked. Finally, *for in doing this thou shalt both save thyself, and them that hear thee* (16). According to this pattern the pastor who would successfully evangelize others must first, and continually, evangelize himself. There is no such being as an "unsaved savior."

Pastoral Administration and Behavior

1 Timothy 5:1-25

1 TIMOTHY 5

Relationships Within the Church Family

1 Tim. 5:1-2

> 1 Rebuke not an elder, but intreat him as a father; and the younger men as brethren;
> 2 The elder women as mothers; the younger as sisters, with all purity.

Very few of the matters which divide the churches of today are given any space in the Pastorals. It may seem surprising, for example, that nothing is said about baptism, and forms of worship and government are almost entirely ignored. Baptism was important then, as it is now, and worship and government there had to be, but the exact forms of these evidently mattered far less to the apostle than the regulating and maintenance of relationships between the believers. The result was that he devoted a great deal of attention to questions relating to this. Understandably so, for a church is people, and it is often in the course of dealing with people that the church leader faces some of his sternest tests.

This would explain why Paul began this section by advising Timothy of the need to deal faithfully, yet discreetly, with all age-groups and both sexes. He must not shrink from the delicate task of administering discipline even though, as a younger man, problems in this direction might well be aggravated. Paul is sure that these are unlikely to get out of hand provided Timothy will observe an important principle, that is, to preserve the spirit of the family within what is, after all, the household of God. In so doing he will avoid reprimanding a senior with unseemly harshness, instead he will "appeal to an older man as if he were [his] father" (1, Phillips); his contemporaries he will treat as brothers, the older women as mothers, and the younger as sisters, being especially mindful in this last instance of the need to act with perfect propriety.

This family image sets the tone for much that follows, and as Paul proceeds to deal with the first of a number of specialized groups in the church, the widows, he bases his instructions upon it.

Responsibilities Within Church Families

1 Tim. 5:3-16

3 Honour widows that are widows indeed.
4 But if any widow have children or nephews, let them learn first to shew piety at home, and to requite their parents: for that is good and acceptable before God.
5 Now she that is a widow indeed, and desolate, trusteth in God, and continueth in supplications and prayers night and day.
6 But she that liveth in pleasure is dead while she liveth.
7 And these things give in charge, that they may be blameless.
8 But if any provide not for his own, and specially for those of his own house, he hath denied the faith, and is worse than an infidel.
9 Let not a widow be taken into the number under threescore years old, having been the wife of one man,
10 Well reported of for good works; if she have brought up children, if she have lodged strangers, if she have washed the saints' feet, if she have relieved the afflicted, if she have diligently followed every good work.
11 But the younger widows refuse: for when they have begun to wax wanton against Christ, they will marry;
12 Having damnation, because they have cast off their first faith.
13 And withal they learn to be idle, wandering about from house to house; and not only idle, but tattlers also and busybodies, speaking things which they ought not.
14 I will therefore that the younger women marry, bear children, guide the house, give none occasion to the adversary to speak reproachfully.
15 For some are already turned aside after Satan.
16 If any man or woman that believeth have widows, let them relieve them, and let not the church be charged; that it may relieve them that are widows indeed.

1. *Widows who are "widows indeed"* (3-8). Here the Church is seen continuing a fine tradition inherited from the Jewish system, that of caring for those in material need, but since she had to operate such a scheme on a

budget far more modest than the Jews could boast, it was essential that she practise a wise economy. First of all, the apostle lists certain details which constitute genuine widowhood within the special understanding of the term.

a. *The widow must be genuinely destitute* (3, 4, 8); "really alone in the world," as Phillips translates verse 3. This meant disqualifying from benevolence any widow who had close relatives. In such a case the burden of care must be assumed by those relatives, thus would pressure be relieved upon the church treasury. However, Paul's reason for this insistence was religious and not economic: "But if a widow has children or grandchildren, these should learn first of all to put their religion into practice by caring for their own family and so repaying their parents and grandparents, for this is pleasing to God" (4, NIV). "This is a reference to the Fifth Commandment and, more generally, to the high valuation placed in the O.T. on the duty of children to provide for their parents."[52]

But the apostle backs his assertion with even more forceful language in verse 8: "If anyone does not provide for his relatives, and especially for his immediate family, he has denied the faith and is worse than an unbeliever" (NIV). This was no overstatement. For instance, according to the Greek law of the time sons and daughters were not only morally but legally bound to support their parents. Anyone who refused to do so lost his civil rights. To Paul it was unthinkable that Christian love should lag behind pagan law.

This still demands serious thought by Christians, even though in many "enlightened" societies public charity is expected to do what private piety ought to do. At this point an observation injected by Barclay is not out of place, even though it is not in the biblical context. He says, "If a person is to be supported, that person must be supportable . . . There is a double duty here; it is the duty of the child to support the parent, but it is the duty of the parent to be sure that that support is possible within the structure of the home."[53] Sometimes, as the proverb says, "Home is the place where we are loved the best and behave the worst." This should never be true of either parent or child in a Christian family.

b. *The widow must be genuinely Christian* (5-7). In these verses Paul goes on to say that while a woman may be genuinely widowed and entirely devoid of family support, something more is required if she is to qualify for church benevolence. "A widow, however, in the full sense, one who is alone in the world, has all her hope set on God, and regularly attends the meetings for prayer and worship night and day" (5, NEB). Here again, if we consider the reference to Anna (Luke 2:37), it is evident that the Church was carrying on an established Jewish tradition, and Paul was determined to maintain the traditional safeguards. A deserving widow must be a godly woman, and among other things that meant showing her dependence upon God in a life of consistent prayer. In so doing she bore witness that God was her sole Help. Thus the Church, as the household of God, would be placed under obligation to act on her behalf, and in His name.

Doubtless such stringent conditions would be frowned upon by the present-day exponents of a virtually indiscriminate social aid program. And probably such people could make out a logical case in defence of the principle of granting assistance without attaching a "moral carrot" to it. But in consequence, as already mentioned, immense sums of money are being expended annually in granting aid to some who have no intention of working. Not only so, but in the course of supporting deserving "one-parent families," the state is maintaining a very large number of so-called illegitimate children and their mothers.

Perhaps the social experts are right in insisting that the state is not the guardian of personal morals, and that, after all, those who are happy to allow the state to finance their indolence and moral laxity are a small minority. But Paul was determined that the church treasury would not be exposed to such abuse, hence his rugged statement in verse 6.

Some commentators have declared that the reference here is to widows who were living on the proceeds of prostitution. While this was common enough in those days when, to be fair, one must recognize that the widow could be left literally penniless, B. S. Easton is probably right when he insists that it is quite unnecessary to infer that such was the case here. Nevertheless, the reference is unquestionably to widows who, living self-indulgently, make pleasure their one aim. Using a characteristic paradox, Paul declares such women to be dead while they live. E. K. Simpson describes such a woman as "a religious corpse." In the apostle's estimation she had no claim on the church's alms.

2. *Widows who are Christian workers* (9-10). While there is insufficient evidence for maintaining that *Let not a widow be taken into the number* implies an official order of widows, it seems clear that the total of those receiving benefit must have exceeded this "number," otherwise the age restriction was manifestly unjust. For instance, among those most deserving assistance would be women with small children and the minimum age of these could hardly have been 60!

What Paul had in mind was almost certainly a body of carefully selected older women to whom particular religious duties were assigned. It is more than likely that this body subsequently evolved into a formal order of widows and that this, in turn, provided the nucleus around which the official order of deaconesses was built.

Besides the age restriction of 60 two other fundamental requirements were laid upon those who offered for such service. First, the widow must have been *the wife of one man*. This was similar to the condition imposed upon applicants for the eldership. E. F. Scott writes that "ancient sentiment allowed a special credit to the widow who refrained from second marriage. A well-known biblical instance is that of Anna the prophetess in Luke 2:36."[54] Secondly, she must have *diligently followed every good work*. Specific examples included ability to care for and rear young children. This was placed high on the list, for in those days, when the marriage bond was extremely lax, there were large numbers of unwanted infants. These were often procured for immoral purposes, so that the Church was quick to see and seize this opportunity to rescue and train these young unfortunates. Each of the remaining requirements, essentially practical and commonplace enough, would, nevertheless, be complementary to the work of the elders and deacons. In all, the primitive Church engaged in a wealth of service which was a reflection of Christ's own and which must have commended His Church to all but her most sullen and biased critics.

The modern Church has much to learn from her early counterpart in terms of social concern, and the modern welfare state could well take heed of the principle which encourages voluntary public service as a return for benefits received.

3. *Widows ineligible for such service* (11-16). Apart from those unable, or unwilling, to measure up to the requirements already listed, Paul barred all younger women from applying for office. He cites two main reasons for doing so.

a. Because he considered that they were likely to have difficulty in holding to their vows, "for when their passions draw them away from Christ, they hanker after marriage and stand condemned for breaking their troth with him" (11, NEB). While not stated, it is implied that a vow of chastity was expected of candidates.

Well the apostle knew that, not infrequently, following the initial shock of her bereavement, the young widow might in all sincerity wish to pursue a life of celibacy, espousing herself, as it were, to Christ. But he also realized the strong likelihood of some such women being caught on a "counter rebound," breaking their widow's vow and bringing judgment upon themselves. On this account he strongly advocated remarriage (14).

This has been taken as evidence against the Pauline authorship of the Epistle since, it is alleged, it contradicts the Corinthian ruling (1 Cor. 7:25 ff.). This latter position has already been discussed in connection with 4:3, but the fact is that here Paul is taking a position substantially similar to that of 1 Cor. 7:9, 36-38. In both cases it is clearly the apostle's view that, ideally, it is better for a Christian whose partner has died to refrain from a second marriage. In this his thinking was in line with ancient sentiment, though he is careful not to claim definite divine inspiration for this view (see 1 Cor. 7:40). But just as clearly does Paul feel it incumbent upon him not only to permit, but to recommend remarriage in cases where those concerned find it impossible to control their passions. "This commonsense advice is in striking contrast to the rage for celibacy which developed in the later history of the Church."[55] Judging from verse 15, one would assume that his ruling had been strengthened as a result of some known instance where a younger woman had taken her vows with regrettable consequences.

b. A second reason for excluding younger widows was because Paul also considered that they were likely to have difficulty in holding their tongues. He feared that they might exploit the office by gadding round from house to house, idling, and busybodying with dangerous tongues (13). This may appear to be an unwonted discrimination against younger women for, as any experienced pastor might confirm, the weaknesses that the apostle names here are not peculiar to younger women, nor, indeed, to the female sex. Yet one should recall that, in New Testament times, with the general exception of those in the more privileged classes, most young women were relatively uneducated, unsophisticated, and unused to the more intimate contacts with the outside world. Paul was simply seeking to anticipate certain hazards that were bound to follow in the wake of that very new social phenomenon, a thoroughly Christian brand of women's liberation.

In connection with verse 16 it should be said that a number of well-attested texts omit the reference to the man. This omission seems to give better sense to Paul's instruction, as J. N. D. Kelly has suggested: "Paul is envisaging the case of a comfortably off female member of the community, whether married herself or single or a widow, whose household includes one or more widows, not close relatives . . . but servants or dependants or friends. Such a woman is encouraged to make herself responsible for their welfare instead of handing them over to the church's charity. . . . The reason why Paul does not impose the same obligation on a Christian man of similar position should be obvious."[56]

Responsibilities Regarding Elders

1 Tim. 5:17-25

> 17 Let the elders that rule well be counted worthy of double honour, especially they who labour in the word and doctrine.
> 18 For the scripture saith, Thou shalt not muzzle the ox that treadeth out the corn. And, The labourer is worthy of his reward.
> 19 Against an elder receive not an accusation, but before two or three witnesses.
> 20 Them that sin rebuke before all, that others also may fear.
> 21 I charge thee before God, and the Lord Jesus Christ, and the elect angels, that thou observe these things without preferring one before another, doing nothing by partiality.
> 22 Lay hands suddenly on no man, neither be partaker of other men's sins: keep thyself pure.
> 23 Drink no longer water, but use a little wine for thy stomach's sake and thine often infirmities.
> 24 Some men's sins are open beforehand, going before to judgment; and some men they follow after.
> 25 Likewise also the good works of some are manifest beforehand; and they that are otherwise cannot be hid.

1. *Concerning remuneration* (17-18). Apart from 4:14 this is the first reference Paul has made in the Pastorals to elder *(presbuteros)* as a title of office (the word is used in 5:1 to denote an older member of the congregation). The use of the word here is of particular significance, for it points to "the embryonic beginnings of the ministry itself."[57] However, there is no justification for using this verse as if it taught a division of responsibility within the eldership resulting in two classes, that is of "ruling elder" and "teaching elder." That all elders were meant to assist in directing the affairs of the church is implied in 3:4-5,

and that the entire eldership had teaching responsibilities is apparent from 3:2 and Titus 1:9.

The particular reference in this verse is to those who "direct the affairs of the church well" (NIV), and who also *labour in the word and doctrine.* It is these officers, who show an aptitude for leadership combined with a single-minded dedication to preaching and teaching, that Paul singles out for special consideration. The importance attached to the ministry of the Word was no doubt due to the prevalence of false teaching. This necessitated the exercise of a precise and powerful presentation of the truth, and elders giving evidence of such ability were to be *counted worthy of double honour.* The exact meaning of this phrase is difficult to determine. Chrysostom interpreted it as granting both honor and honorarium. Tertullian favored the idea of giving honor as to both a brother and a ruler. Calvin thought it meant that from church alms the elders in question should receive twice the "honour" allocated to widows. Most recent translators incline to render "honour" in terms of material reward and, on the whole, Moffatt's version, "worthy of ample remuneration," seems most reasonable.

Paul's citations of scripture in verse 18 would certainly suggest that he had in mind God's sanction of adequate provision for those who serve in this larger capacity. Perhaps few would go so far as to say that "although ministers may be reluctant to suggest that 'double honour' may be expressed in money, that seems to me to be the context of the statement. . . . If this interpretation is correct, the absolute minimum for any minister should be double the average wage in his community."[58] However, this opinion is expressed seriously by a prominent and most able layman who serves as a deacon in one of London's largest and most influential churches.[59] At least no one could fault this writer's question, "How can we expect the world to take notice of us when we keep our ministers in penury?"[60] and none could doubt that such congregational parsimony is a flat contradiction of apostolic policy.

Nevertheless, it is notable that Paul links ample remuneration with *labour in the word and doctrine*. This word translated "labour" (Gk., *kopaiō*) suggests work of the most demanding sort in which, presumably, not all elders felt inclined, or called, to engage. But no preacher and teacher can justify his support, let alone his claim to a call, who is not prepared to toil in such a fashion.

One of the most effective preachers on either side of the Atlantic has written, "The ministry . . . is unique in this respect—that it is the one profession which a lazy, incompetent or unprincipled man can exploit for his own advantage and through which he can bluff his way for a lifetime. Let him compile a minimum of basic sermons to which he adds from time to time and, if he changes his pastorate often enough, he can enjoy a forty-year ministry without ever doing a hard day's work in his life. Only to God must he give account of his stewardship and, if he can square that with his conscience, he can get away with anything."[61]

This may sound like a hard saying, but the man responsible has calculated that the average number of man-hours required in the preparation of one of his Sunday sermons is just under 20. These include everything from the first bout of wrestling with his text to the final delivery of the message. While it may appear to be a counsel of perfection to suggest that we all cut our sermonic cloth by that pattern, the fact remains that it is a master of his craft who finds such a pattern essential.

2. *Concerning litigation* (19-21). From the rewarding of elders who have faithfully served, Paul now turns to the reprimanding of those who have fallen short. Once again we are reminded of the indebtedness of the Christian Church to Jewish tradition, this time in the sphere of jurisprudence. Applied to the discipline of elders the enlightened law, which demanded that an accusation against an elder be supported by two or three witnesses, was a safeguard against frivolous or malicious charges. Where the

elder was proved guilty, rebuke was to be publicly administered and in a most solemn charge, invoking *God, and the Lord Jesus Christ, and the elect angels,* Timothy is instructed to observe and apply such regulations without prejudice and with the strictest impartiality.

3. *Concerning ordination* (22, 24-25).

a. While every conceivable care must be taken in the selection of ordinands, the apostle concedes that assessment may be exceedingly difficult. This is why he advises, "Never be in a hurry to ordain a man" (22, Phillips). The reason for caution is twofold, first, because a candidate's unworthiness may not be immediately apparent. "Remember that some men's sins are obvious, and are equally obviously bringing them to judgment. The sins of other men are not apparent, but are dogging them, nevertheless, under the surface" (24, Phillips). Paul has solemnly prefaced this by declaring that those who ignore the possibility of this insidious process and ordain a man in undue haste "may be making [themselves] responsible for his sins" (22, Phillips). On the other hand, "Similarly some virtues are plain to see, while others, though not at all conspicuous, will eventually make themselves felt" (25, Phillips).

Paul could not have written more convincingly of the need for the most thoroughgoing scrutiny of candidates for the ministry.

b. It remains to examine a verse which contains an oft-debated word of advice—verse 23. While parenthetical it is by no means incidental, for it would appear that Paul, in the course of admonishing Timothy to keep himself pure, advises him against the unwisdom of extreme asceticism. Such an interpretation accords with the wider context of the Epistle (see especially 4:1-6), and this is certainly the sense of the NIV, "Stop drinking only water, and use a little wine because of your stomach and your frequent illnesses." Viewed fairly, this cannot possibly be quoted as justifying so-called moderate drinking. As Barclay has commented, Paul's word "simply approves the use of wine when wine may be medicinally helpful."[62]

But how are we to understand the term "wine"? This cannot be finally determined by appealing to the Greek *oinos,* since this word is used to designate wine both in its fermented and unfermented states. In stating this, it is recognized that, according to the *Pulpit Commentary,* "wine, to be wine, must undergo fermentation," and *Hastings Dictionary* goes so far as to dismiss as "special pleading" the arguments of those who advance a scriptural basis for total abstinence by differentiating intoxicating from nonintoxicating wine in the biblical terminology.[63] But the observation of Ferrar Fenton is particularly relevant:

> As in the Hebrew, *yain,* the word *(oinos)* does not always . . . signify fermented, intoxicating drink, but grapes as fresh fruit, dried as raisins, or prepared as jam, or preserved by boiling for storage, or as a thick syrup for spreading upon bread as we do butter; and that syrup dissolved in water for a beverage at meals, as described in the Hebrew Bible by Solomon and others, and among Greek writers by Aristotle, and Pliny among the Roman ones. This mixing of the syrup with water ready for use at meals is alluded to in more than one of our Lord's parables. The liquid was absolutely non-alcoholic and not intoxicating.[64]

On the strength of such evidence Robertson has concluded that Paul was saying of Timothy, "Water alone . . . is not sufficient to cleanse the toxins from his system which were causing his physical ailments: a little grape-juice mingled with water would have this salutary effect."[65]

Nevertheless, if it be argued that *oinos* here does refer to alcoholic wine, it is essential to note such a comment as J. Glenn Gould has quoted: "D. Miall Edwards points out that 'the drink question is far more complex and acute in modern than in Bible times, and that the conditions of the modern world have given rise to problems which were not within the horizon of New Testament writers.'"[66] In a day when alcoholism is increasing at an unprecedented and frightening rate, Christians must avoid giving even tacit approval of even a limited use of alcoholic drinks as beverages.

Fitzsimmonds has well made the point as representative of those scholars who would take Miall Edwards' position:

> It may be said that while wine is not condemned as being without usefulness, it brings in the hands of sinful men such dangers of becoming uncontrolled that even those who count themselves to be strong would be wise to abstain, if not for their own sake, yet for the sake of weaker brethren (Rom. 14:21). If it is argued that there are many other things which may be abused besides wine, the point may be immediately conceded, but wine has so often proved itself to be peculiarly fraught with danger that Paul names it specifically at the same time as he lays down the general principle.[67]

Perhaps one thing further may be added. Since the apostle specifically mentioned a stomach ailment, it is highly improbable that a doctor today would prescribe alcohol, even in limited amounts, for such a condition. On the other hand, the unfermented juice of grapes does possess decided therapeutic properties, and this would give credence to the view that it was this that Paul had in mind.

1 TIMOTHY 6

Relations Between Slaves and Masters

1 Tim. 6:1-2a

> 1 Let as many servants as are under the yoke count their own masters worthy of all honour, that the name of God and his doctrine be not blasphemed.
> 2 And they that have believing masters, let them not despise them, because they are brethren; but rather do them service, because they are faithful and beloved, partakers of the benefit.

It was inevitable that as Christianity began to make inroads into Roman society it would precipitate problems. It was not for nothing that the early Christians gained the reputation of turning the world upside down. And it was inconceivable that slavery should escape the upturning impact of the gospel, for a message which proclaimed the equality of all men before God, and their equal right to become partakers of His grace, was totally incompatible with any form or degree of slavery.

But true to the Christian method, Paul approached the problem from the personal and not the political standpoint, insisting that Christian slaves must obey their masters and treat them with all honor. An unbelieving master might be tyrannical, but an attitude of disrespect towards him on the part of a Christian slave would bring both God's name and Christ's teaching into disrepute. Where Christian slaves had believing masters, they must learn that spiritual equality did not efface Christian responsibility. Far from taking advantage in such a situation, the believing slave must serve all the better since "those who benefit by their services are believers and beloved" (2, RSV). Here we are given an invaluable insight into how Christianity effected social change.

1. Without doubt, such a principle as Paul applied, which operated according to what has been called "the law of indirectness," would be repudiated by many today, some Christians included. Yet it has been widely agreed that, in New Testament times, any direct action against the system of slavery would almost certainly have been doomed to failure, since it had become essential to the very fabric of Roman society. It has been estimated that something like one-third of the population of Rome were slaves, and even some slaves had slaves of their own! It is hardly surprising that any attempt to overthrow the system was ruthlessly put down.

2. But is the Christian today justified, as Paul, in tacitly recognizing an existing social evil in the belief that the

patient application of Christian principles will slowly but surely erode it? To say the least, such an idea is intensely unpopular with many Christians, and totally unacceptable to some. Indeed, the present tendency in certain sections of the Christian Church is to emphasize social justice even to the exclusion of authority, discipline, and law, a position which is the direct antithesis of Paul's position. Yet is there a Christian alternative? Not if that alternative involves the Christian in violent revolution and anarchy. "The Christian cannot seek the limited objectives of the protestors regardless of everything else. He has to keep a balance. The Christian faith is a comprehensive and systematic faith. It is a total way of life where every part is balanced with every other. He cannot find quick solutions to one problem at the cost of raising half a dozen others. . . . And in the Christian way there are no short cuts, especially not the short cut of violence."[68]

However, it should be added that the Christian cannot adopt a position of smug complacency and, playing a totally passive role, even in the face of the most outrageous examples of social and moral depredation and public and political corruption, assume that everything will work out right in the end. As Brian Griffiths has said, "While [the Christian] must support the police, the executive, and the judiciary in their task of enforcing the law, at the same time he must not hesitate to denounce and protest at individual and social injustice. His mandate is to be a light in society—not a mirror, simply reflecting it."[69]

3. Were it not for the fact that, in the words of Hegel, "history teaches us that history teaches us nothing," it would be plain that the principle of violent revolution is basically and incurably weak. "The French have as much experience of revolution as anyone in Europe, and . . . the revolution of 1789 produced the emperor Napoleon—which was certainly not the object of the exercise. The revolution of 1848 produced another emperor, Louis Napoleon, which was certainly not the object of that exercise, either. The Russian revolution produced Stalin. The Germans threw

over the Kaiser only to land themselves with Hitler. This is not a series of coincidences."[70] And the principle of violent change is fundamentally weak because it is theologically weak. It is built largely upon the premise that new social institutions will produce new men, a notion which discounts man's inherited depravity and his utter need of divine redemption, and is therefore manifestly impracticable.

Perhaps no section of the Pastorals has more to teach contemporary man than this one. Properly understood there is nothing effete, and there is certainly nothing bourgeois, about Paul's principles. They do demand a true Christian courage and patience in their application, and these are fearfully demanding, but there is no other way.

A Final Miscellany
1 Timothy 6:2*b*-21

Untruth and Its Consequences

1 Tim. 6:2b-10

> These things teach and exhort.
> 3 If any man teach otherwise, and consent not to wholesome words, even the words of our Lord Jesus Christ, and to the doctrine which is according to godliness;
> 4 He is proud, knowing nothing, but doting about questions and strifes of words, whereof cometh envy, strife, railings, evil surmisings.
> 5 Perverse disputings of men of corrupt minds, and destitute of the truth, supposing that gain is godliness: from such withdraw thyself.
> 6 But godliness with contentment is great gain.
> 7 For we brought nothing into this world, and it is certain we can carry nothing out.
> 8 And having food and raiment let us be therewith content.
> 9 But they that will be rich fall into temptation and a snare, and into many foolish and hurtful lusts, which drown men in destruction and perdition.
> 10 For the love of money is the root of all evil: which while some coveted after, they have erred from the faith, and pierced themselves through with many sorrows.

In drawing his Epistle to a close, Paul has left us in some doubt as to whether his admonition *These things teach and exhort* (2*b*) should be applied to the foregoing or to the remainder of this final chapter. It seems most probable that he intended it to serve as a link between the teaching already given and the miscellaneous injunctions following, some of which contain material not previously discussed. In any case the apostle made it plain that Timothy was to take an uncompromising stand against "anyone [who] teaches otherwise and does not agree with the sound words of our Lord Jesus Christ and the teaching which accords with godliness" (3, RSV). Paul then proceeds to give a profile of the false teacher in terms which J. Glenn Gould has described as being as close to invective as the apostle ever comes. This is very apparent in the NEB where the one in error is denounced as a "pompous ignoramus." The writer goes on to trace the tragic course of such a man.

1. *Preoccupation with false teaching impairs the mind* (3-5a). In verse 4 the word *noseō,* translated "doting" in the KJV, means, literally, "to be sick," a condition which is inevitable where one has turned aside from *the wholesome words . . . of our Lord Jesus Christ* (3). The symptoms of such a mental malaise include "jealousy, quarrelling, slander, base suspicions, and endless wrangles: all typical of men who have let their reasoning powers become atrophied and have lost grip of the truth" (4-5a, NEB). Scott's observation is most apposite at this point: "It has often been noticed that the partisans of some eccentric theory . . . are shortly at daggers drawn with one another."[71]

2. *Such mental aberration impairs the morals* (5b-8). For those who peddle their high-flown heresies come to regard religion as a source of profit. "They think religion should yield dividends" (5, NEB). Paul has already taught that "godliness is profitable" (8), but its profit has nothing to do with external, material possessions. As the NEB continues, "And of course religion does yield high dividends, but only to the man whose resources are within him." This translation reflects the meaning of the Greek, *autarkeia,*

or "self-sufficiency." As Kelly comments, "This was a technical term in Greek philosophy, particularly favoured in the Cynic-Stoic tradition, which used it to denote the wise man's independence of circumstances. . . . But the deeper, more characteristically Christian meaning which it has here is illustrated by Phil. 4:11."[72] See also verses 6 and 7.

3. *The false teacher becomes the prey of his own inordinate desires* (9-10). Their love of money, and their prostituting of religion as a means of gaining it, brings them ultimately to their doom. In describing this Paul employs the most vivid of metaphors. In verse 9 he likens these money-grubbing teachers to animals lured from the safe track into a snare, from whence the helpless victim is taken by his captors to be drowned in the ocean of total disaster. In verse 10, while the metaphor changes, a similar sequence is presented for here, having taken a wrong turning, the victim finds himself impaled upon the murderous barbs of his own making. In both instances we see illustrated "the lust, the lure, and the loss" sustained by those who are dedicated to the spread of false teaching.

Faith and Its Challenges

1 Tim. 6:11-12

> 11 But thou, O man of God, flee these things; and follow after righteousness, godliness, faith, love, patience, meekness.
> 12 Fight the good fight of faith, lay hold on eternal life, whereunto thou art also called, and hast professed a good profession before many witnesses.

Just as the "man of the world" or the "man of business" has earned his title through a single-minded loyalty to the object of his devotion, so with the "man of God" (11). That Paul should have so named Timothy was a credit to him; yet if he was to retain that title, he must accept the rigors that go with it. Three key words outline the pattern of life which he must pursue in this connection—*flee, follow,* and *fight.*

1. *Flee the evil* (11*a*). In verse 5 Timothy had been admonished to withdraw himself from the sectaries; here, in still stronger terms, he is commanded to shun their every evil way. The *thou* of verse 11 is emphatic and, since it is set in the immediate context of greed for gain, we may assume that this was in the apostle's mind. Not that there was even a breath of a suggestion that his young reader had any tendency to seek monetary gain but, as we have seen in verse 5, one of the root sins of the sectaries sprang from the notion that godliness was a means of gain, and the enemy baits this particular snare with things other than gold.

Whenever religion is considered as a means of personal enrichment, either in terms of money, goods, or status, the process of seduction from the faith is already operating. The only true safeguard is to live by the formula in verse 6.

2. *Follow the good* (11*b*). The word translated *follow after* ("pursue," NEB) is a hunter's word, and the "prey" in this case is a concatenation of virtues indispensable to the man of God—"justice, piety, fidelity, love, fortitude, and gentleness" (11, NEB). Hanson, in common with others who contend that the Pastorals are pseudonymous, objects, "This is not very like the way Paul writes. For Paul . . . all good qualities were the gift of God rather than the object of man's pursuit."[73]

But such a statement loses sight of the typical Pauline paradox. Elsewhere, while he teaches that love is the fruit of the Spirit (Gal. 5:22), he exhorts the Corinthians to pursue it (1 Cor. 14:1), for whatever the Spirit imparts gratuitously is capable of development, enlargement, improvement. Herein is a process to which the devoted Christian is committed and which is meant to continue throughout life.

Dr. Wiley, discussing the same word in Heb. 12:14 in relation to holiness, has made a comment relevant to the present case: "The word 'follow' is sometimes interpreted to mean the pursuit of a flying goal . . . which can never be realized. Nothing is further from the truth. The word has reference to a course of action to be followed or a pattern of life to be realized, and with all diligence."[74]

3. *Fight the good fight* (12). While the command to *fight* continues the athletic analogy, military overtones are also implied, a reminder that, whether in contest or conflict, Christian service involves one in continuous struggle. Here is that "moral equivalent of war" that William James declared to be so essential an element in modern society.

As regards the phrase *lay hold on eternal life,* Kelly has commented that while the command to fight is in the present imperative, indicating a continuous process, the verb translated *lay hold on* is in the aorist imperative, suggesting immediate possession of eternal life.[75] G. Campbell Morgan has put it succinctly, "The charge of the Apostle here is not that a man shall fight in order to lay hold on eternal life, but that a man shall lay hold on life eternal in order to fight."[76] To such an ongoing conflict Timothy had been called in the hour of his baptism (13), and nothing is more pathetic than the sight of one who has lost sight of the fact that eternal life is given to provide equipment as well as enjoyment.

> *When I was young and bold and strong,*
> *Oh, right was right and wrong was wrong!*
> *My plume on high, my flag unfurled,*
> *I rode away to right the world.*
>
> *Now I am old; and good and bad*
> *Are woven in a crazy plaid.*
> *I sit and say, "The world is so;*
> *And he is wise who lets it go."*

(*The Veteran,* by Dorothy Parker)

Final Charges

1 Tim. 6:13-21

> 13 I give thee charge in the sight of God, who quickeneth all things, and before Christ Jesus, who before Pontius Pilate witnessed a good confession;
> 14 That thou keep this commandment without spot, unrebukeable, until the appearing of our Lord Jesus Christ:
> 15 Which in his times he shall shew, who is the blessed and only Potentate, the King of kings, and Lord of lords;
> 16 Who only hath immortality, dwelling in the light which no man can approach unto; whom no man hath seen, nor can see: to whom be honour and power everlasting. Amen.
> 17 Charge them that are rich in this world, that they be not high-minded, nor trust in uncertain riches, but in the living God, who giveth us richly all things to enjoy;
> 18 That they do good, that they be rich in good works, ready to distribute, willing to communicate;
> 19 Laying up in store for themselves a good foundation against the time to come, that they may lay hold on eternal life.
> 20 O Timothy, keep that which is committed to thy trust, avoiding profane and vain babblings, and oppositions of science falsely so called:
> 21 Which some professing have erred concerning the faith. Grace be with thee. Amen.

1. *To Timothy* (13-16). Thinking of Timothy's baptism, Paul is moved to remind his young colleague that the confession he had made on that solemn occasion amounted, in fact, to a commission, for baptism involved the candidate in the high resolve to serve his Lord and Master. Now, in the presence of two awesome witnesses, "the quickening God and the confessing Christ," Paul declares, "I charge you to obey your orders irreproachably and without fault until our Lord Jesus appears" (14, NEB). In so doing he assures his son in the faith that "that appearance God will bring to pass in his own good time" (NEB). This may well amount to a confession on the apostle's part that there is little prospect now of the Lord's return in his lifetime, but his words strongly suggest that Timothy may live to see it.

Nevertheless, the writer's confidence has not wavered in the fact that, early or late, God's appointed moment for His Son's appearance will arrive. This now moves the apostle to extol, in words that may well have been taken from a Christian hymn of the period, the unique sovereignty of God.

Kelly sees in these sonorous lines (15-16) an implied

rebuttal of two claims that were being currently pressed by protagonists of the imperial cult, one involving emperor worship and the other the belief that the deceased emperor was immortal. However, the phrase *who only hath immortality* does not deny it to anyone other than God but brings out the truth that God alone possesses it inherently and by right. He is the God immortal, unapproachable, invisible, unrivalled, and worthy of all honor.

2. *To the Wealthy* (17-19). It is typical of Paul that, hard upon the heels of such a majestic ascription of praise to God, he could address his fellow mortal on monetary matters (compare 1 Corinthians 15 and 16:1). However, since it is possible that verses 11 to 16 constitute a digression, this may be a resumption of his discourse on wealth, though this charge concerns those who are already wealthy, as distinct from those who covetously aspire to riches. It is assumed, of course, that the accumulation of such wealth will have been by honest means, but, as elsewhere in the New Testament, Paul's attitude towards affluence is strikingly moderate, to use Guthrie's phrase.

The man who possesses wealth is not denounced on that account, though he is straitly warned that it can lead to arrogance and a foolish dependence upon what is essentially transitory. So, after admonishing the wealthy to *trust in the living God, who giveth us richly all things to enjoy*—a timely hint to the extreme ascetics!—the apostle continues with a series of positive injunctions, well rendered by the NEB, "Tell them to hoard a wealth of noble actions by doing good, to be ready to give away and to share, and so acquire a treasure which will form a good foundation for the future" (18-19). By so doing, the man of wealth may also be a man of God, being a partaker of that eternal life available to rich and poor alike, and common to all who are wholly committed to His will.

3. *A closing exhortation* (20-21). This is so much in the nature of a heart cry that the lines must surely have been penned to Timothy by Paul's own hand. They express both

passionately and pointedly the apostle's utter abhorrence of the heresy against which the younger man had to contend. This was a conglomeration of pseudotheological and pseudoscientific jargon, falsely so-called "knowledge." No wonder that "by professing it some . . . missed the mark as regards the faith" (21, RSV), since they had aimed at nothing but to contradict the true beliefs as taught by the apostle. In face of all such oppositions Timothy was admonished to guard what had been entrusted to his care.

We may deduce from this that, while the "rule of faith" still had to be given its final shape and order, Paul had committed its substance to his young lieutenant. It was to be secured, like treasure deposited for safekeeping in a bank. This analogy should not be overapplied, however, since he who possesses such truth is committed to sharing it. But he has absolutely no right to interfere with it in any way. It is the sin of the errorist to teach doctrinal novelties. What the messenger of Christ must proclaim is nothing less than a divine revelation. Man did not invent it; he must neither take from it nor add to it but communicate it unimpaired.

Now, concludes Paul, "Grace be with you all!" (NEB). The plural address confirms what has already been apparent, namely, that the letter was to be read to the assembled congregation. Thus would they be made aware that pastor and people must labor together so that the life-giving, wholesome truth of God might be preserved and proclaimed.

The Second Epistle to
TIMOTHY

Topical Outline of Second Timothy

Introduction and Salutation (1:1-2)
From Paul the Apostle to Timothy (1:1-2)

The Privilege of Spiritual Parentage (1:3-5)
In the Case of Timothy (1:3-5)
In the Case of Paul (1:3)

The Provision for Spiritual Courage (1:6—2:26)
An Adequate Gift (1:6-8)
An Adequate Gospel (1:9-12)
An Adequate God (1:13-18)
An Unbindable Word (2:1-18)
An Unshakeable Foundation (2:19-26)

The Prospects Calling for Spiritual Courage (3:1—4:22)
The Last Days (3:1-17)
The Charge to Preach (4:1-5)
The Valediction of a Preacher (4:6-8)
The Dereliction of a Preacher (4:9-21)
The Apostle's Last Word (4:22)

Introduction and Salutation

2 Timothy 1:1-2

2 TIMOTHY 1

From Paul the Apostle to Timothy

2 Tim. 1:1-2

> 1 Paul, an apostle of Jesus Christ by the will of God, according to the promise of life which is in Christ Jesus,
> 2 To Timothy, my dearly beloved son: Grace, mercy, and peace, from God the Father and Christ Jesus our Lord.

While in the introduction to his other Epistles, as here, Paul frequently quoted the *authority* of his apostleship, it is fitting that in this, his last, he should also mention its *object—according to the promise of life in Christ Jesus.* For as he wrote, death stared him in the face, and in such times of supreme crisis how immensely heartening it is for the preacher to rehearse to himself, as well as to others, the precious promises of God.

Appropriate also to the present situation is the description of Timothy as *my dearly beloved son.* Always, when the aged apostle has addressed his young helper, we have sensed the warmth of a deep affection in his words, and even when referring to him in a letter to others (see 1 Cor. 4:17), the same is true. But as he begins this final letter, he uses the tenderest terms of all. Also significant is the addition of *mercy* to the more usual salutation of *grace* and *peace.* While grace is for the worthless and peace is for the restless, mercy is indispensable to the helpless, to such as this young pastor who felt so keenly his manifold limitations.

The Privileges of Spiritual Parentage
2 Timothy 1:3-5

In the Case of Timothy

2 Tim. 1:3-5

> 3 I thank God, whom I serve from my forefathers with pure conscience, that without ceasing I have remembrance of thee in my prayers night and day;
> 4 Greatly desiring to see thee, being mindful of thy tears, that I may be filled with joy;
> 5 When I call to remembrance the unfeigned faith that is in thee, which dwelt first in thy grandmother Lois, and thy mother Eunice; and I am persuaded that in thee also.

Before he recommends an antidote for Timothy's fear, Paul first commends him for his faith. He calls it *unfeigned faith,* a phrase he has already used (1 Tim. 1:5), in which instance it is used in conjunction with a *good conscience.* We may understand, therefore, that even within the trembling heart there can dwell a genuine faith, a faith without vestige of pretence and perfectly at home with a good conscience. What is more, we may gather from this passage that there is a sense in which such a faith may be transmitted from parent to child, for it had *dwelt first in [Timothy's] grandmother Lois, and [his] mother Eunice.* This is a truth to be treated with discretion for, as Samuel Chadwick insisted, "We cannot live on other people's goodness. We must have salt in ourselves. Religion is a personal matter. One man's grace is never enough for two."[1]

Yet there are those who, if ever they enter a lost eternity, will have to do so against the accumulated forces of parental piety, and their judgment will be the severer on that account. Dr. Arthur Gossip has written, "Only a short time ago I was shown an old bundle of letters faded with age, in which a mother—long dead now—set down her longings for her wonderful baby boy; and as I read my soul blushed red, because that writer was my mother, and the baby boy was I."[2]

One of the most memorable testimonies I ever heard was given by a young man who confessed that he couldn't recall when he actually became a child of God and, even more strikingly, he declared that he couldn't remember a time when he hadn't loved Jesus. "But," he went on, "I do love Him, I do know that He is my present Savior, and the reason is to be found in the faith of my godly mother. The very first word she taught me to speak was not 'Dad,' or 'Mother,' but 'Jesus.'" Happy child! Blessed mother! One can imagine Eunice being such a mother, and Lois before her. Nor did the faith of Eunice blossom in the most congenial kind of soil, for hers was a "mixed marriage." And the value of Lois' faith can be all the better appreciated in the light of a comment made by a missionary to India, "To make a sound Christian of a Hindu you have got to convert his grandmother."

In the Case of Paul

It would seem that Paul could not think of Timothy's spiritual heritage without his memory being stimulated to recollect his own. Unlike that of his spiritual son's, his ancestral piety had been Jewish, but by it he had been trained to serve God with a pure conscience within the limits of the law. Of this he invariably spoke with respect, even acknowledging that, though now superseded by grace, it had served its purpose in leading him to Christ (Gal. 3:24). Continuing his reminiscing, he harks back to his last deeply emotional parting with Timothy, probably prior to his present imprisonment, and he speaks of his ceaseless longing and prayer for a joyous reunion (4). He then stirs the young man's memory so that, recalling his rich heritage, he might brace himself for the demands that await him.

The Provision for Spiritual Courage

2 Timothy 1:6—2:26

An Adequate Gift

2 Tim. 1:6-8

> 6 Wherefore I put thee in remembrance that thou stir up the gift of God, which is in thee by the putting on of my hands.
> 7 For God hath not given us the spirit of fear; but of power, and of love, and of a sound mind.
> 8 Be not thou therefore ashamed of the testimony of our Lord, nor of me his prisoner: but be thou partaker of the afflictions of the gospel according to the power of God;

"A teacher who experimented with an 'ergograph machine,' an instrument designed to measure fatigue, tells how when a tired child was told, 'You're doing fine,' the boy's energy curve soared."[3] Discouragement and fault-finding have exactly the opposite effect; this is why the wise leader will avoid administering an ill-timed rebuke even when it is called for.

Abraham Lincoln would often delay such action until he could write an encouraging letter. To one officer he wrote, "Although what I am now going to say to you is in the form of a reprimand, it is not intended to add a pang to what you have already suffered. You have shown too much promise for your future to be lightly surrendered."[4]

What Paul is about to say is a reminder rather than a reprimand but, even so, in the previous verses he has first of all sought to build up his young reader's confidence. He continues to do so: "That is why I now remind you to stir into flame the gift of God which is within you" (6, NEB). This was not the gift of faith, for, as we saw in 1 Tim. 4:14, it was connected with his ordination and was almost certainly a special enduement of the Spirit enabling him to serve effectively as a minister of Christ. It was not a gift that needed to be repeated but revived, for it had a particular relevance to his present need. Timothy was being reminded of the lesson which William Booth taught his officers in the early days of the Salvation Army, that "the tendency of fire is to go out."

With reference to the *spirit* in this verse, most commentators and translators favor retaining the small *s*, but this does not alter the fact that it is the Holy Spirit alone who can impart to the natural man a true, spiritual courage. Such courage consists of three elements: *power* to give enablement; *love* which ensures that such power will be used in the service of others; and *self-control* which enables one to exercise power with a God-glorifying restraint. "Let such a spirit prevail," Paul was saying, in effect, "and you will never be ashamed of witnessing to our Lord nor of identifying yourself with me, His prisoner" (8a). Incidentally, Paul did not consider himself to be the prisoner of the emperor but of his Savior. In fact, Paul in his dungeon was infinitely freer than the emperor on his throne. He was proving the truth George Matheson so vividly expressed—

> *Make me a captive, Lord,*
> *And then I shall be free;*
> *Force me to render up my sword,*
> *And I shall conqueror be.*
> *I sink in life's alarms*
> *When by myself I stand;*
> *Imprison me within Thine arms,*
> *And strong shall be my hand.*

There is reason to believe that Timothy proved this too. Paul went on, "Take your share of suffering for the sake of the Gospel, in the strength that comes from God" (8, NEB), and Heb. 13:23 gives more than a hint that he did just that when the great test finally came.

An Adequate Gospel

2 Tim. 1:9-12

> 9 Who hath saved us, and called us with an holy calling, not according to our works, but according to his own purpose and grace, which was given us in Christ Jesus before the world began,
> 10 But is now made manifest by the appearing of our Saviour Jesus Christ, who hath abolished death, and hath brought life and immortality to light through the gospel:
> 11 Whereunto I am appointed a preacher, and an apostle, and a teacher of the Gentiles.
> 12 For the which cause I also suffer these things: nevertheless I am not ashamed: for I know whom I have believed, and am persuaded that he is able to keep that which I have committed unto him against that day.

It is typical of the devil's subtlety and skill that he has made the gospel, of which Paul was so immensely proud, for so many an object of shame and even contempt. In his *Ring of Truth,* J. B. Phillips has written, "It is part of our incredible modern blindness that we fail to see [the gospel] as the best of good news! And such is the prevailing de-Godded atmosphere that most men see no need for the Gospel at all, and even Christians to some degree miss the wonder of the divine invasion."[5] Nothing could be more diametrically opposed to the view of the apostle, for here he describes a gospel stupendous in its purpose and power.

1. *A gospel of full salvation* (9). The God *who hath saved us* has also *called us with an holy calling* (9). Any man who sees salvation as no more than forgiveness of sins has a woefully inadequate view of the gospel. Nor need the believer shrink from its demands for, as Paul assured the Thessalonian believers, "He who calls you is faithful, and He will do it" (1 Thess. 5:24, RSV).

2. *A gospel purposed in eternity* (9). The NIV has rendered verse 9—"God . . . has saved us and called us to a holy life —not because of anything we have done but because of his own purpose and grace. This grace was given us in Christ Jesus before the beginning of time." Thus Paul, in rooting the grace of God in eternity, has left absolutely no room for human merit in the scheme of salvation. As E. K. Simpson

writes, "The Lord's choices have their unfathomable grounds, but they are not founded on the innate eligibility of the chosen."[6] Nevertheless, those who are called must themselves believe. The divine initiative does not preclude the human response. God has done literally everything essential to our salvation, even to the bestowal of faith (Eph. 2:8-9), but God does not believe for any man.

3. *A gospel revealed in time* (10); that is, as an act of God in history. Commenting upon what he calls "the percolated influence" of Rudolf Bultmann, J. B. Phillips has said: "His idea, which amounts to an obsession, is that 'the life of Jesus is set in such a mythological framework that its real meaning can only be found when we get rid of the whole first century background.'"[7] But, according to Paul, the very opposite is the case. The birth, life, death, and resurrection of Jesus Christ were not mythological abstractions but historical events.

4. *A gospel of life and immortality* (10-12). Christ *hath abolished death.* Paul has used the same verb, "abolished" (Gk., *katargeō*), in a similar way in 1 Cor. 15:26 except that, while in the Corinthian case the thought is future, here, since the aorist is used, a completed event is in view. There is, however, no contradiction for, as Donald Guthrie has pointed out, here the whole range of Christ's work is presented as an accomplished fact, while in Corinthians Paul is pointing to the final consummation.[8] Naturally, verse 10 does not imply that Christians are exempt from dying, but because "Christ has broken the power of death" (NEB) it is no longer to be feared by the believer (Heb. 2: 14-15); hence it has been robbed of its sting (1 Cor. 15:55).

Furthermore, Christ *hath brought life and immortality to light* (10). Even to the saintliest of the Old Testament worthies life beyond the grave was what Bishop Handley Moule described as a "comparative dusk," but Christ is the great Illuminator as well as the great Destroyer. In doing away with death, through His own death and resurrection, He has brought life and immortality into clear view and within the reach of faith.

To the proclamation of such a message Paul was appointed a "herald, apostle and teacher" (12a, NEB), hence he announced it publicly and boldly, he declared it with full authority, and he taught it thoroughly and systematically. He suffered in the process, but who could be ashamed of paying such a price in the announcing of the only gospel adequate for man, in this life and the next?

An Adequate God

2 Tim. 1:13-18

> 13 Hold fast the form of sound words, which thou hast heard of me, in faith and love which is in Christ Jesus.
> 14 That good thing which was committed unto thee keep by the Holy Ghost which dwelleth in us.
> 15 This thou knowest, that all they which are in Asia be turned away from me; of whom are Phygellus and Hermogenes.
> 16 The Lord give mercy unto the house of Onesiphorus; for he oft refreshed me, and was not ashamed of my chain:
> 17 But, when he was in Rome, he sought me out very diligently, and found me.
> 18 The Lord grant unto him that he may find mercy of the Lord in that day: and in how many things he ministered unto me at Ephesus, thou knowest very well.

1. *Paul had proved Him* (12b, 15-18). Paul here states that on the basis of *whom* he had believed—not "what"— he is convinced that he will be sustained until the Great Day. As regards the phrase *that which I have committed unto him,* there is some ambiguity, for this could have reference either to what Paul had committed to God or what God had committed to him. The latter would seem to be the better rendering, for it aligns more closely to the thought of verse 14. But both interpretations lead to the one conclusion.

Scott illustrates this: "The man entrusted with a valuable jewel or document is careful to have it placed in some strong room where it will be guarded night and day. He is nervous and anxious until it has passed out of his own doubtful keeping into one that he can depend upon. Paul thus conceives of the trust that has been laid upon him as guarded by God."[9] What a blessed assurance this is for those who have been entrusted with the Word of God! As Barrett observes, "On no other ground would the work of preaching be for a moment endurable."[10] But with God as his Guard Paul knows neither shame nor fear, not even when almost everyone in the ranks of his associates had been ashamed of him.

In this connection we do not know the identity of Phygellus or Hermogenes, but they would appear to have been the main instigators of the defection from Paul (15). This probably arose out of his second imprisonment, for he has mentioned specifically the one man who did stand firmly by his side, *Onesiphorus . . . was not ashamed of my chain* (16). He even went to the length of tracking the apostle down in his prison (17).

Incidentally, since Paul's prayer in verse 16 was made, not for Onesiphorus but for his household, it has been assumed by some that by this time he had died. On the basis of this assumption the apostle's spontaneous petition on behalf of his friend (18) has been quoted as a precedent for intercession for the dead. Guthrie rightly observes, "It is precarious to base a doctrine, which finds no sanction anywhere else in the New Testament, upon the mere inference that Onesiphorus was dead."[11]

2. *Timothy had, therefore, every reason to prove God* (13-14). Considering Paul's experience of God's faithfulness, and with a gospel of such fullness, he has no hesitation in exhorting young Timothy, in his turn, to keep *that good thing which was committed unto* him, especially since to him also had been promised the aid of the indwelling Spirit (14). His was the same gift, the same gospel, and the same God. Perhaps it might be as well to emphasize the same gospel, for the word in verse 13 translated "form" (Gk., *hupotupōsis*), is sometimes used to describe the outline sketch which an architect makes before preparing his detailed plan.

It has been suggested that in using this word the apostle looked upon his own teaching as no more than a starting point of truth. For example, Guthrie comments, "Timothy is not told merely to repeat what Paul taught, but to follow that teaching as a basis."[12] While this is a perfectly valid interpretation, it must be treated with appropriate caution for, in doctrine, narrow deviations have a way of developing into wide divergences. We may be certain that Paul would not have wished the word *form* to be understood in the sense of a set, lifeless formula, for it was he who wrote of God as "having qualified us to be ministers of a new covenant, not in a written code but in the Spirit; for the written code kills, but the Spirit gives life" (2 Cor. 3:6, RSV). Nevertheless, it is good to remember, as John Stott has observed, that *hupotupōsis* is also used to denote a prototype.[13] Moffatt's version helps to convey this thought—"Keep the great securities of your faith intact, by aid of the Holy Spirit that dwells within us" (14). This would also seem to be in harmony with the apostolic thinking in 2:2.

2 TIMOTHY 2

An Unbindable Word

2 Tim. 2:1-18

> 1 Thou therefore, my son, be strong in the grace that is in Christ Jesus.
> 2 And the things that thou hast heard of me among many witnesses, the same commit thou to faithful men, who shall be able to teach others also.
> 3 Thou therefore endure hardness, as a good soldier of Jesus Christ.
> 4 No man that warreth entangleth himself with the affairs of this life; that he may please him who hath chosen him to be a soldier.
> 5 And if a man also strive for masteries, yet is he not crowned, except he strive lawfully.
> 6 The husbandman that laboureth must be first partaker of the fruits.
> 7 Consider what I say; and the Lord give thee understanding in all things.
> 8 Remember that Jesus Christ of the seed of David was raised from the dead according to my gospel:
> 9 Wherein I suffer trouble, as an evil doer, even unto bonds; but the word of God is not bound.

10 Therefore I endure all things for the elect's sakes, that they may also obtain the salvation which is in Christ Jesus with eternal glory.
11 It is a faithful saying: For if we be dead with him, we shall also live with him:
12 If we suffer, we shall also reign with him: if we deny him, he also will deny us:
13 If we believe not, yet he abideth faithful: he cannot deny himself.
14 Of these things put them in remembrance, charging them before the Lord that they strive not about words to no profit, but to the subverting of the hearers.
15 Study to shew thyself approved unto God, a workman that needeth not to be ashamed, rightly dividing the word of truth.
16 But shun profane and vain babblings: for they will increase unto more ungodliness.
17 And their word will eat as doth a canker: of whom is Hymenaeus and Philetus;
18 Who concerning the truth have erred, saying that the resurrection is past already; and overthrow the faith of some.

Early in this century Robert Blatchford, one of Britain's most aggressive socialists, declared that the Church would not live to see the beginning of another century. When G. K. Chesterton was asked how he felt about such a dismal prospect, he replied, "I am simply prancing with belief!" That was a typical Chestertonian reaction. It was also typically Pauline, for in the previous chapter the apostle had recorded what would have been seen by some as the death knell of the Church in Asia.

In the chapter ahead he is about to describe the future of human society in the most sombre terms. And before the letter ends he will have announced his own impending execution. Yet he opens the present chapter by deliberately giving directions to a relatively ill-equipped successor, but in the full assurance that he, Timothy, will be but one link in a chain of valiant witness that will endure as long as time extends. Paul bases his confidence on two great certainties. First, *that the word of God is not bound.* Moffatt has translated this section of verse 9 as, "But there is no prison for the word of God." The teaching which surrounds this verse is of great importance, and it is presented in a variety of metaphors. But in each one the central thought prevails and this is that, if the Word is to have free course, human channels must be made available; and if these are to be effective, they must be subject to certain disciplines.

1. *The discipline of the teacher* (1-2). So far Timothy's responsibility had consisted largely in holding fast the authentic Word, a Word that had been confirmed "in the presence of many witnesses" (2, NIV). This phrase reminds us that, unlike the secret communication of the private revelations of the errorists, the truth had been committed to him publicly. There is nothing surreptitious in the delivery of the Word of Truth (see Acts 26:26). But now Timothy is to do more than preserve the truth, he is to pass it on. This will necessitate the appointing of suitable teachers, men of unquestioned integrity and ability.

This is still one of the Church's most pressing needs as she seeks to bridge the so-called generation gap. The Church must have men faithful to God's unchanging Word and yet skilled in the art of making it relevant and intelligible to their contemporaries. As in Timothy's day, one of the Church's prior disciplines is to maintain a teaching continuity that is at once conservative and imaginative, but God still promises needed grace (2:1).

2. *The discipline of the soldier* (3-4). "A soldier on active service will not let himself be involved in civilian affairs" (4, NEB). There is not a thing wrong with civilian affairs —for the civilian. But the Christian pastor and teacher is a soldier on active service. Several commentators see in this rule a recommendation against the minister of the gospel becoming involved in "secular" work, but there are other external interests that can hinder a man from giving himself concentratedly and with true sacrifice to gaining skill in wielding the Sword of the Spirit.

Griffiths tells how a church called a man to be their pastor because he appealed to them as a preacher, and then proceeded to destroy him as a preacher. They laid on his conscience so many burdens, unrelated to the pulpit, that it became impossible for him to read and study. He scarcely had time to say his prayers. One day, to the astonishment of all, he suffered a nervous breakdown—and nobody guessed the reason why.[14]

No pastor dare become a recluse or a mere academic remote from his own people and the community to which he has been called. But if he knows not how to use his Sword, he will never be a soldier; and if he is not a soldier of the Word, he will be no true pastor. Nevertheless, soldiering belongs to Christians in all kinds of places and service. Browning was so right when he wrote that "It is so very hard to be a Christian."

3. *The discipline of the runner* (5). This is another favorite Pauline metaphor and the NEB has rendered it most accurately, "No athlete can win a prize unless he has kept the rules." The tense is important, for it reminds us that no athlete was allowed even to enter for a race in the Olympiad who could not swear on oath that he had completed 10 consecutive months of training during the previous year —and this to gain a fading crown! As John Stott has put it: "No rules, no wreath." And there are no exceptions in the Christian race.

4. *The discipline of the farmer* (6). As no athlete is worthy unless he aims for the crown, no farmer is worthy unless he aims for a crop. At this point Bishop Handley Moule has a most perceptive comment to the effect that the labor of the farmer is "strenuous and prosaic toil, totally devoid of excitement, remote from all glamour of peril and applause."[15] For this reason some neglect adequate preparation for preaching and teaching. Shrinking from the grueling, unspectacular disciplines of the study, they prefer to depend upon the inspiration of the moment. Yet in one of his books J. H. Jowett declared, "Men are not deeply influenced by extemporized thought—preaching that costs nothing accomplishes nothing. If the study is a lounge, the pulpit will be an impertinence. It is imperative that the preacher goes into the study to do hard work."[16] Not that study is the be-all and end-all of spiritual farming, for the pastor must do a great deal more than occupy the pulpit.

Prayer and personal evangelism have their own vital places in his program, for spiritual harvests are frequently tear-irrigated and hand-cultivated.

Some scholars, with the full-time ministry in view, have linked verse 6 with 1 Cor. 9:10, drawing attention to Paul's principle "that they which preach the gospel should live of the gospel."

5. *The discipline of the thinker* (7). "Think over what I say, for the Lord will grant you understanding in everything" (RSV). Kelly renders the first part of this verse as, "Work out what I am getting at." This could have been a tactful reminder to Timothy that, while the Lord had promised that the Spirit would lead into all truth, this was not meant to dispense with mental sweat. On the other hand, intellectual perspiration is no substitute for spiritual inspiration. After all our thinking has been done, we must depend upon the Spirit for a true understanding of God's will and Word.

6. *The discipline of the sufferer* (8-13). In verses 8 and 9 Paul reminds Timothy that throughout his ministry he has suffered persecution and ridicule for preaching "Jesus Christ, risen from the dead, descended from David" (8, RSV). Even now he is "suffering and wearing fetters like a criminal" (9, RSV). Nonetheless, "The Word doth win its wid'ning way." But the apostle goes on to impress upon his young successor that suffering is not merely a consequence of such a ministry, it is a decided factor in its success. Such a discipline has a part to play in the saving of God's elect (10). This is quite an astonishing statement, yet it is by no means alone in Paul's teaching, for he has struck the identical note in Col. 1:24. Well might Oswald Chambers speak so frequently of the necessity of Christ's disciples being made "broken bread and poured out wine" for others. And Jowett often reminded us that unless we bleed, we are unlikely to bless.

It is at this point that we reach the fourth "trust-worthy saying" of the Pastorals. Again it is taken from a primitive Christian hymn. Some see it as a commendation of martyrdom, though it is much more likely to be an excerpt from a baptismal hymn. It echoes the teaching of Rom. 6:1-11 and is a further reminder that the bearing of the cross is essential to the wearing of the crown. This is particularly the theme of the first two lines, *For if we be dead with him, we shall also live with him: if we suffer, we shall also reign with him* (11-12a).

Developing his thought on the inevitability of Christian suffering, Paul proceeds, in the second couple of epigrams, to face his readers with the solemn consequences of disloyalty to Christ—"If we deny him, he also will deny us; if we are faithless, he remains faithful—for he cannot deny himself" (12b-13, RSV). Of this last, A. T. Hanson asks, "Is this a threat or a promise?" and he answers by saying that "on the whole it seems better to follow those who take it as an encouraging promise. The author is no grim rigorist and always emphasizes the wideness of God's mercy."[17]

While one can appreciate this preference, such an interpretation is not consistent with the progress of Paul's thought. Surprisingly perhaps, William Hendriksen, a convinced Calvinist, has stressed this. He writes: "It is hardly necessary to add that the meaning of the last line cannot be, 'If we are faithless and deny him, nevertheless he, remaining faithful to his promise, will give us everlasting life.' Aside from being wrong for other reasons, such an interpretation destroys the evident implication of the parallelism between lines three and four. If Christ failed to remain faithful to his threat as well as to his promise, he would be denying *himself,* for in that case he would cease to be the Truth."[18]

7. *The discipline of the builder* (14-18). Applying the analogy of the builder:

a. *The teacher himself must be straight and true* (15). *Study to shew thyself approved unto God.* The Greek word translated "approved" *(dokimos),* was used with reference to "a stone which had been cut and tested . . . fit to be fitted into its place in a building."[19]

b. His teaching must be straight and true (15). *A workman that needeth not to be ashamed, rightly dividing the word of truth.* While some scholars have understood *workman* to denote an agricultural laborer, the word was actually used in a general sense. Scott observes that "in this comparison of the teacher to a *workman* the writer may have in mind some form of labour which is indicated in the latter part of the verse by the word *handle* (lit. 'cutting rightly'). In the KJV we have *rightly dividing.* . . . If a definite craft is indicated, it is most probably that of a mason. . . . As the mason hews the stones and fits them into each other, so the teacher must fashion his message into a structure that will stand foursquare."[20] But, as Paul points out, the teacher must not only build straight and true, he must guard his structure of truth against those who would distort and destroy it.

c. He must prohibit pointless disputation (14). Discussing the word *subverting* in this verse, Donald Guthrie remarks that "the Christian teacher must never forget his responsibility to those who listen. The word *katastrophē,* used here for subversion, which means literally 'turning upside down,' is the antithesis of edification."[21] In other words, while the true teacher builds, the false teacher tears down. In this connection some words of Barclay are worth noting, referring as they do to the apparently innocent setting of the Sunday school class or discussion group. He writes, "It sometimes happens that a simple-minded person finds himself in a group which is tossing heresies about . . . And it may well happen that clever, subtle, speculative, destructive, intellectually reckless discussion may have the effect of demolishing, and not building up, the faith of [that] simple person."[22]

d. He must avoid godless chatter (16-18). "It [such chatter] will lead people into more and more ungodliness, and their talk will eat its way like gangrene. Among them are Hymenaeus and Philetus, who have swerved from the truth by holding that the resurrection is past already" (RSV). Again Paul shows that he is not above changing his metaphor when it suits his purpose, and his aim here is to impress upon Timothy that false teachings are "as dangerous as blood poisoning to the body, and spread like sepsis from a wound" (Phillips). This had been the effect of the work of the two culprit teachers mentioned. Hymenaeus we have met before (1 Tim. 1:20), and we might be surprised that he was still in the church. Evidently he had remained unchastened in spite of having been disciplined, and this intransigence might well have aggravated the doctrinal situation. In any event, the root heresy that he and his partner were disseminating was that "our resurrection has already taken place" (18, NEB).

This betrays the Gnostic inclination of these false teachers and one can understand that, because of this, their teaching might have appealed to the less stable of the Ephesian believers. This would be especially true for those who had not been fully delivered from the instinctive repugnance of the Greek towards any suggestion of physical resurrection. To him true happiness in the future state would be contingent upon the soul being released from the "prison of the body." Repudiation of this heresy does not preclude the enjoyment of a present spiritual resurrection such as Paul teaches, for example, in Romans 6.

The apostle now introduces the second of the two massive certainties upon which he bases his confidence.

An Unshakeable Foundation

2 Tim. 2:19-26

19 Nevertheless the foundation of God standeth sure, having this seal, The Lord knoweth them that are his. And, Let every one that nameth the name of Christ depart from iniquity.
20 But in a great house there are not only vessels of gold and of silver, but also of wood and of earth; and some to honour, and some to dishonour.
21 If a man therefore purge himself from these, he shall be a vessel unto honour, sanctified, and meet for the master's use, and prepared unto every good work.
22 Flee also youthful lusts: but follow righteousness, faith, charity, peace, with them that call on the Lord out of a pure heart.

23 But foolish and unlearned questions avoid, knowing that they do gender strifes.
24 And the servant of the Lord must not strive; but be gentle unto all men, apt to teach, patient,
25 In meekness instructing those that oppose themselves; if God peradventure will give them repentance to the acknowledging of the truth;
26 And that they may recover themselves out of the snare of the devil, who are taken captive by him at his will.

1. *The Church and its true security* (19*a*). In contrast to these defaulting brethren, Hymenaeus and Philetus, who had been "dislodged like ill-fastened stones from the church's structure," Paul affirms, "God's solid foundation stands firm" (NIV). The Church is secure because it is built *upon* a Divine Foundation (1 Cor. 3:10-11; Eph. 2:20), but also because it *is* a Divine Foundation, a God-wrought society. In 1940, Hitler boasted that he would "tear up the Christian Church by the roots." He didn't; he couldn't; for those roots lie beyond the reach of man.

2. *The Church and its true identity* (19*b*). For Paul, the Church's security cannot be divorced from its identity. He proceeds to list these marks or seals of identity.

a. The seal of possession. Having this seal, The Lord knoweth them that are his. This is probably a citation from Num. 16:5, with its reference to the rebellion of Korah. Now, as then, the Lord alone is able to perfectly discern between the precious and the vile, the wheat and the tares within the one field and the sheep and goats within the one fold. Yet this seal is not altogether secret. It is double-sided, and on its reverse it carries the next seal.

b. The seal of profession. Let every one that nameth the name of Christ depart from iniquity. A little Scots girl had the temerity to apply for church membership. A dour kirk elder was doubtful as to her fitness since she was of such tender age, and he subjected her to a close questioning.

"Did you ever find out that you were a sinner?" he asked.

"Indeed, sir, I did," was the reply.

The elder continued, "Do you think you have undergone a change?"

"Yes, sir, I believe I have," came the answer.

"And what makes you so sure?" persisted the elder.

The girl replied, "Before I was running after sin, now I'm running away from it." Here is the unmistakeable identity apart from which there can be no unshakeable security.

3. *The vessels and their essential purity* (20-26). In verses 20 and 21 the apostle is facing squarely the fact that within the fellowship of the Church there will be found those who do not bear the seal of God. To illustrate their position he draws an analogy between any great house and the household of God. But the analogy is not a perfect one for, in the former, there will be found vessels of differing values each with its particular function, whereas, in the latter case, only the vessel unto honor, sanctified and prepared unto every good work, is fit for the Master's use. Timothy is therefore admonished to keep himself pure.

First, he must *purge himself from these* (21). This means, presumably, that he is to separate himself strictly from such as Hymenaeus and Philetus, false teachers who deny, and persist in denying, fundamental Christian truth. In this instance Timothy must himself take action against the errorists (cf. 1 Tim. 1:19-20).

Secondly, he must "shun youthful passion and aim at righteousness" (22, RSV). Thus to be a true servant of the Lord (note the change of metaphor at v. 24), nothing less than purity, both of doctrine and life, will qualify. Moreover, the servant of God must be as diligent in following the good as in fleeing the evil. Wesley must have had something like this in mind when he wrote—

> *Superior sense may I display*
> *By shunning every evil way,*
> *And walking in the good.*

But the final verses of this chapter indicate that the "youthful passions" against which Paul warned Timothy were not of the more usual kind. First of all he mentioned the tendency to quarrel and to be drawn into pointless arguments. Despite such a youthful proclivity, Timothy was to avoid being quarrelsome, instead he was to be "kindly to everyone, an apt teacher, forbearing, correcting his opponents with gentleness" (24, RSV). These are among the more difficult of those demands which the teacher must meet, yet they were exemplified in the ministry of One who did not break the bruised reed nor quench the smoking flax. And where such true gentleness is practised towards those who have begun to stray, "God may perhaps grant that they will repent and come to know the truth, and they may escape from the snare of the devil, after being captured by him to do his will" (25-26, RSV).

The Prospects Calling for Spiritual Courage
2 Timothy 3:1—4:22

2 TIMOTHY 3

The Last Days

2 Tim. 3:1-17

1 This know also, that in the last days perilous times shall come.
2 For men shall be lovers of their own selves, covetous, boasters, proud, blasphemers, disobedient to parents, unthankful, unholy,
3 Without natural affection, trucebreakers, false accusers, incontinent, fierce, despisers of those that are good,
4 Traitors, heady, highminded, lovers of pleasures more than lovers of God;
5 Having a form of godliness, but denying the power thereof: from such turn away.
6 For of this sort are they which creep into houses, and lead captive silly women laden with sins, led away with divers lusts,
7 Ever learning, and never able to come to the knowledge of the truth.
8 Now as Jannes and Jambres withstood Moses, so do these also resist the truth: men of corrupt minds, reprobate concerning the faith.
9 But they shall proceed no further: for their folly shall be manifest unto all men, as theirs also was.
10 But thou hast fully known my doctrine, manner of life, purpose, faith, longsuffering, charity, patience,

11 Persecutions, afflictions, which came unto me at Antioch, at Iconium, at Lystra; what persecutions I endured: but out of them all the Lord delivered me.

12 Yea, and all that will live godly in Christ Jesus shall suffer persecution.

13 But evil men and seducers shall wax worse and worse, deceiving, and being deceived.

14 But continue thou in the things which thou hast learned and hast been assured of, knowing of whom thou hast learned them;

15 And that from a child thou hast known the holy scriptures, which are able to make thee wise unto salvation through faith which is in Christ Jesus.

16 All scripture is given by inspiration of God, and is profitable for doctrine, for reproof, for correction, for instruction in righteousness:

17 That the man of God may be perfect, throughly furnished unto all good works.

As we have seen, Paul was a realist, and he was concerned that his young colleague should share his realism. Consequently he begins this penultimate chapter of his last letter with the words, "You must face the fact: the final age of this world is to be a time of trouble" (1, NEB).

1. *The depravity of the period* (1-9). The *last days* should be distinguished from the "last day." While the latter might be said to denote a point in time, the former indicates the period leading up to that point. This period was inaugurated by the birth of Christ (Heb. 1:2); it very soon saw the birth of the Church of Christ (Acts 2:16-17); and it will continue until the return of Christ.

According to the apostle, within this period there will come "times of stress" (RSV); "terrible times" (NIV); and these are described in all their sordid detail. While, as Guthrie has noted, the list itself seems to lack any premeditated order, it is probably not without intention that at the extremities of this dreadful catalogue of depravity there are references to misplaced love. In v. 2 "men will be lovers of self, lovers of money," and in v. 4, "lovers of pleasure rather than lovers of God" (RSV).

It is no coincidence that another similar list of sins, in Romans 1, is related directly to the giving to other things the place in the affections and attentions which God himself is meant to occupy. It has been well said that "when religion flies out of the window, something else comes up through the drains." According to *The Living Bible* this something produces people who are "proud and boastful, sneering at God, disobedient to parents, ungrateful to them and God . . . hard-hearted and never [giving] in to others; . . . constant liars and troublemakers . . . [thinking] nothing of immorality" (2-4).

Yet perhaps the most shocking feature of this period will be that such people have a form of religion (5). As John Stott has commented, "In the history of mankind, although this is a shameful thing to confess, religion and morality have been more often divorced than married."[23] As regards "holding the form of religion but denying the power of it" (RSV), Guthrie shows how farcical it is when he says, "It is not simply a matter of an organized religion which has ceased to function but a religion which is not intended to function."[24]

At this point the apostle refocusses his attention upon the false teachers and in doing so, in verses 6 and 7, he reveals the cunning, unscrupulous tactics that have characterized the proselytizing methods of the sectaries of every age. These "tradesmen of heresy" are skilled at concentrating their attentions upon "weak women" (6, RSV), an expedient as old as the fall of man. The false teachers well know how susceptible such listeners are, "burdened with sins and swayed by various impulses" (RSV), and how ready to grasp at any specious religious panacea that might be offered. But because they are "always wanting to be taught [they render themselves] incapable of reaching a knowledge of the truth" (NEB).

As examples of such spurious teachers Paul refers to Jannes and Jambres, reputed to have been two of Pharaoh's magicians who, performing their counterfeit miracles, had defied Moses much as their Ephesian counterparts were now defying him. But the apostle assures Timothy that since, like these Old Testament charlatans, the errorists of Ephesus cannot pass the tests of faith, they too will eventually "run out of tricks," thus revealing their folly to all men.

2. *The inevitability of persecution* (10-13). Paul seems determined to leave his successor with no illusions about the rigors that await him. Accordingly, he calls upon Timothy to face up to two other features of these last days. For while the denouement of the errorists may be certain, there are other factors no less sure.

a. *All that will live godly in Christ Jesus shall suffer persecution* (12). To prove this the apostle quotes his own experience. Before ever the present situation developed in Ephesus he had run the gauntlet of suffering and affliction in Antioch, Iconium, and Lystra. In the last-named city Timothy, but a youth at the time, had been a witness of this, and there is good reason to believe that he had been so profoundly impressed as he had beheld Paul's fortitude that he had become a disciple. But Paul makes bold to say that not only had his son in the faith witnessed his example in those spectacular crises when, quite often, special grace seems to be given, but in many and varied circumstances a consistent testimony had been borne. So he could write, "But you, my son, have followed, step by step, my teaching and my manner of life, my resolution, my faith, patience, and spirit of love" (NEB).

Some have expressed surprise at what they consider to be the apostle's lack of modesty in thus enumerating his own Christian graces, but this is no vain or empty boasting. Paul is simply stating incontrovertible facts to illustrate a lesson that a man must learn if he is to be a true disciple of Christ. A true Christian witness will draw persecution in some measure or kind as honey draws bees, and the fact that under such pressures he will be able to maintain his witness reflects no glory upon himself. For "the will of God never leads us where the grace of God cannot keep us."

b. *Evil men and seducers shall wax worse and worse, deceiving and being deceived* (13). Commenting on this verse, Blaiklock observes how the various translators "list a shocking catalogue of terms: 'impostors'; 'pretenders'; 'swindlers'; 'charlatans'; 'mountebanks'—how they swarm."[25] How indeed! But, as Paul has mentioned, not only do they carry within themselves the seeds of their own destruction, those seeds spread infection. The only adequate preventive against that infection, according to the apostle, is to continue in the sound truths already learned and to become increasingly proficient in the understanding and use of them.

3. *The necessity for proficiency* (14-17). Moffatt renders this passage: "But hold you to what you have been taught, hold to your convictions. . . . All scripture is inspired by God and profitable . . . to make the man of God proficient and equip him for good work of every kind."

Paul's command to Timothy runs counter to a great deal being taught today by the so-called religious progressives which, incidentally, is what these false teachers were, for they made "progress from bad to worse" (13, NEB). This "advance in reverse" has been an all too familiar phenomenon for far too long in some theological circles. Nor will it be halted until it is more widely appreciated that the question which matters is not "what is new?" but "what is true?"

So, like Timothy, disregarding the scorn of contemporary Gnostics, we must hold to what we have been taught, frankly confessing that "Christianity has come down to us by inheritance. No man is a spiritual Columbus sailing out into the unknown uncharted seas of the soul on his own. What we know initially about God has come to us through the media of family, Church and community."[26]

In this connection we note that Paul links the knowledge of the truth with the knowledge of the teacher (14), for the dependability of the one is so closely related to the dependability of the other. In Timothy's case the integrity of his teachers had been beyond question. His mother and grandmother had instructed him faithfully in the scriptures of the Old Testament, while Paul, a true apostle of Jesus Christ, through his "sound words," had given him a deep understanding of Christian truth. But the apostle's mention of *the holy scriptures* leads him to a discussion of the purpose and features of sacred truth.

a. The purpose of Holy Scripture (15*b*) is *to make thee wise unto salvation through faith which is in Christ Jesus.* The Bible is a specialized book. In no sense unscientific, by no means antiscientific, it is, nevertheless, a handbook on salvation and not on science. Paul consistently taught that this was the chief purpose of the Old Testament. He did not see the Scriptures of his fathers merely as a compilation of ancient records, laws, usages, and prophecies but supremely as a revelation of God's saving purpose (see, e.g., Rom. 1:1-3; 4:1-8; 10:5).

b. The inspiration of Holy Scripture (16). Some scholars have rendered the opening words of this verse as "every inspired scripture has its use" (NEB), thus allowing, by implication, that some scriptures may not be inspired. In fairness it should be said that both the KJV and NEB translations are textually valid though we have seen Moffatt's preference, and this is shared by most modern translators. Guthrie, after having discussed the question with scholarly care, has given his reason for this: "While not ruling out the possibility of the alternative interpretation, it is rather more in harmony with grammar and syntax to translate, 'All scripture is inspired by God and profitable . . .' (RSV)."[27] No theory of inspiration is propounded by Paul, but the NIV has conveyed the essential emphasis, "All scripture is God-breathed."

One further question about the inspiration of Scripture relates to what Paul meant by the phrase *all scripture.* About its referring to the Old Testament there is no doubt, but what of his own "sound words"? Evidently Peter accorded to these the status of Scripture (see 2 Pet. 3:16). As to the inspiration of the entire New Testament it is interesting to read the testimony of a renowned contemporary translator, J. B. Phillips. He has written, "The New Testament, given a fair hearing, does not need me or anyone else to defend it. It has the proper ring for anyone who

has not lost his ear for truth. . . . As the years have passed
—and it is now twenty-five years since I began translating
the 'Epistles'—my conviction has grown that the New
Testament is in a quite special sense inspired."[28]

c. *The profit from Holy Scripture* (16). Because it is
concerned with both belief and behavior, having "its uses
for teaching the truth and refuting error . . . for reformation
of manners and discipline in right living" (NEB), it is
God's chief instrument for equipping His servant for life
and ministry. As Stott puts it: "Paul's advice to his young
successor was 'Let the word of God make you a man of
God.'"[29]

2 TIMOTHY 4

The Charge to Preach

2 Tim. 4:1-5

> 1 I charge thee therefore before God, and the Lord Jesus Christ, who
> shall judge the quick and the dead at his appearing and his kingdom;
> 2 Preach the word; be instant in season, out of season; reprove, re-
> buke, exhort with all longsuffering and doctrine.
> 3 For the time will come when they will not endure sound doctrine;
> but after their own lusts shall they heap to themselves teachers, having
> itching ears;
> 4 And they shall turn away their ears from the truth, and shall be
> turned unto fables.
> 5 But watch thou in all things, endure afflictions, do the work of an
> evangelist, make full proof of thy ministry.

"Unless we are to reduce all Christian worship to
ritual spectacle, all evangelism to individual contact, all
Christian education to discussion groups in which 'articu-
late ignorance spreads bewilderment more widely,' preaching will always be needed."[30] According to these opening
verses preaching always has been needed. Indeed, when
Dibelius, in the course of exploring Christian origins pro-
nounced his great dictum, "In the beginning was the sermon," he might well have had the words of Paul in mind.
But the apostle has also reminded us that preaching is not

only indispensable, it is difficult and intensely demanding. This is implied in the solemnity and responsibilities of the charge.

1. *The solemnity of the charge* (1). It is impossible to conceive of a charge more solemn than this, given by an aged preacher so soon himself to be called to account, and reminding his young lieutenant that he too is being called upon to discharge his ministry in the presence of the One who will judge both the living and the dead when He appears.

2. *The responsibilities within the charge* (2-5). These are fivefold, all of them imperatives and all aorists.

   a. Preach the Word (2). This is the basis of the charge, and for a very good reason. For not only does the Word make new men of those who savingly hear it, it makes new men of those who preach it. Even as Paul writes these parting words, he is keenly conscious of Timothy's timidity. How would such a shrinking, retiring young man fare under the exacting burdens that were being thrust upon him? Especially, how would he stand up to the unavoidable confrontation with the sectarians, bold and brash as such men are wont to be? Well, the apostle did not insist that Timothy should stand upon his dignity as an ordained elder, or assert his authority as an appointed leader. Where authority must be asserted much of it has already been lost anyway. Instead he said, *Preach the word,* for well he knew that neither assertiveness, nor dogmatism, nor even rhetorical power will make for effective Christian leadership. In the ministry true authority derives, not from the one who preaches but from what he preaches.

   b. Preach the Word urgently (2). Phillips translates it: "Never lose your sense of urgency, in season or out of season." Someone has called preaching "thirty minutes to raise the dead," but we don't always have that long. During the First World War Bishop Taylor-Smith was chaplain-general to the British forces. When a clergyman came to him applying for a chaplaincy, instead of giving a direct reply the bishop drew his watch from his pocket with a dramatic gesture, glanced at it, and said, "I am a soldier dying on the battlefield; I have three minutes to live. What have you got to say to me?" Taken aback the clergyman stood dumb. "Quickly!" urged the bishop. "Time is fleeting. Only two of my three minutes are left. Is there nothing you can tell me that will help my soul?" Still there was no answer. The bishop's voice grew very grave as he went on: "There is but one minute now between me and eternity. Have you no saving word to speak to me?" Feeling that he must somehow save face, the clergyman fumbled for his prayer book, but the bishop waved it aside. "No, no," he said, "not that . . . now!" The applicant was rejected. Only he who is moved with the sense of urgency is equipped to deal with an emergency.

c. *Preach the Word pertinently* (2). "Use argument, reproof and appeal" (NEB). Such preaching is then addressed to the whole man at each point of need, appealing to the reason, searching the conscience, and moving the will. Macaulay said, "The object of oratory is not truth, but persuasion." But while the preacher is not necessarily an orator, he is in fact more than an orator, for the object of preaching is *both* truth and persuasion. And the preacher must be skilled in applying the latter, for, as Professor Dickie of St. Andrews said, "We preach always in anxiety, always under tension, since we are preaching always for a verdict." This assumes that we shall gain response at mental, emotional, or volitional levels—and, ideally, at all of them.

d. *Preach the Word patiently* (2); "using the utmost patience in your teaching" (Phillips). Guthrie has marked Paul's connection between reproof, long-suffering, and doctrine in his comment on this verse: "Christian reproof without the grace of long-suffering has often led to a harsh, censorious attitude intensely harmful to the cause of Christ. But the other requirement is equally essential, for correction must be intelligently understood and hence based on 'teaching.' To rebuke without instruction is to leave the root cause of the error untouched."[31]

e. *Preach the Word persistently* (3-5). No matter how unpopular or unpalatable biblical truth may be, the man of God must persist in preaching it. He must personify Bunyan's portrait of the preacher: "Christian saw the picture of a very grave person . . . and this was the fashion of it; It had eyes lifted up to heaven, the best of books was in his hand, the law of truth was written upon his lips, the world was behind his back, he stood as if he pleaded with men."

The Valediction of a Preacher

2 Tim. 4:6-8

> 6 For I am now ready to be offered, and the time of my departure is at hand.
> 7 I have fought a good fight, I have finished my course, I have kept the faith:
> 8 Henceforth there is laid up for me a crown of righteousness, which the Lord, the righteous judge, shall give me at that day: and not to me only, but unto all them also that love his appearing.

With these verses the Epistle reaches its climax. Paul's final counsels have been given, his great work is concluded, and "already [his] life is being poured out on the altar" (NEB). This vivid metaphor was probably suggested to Paul by the Jewish practice of pouring a drink-offering of wine at the foot of the altar prior to certain sacrifices being offered (Exod. 29:40; Num. 28:7).

But in verse 6 the apostle has in mind not only a libation but a liberation, for the word translated "departure" (Gk., *analusis*), conjures up the image of a soldier or a traveller striking camp, or of a ship weighing anchor. Thus the fettered veteran missionary sees himself as a vessel about to be loosed from its moorings. Soon his greatest ambition will be realized and he will be with Christ, which is far better. (See Phil. 1:23 where the identical metaphor is used.)

Now, on the eve of this grand adventure, Paul reviews

his long ministry and, in doing so, writes what has been described as "the ideal epitaph," though one preacher has ventured to say that the "I" has been given undue prominence. He suggests that, "It would have been more like Paul to have written, 'I have been kept in the faith . . .', for should God not have been given all the glory?" With due respect one might reply that it was the Paul of the "crucified I" who penned these words. When he declared, *I have kept the faith,* that was about the only thing he had kept. All things else he had counted but refuse that he might gain the goal (Phil. 3:4-11). This was why he was able to face the future without fear. Execution holds no real terrors for the one who has already undergone crucifixion. This also explains why Paul could speak so confidently of the reward awaiting him, for after crucifixion there comes the coronation.

There has been some question as to what the crown, or garland, of righteousness represents, but it is most unlikely that Paul was thinking of a "crown which consists of righteousness" (cf. "crown of life" in Jas. 1:12; Rev. 2:10; and "crown of glory" in 1 Pet. 5:4, where the genitive is one of substance). The apostle had consistently taught that righteousness was the present possession of the believer, it was of God through faith in Christ, so that White is undoubtedly correct when he understands Paul to mean "the crown which belongs to, or is the due reward of, righteousness."[32] Paul declares that it will be given in that day by the One whose judgments, unlike that of a Roman emperor, are altogether righteous.

Nor will such a reward be exclusively Paul's, for he will share the honor with *all them also that love his appearing,* a qualification which is at once encouraging and salutary. Calvin has commented that Paul excludes from the number of the faithful those to whom the advent of Christ is terrible. The degree of ardent longing with which we await His coming is the measure of our fitness to wear His crown.

The Dereliction of a Preacher

2 Tim. 4:9-21

9 Do thy diligence to come shortly unto me:

10 For Demas hath forsaken me, having loved this present world, and is departed unto Thessalonica; Crescens to Galatia, Titus unto Dalmatia.

11 Only Luke is with me. Take Mark, and bring him with thee: for he is profitable to me for the ministry.

12 And Tychicus have I sent to Ephesus.

13 The cloak that I left at Troas with Carpus, when thou comest, bring with thee, and the books, but especially the parchments.

14 Alexander the coppersmith did me much evil: the Lord reward him according to his works:

15 Of whom be thou ware also; for he hath greatly withstood our words.

16 At my first answer no man stood with me, but all men forsook me: I pray God that it may not be laid to their charge.

17 Notwithstanding the Lord stood with me, and strengthened me; that by me the preaching might be fully known, and that all the Gentiles might hear: and I was delivered out of the mouth of the lion.

18 And the Lord shall deliver me from every evil work, and will preserve me unto his heavenly kingdom: to whom be glory for ever and ever. Amen.

19 Salute Prisca and Aquila, and the household of Onesiphorus.

20 Erastus abode at Corinth: but Trophimus have I left at Miletum sick.

21 Do thy diligence to come before winter. Eubulus greeteth thee and Pudens, and Linus, and Claudia, and all the brethren.

So far Timothy must have found the contents of this chapter more than a little daunting. The gravity of Paul's charge, followed by the quality of his testimony, must have caused the younger man almost to despair of ever attaining the heights expected of him. And these present verses would hardly seem calculated to lessen his apprehension, for rarely will one read such compelling evidence of that loneliness which is inseparable from leadership. At this point one can almost feel the winter chill of that Mamertine prison.

Yet there is warmth in these words, the warmth of a genuine humanness. Contrary to what one might expect, as earth recedes and heaven draws near, this warrior of the Cross begins to write of practical concerns. Sometimes one gains an impression that in such an hour the deeply spiritual person loses sight of such mundane matters as books and cloaks, but not Paul. Here he is very much Paul the man, and a very frail man at that, with very human needs. Yet his humanity is no reflection upon his spirituality; in fact, perhaps at no time in his life did he illustrate just so clearly his own words, "We have this treasure in earthen vessels, that the excellency of the power may be of God, and not of us" (2 Cor. 4:7). So one can imagine that Timothy might well have felt his own heart strangely warmed as he realized that Paul, his great spiritual mentor and father, was a man of like passions as himself.

1. *Physical needs* (13). Paul was no false ascetic, as we have seen. He saw no virtue in freezing to death for the glory of God. While he had not much longer to live, for the residue of his days he was still answerable to God for the way in which he treated his body. It was still God's temple and vessel. So, as a true spiritual athlete to the end, he kept his body in its place, but he kept a place for his body, in the will of God.

2. *Mental and spiritual needs* (13). Paul was a writer, one whose works will live on after those of most others will have been forgotten. Yet in such dire circumstances he still felt the need to stretch and refresh his mind—so, he says, *Bring . . . the books.* But he was, in particular, one of that tiny number of divinely inspired writers through whom God himself spoke. Yet he wrote, *Bring . . . especially the parchments.* Unlike some who have boasted of their private revelations, and who therefore have imagined that they have graduated beyond the need for Bible reading and study, the apostle longed earnestly to search the Scriptures. He was sure that "the Lord had for him yet more light and truth to break forth from His Word." One does not deprecate genuine personal divine guidance, but at all times it must be checked in the light of that one and only infallible Word. Otherwise, as one has said, "The inner light can sometimes prove to be the shortest route to outer darkness."

3. *Social needs* (9-12, 14-18).

a. We see, not only from the list of names in this passage, but from those in other Epistles, how wide was Paul's circle of friends. Like his Lord, he was no recluse, no private pietist; he needed and greatly enjoyed the fellowship of kindred minds. Yet, in the interests of Christ's kingdom, he was ready to sacrifice human fellowship. From verses 10 and 11 it would seem that he had despatched Crescens and Titus to various other centres on the Lord's work, leaving only Luke to remain with him.

One can easily imagine that Luke, with his physician's skill, must have been a source of great help and strength to the aged apostle. In verses 19 to 21 reference is made to other friends, among them Prisca (Priscilla) and Aquila, two of Paul's oldest and most devoted helpers. Remarkable tribute is paid to their loyalty and devotion in Rom. 16:4 where Paul wrote that they had "risked their necks" (NEB) for his life, thus laying not only himself but all the Gentile churches under their debt. The household of Onesiphorus we have already met (1:16). Erastus may possibly be identified as the city treasurer of Corinth (Rom. 16:23), although another person bearing this name was sent by the apostle to accompany Timothy, in advance of himself, into Macedonia (Acts 19:22).

The four persons listed in verse 21 are not known, but since these are specifically named and are thus distinguished from the rest of the brethren in Rome, it is thought that perhaps they had plucked up courage to visit Paul in prison. Trophimus (20) was a trusted Gentile helper (Acts 20:4; 21:29; 2 Cor. 8:19-22), but we are not given details of the sickness which had confined him to Miletum, nor why he had not been healed. But Chrysostom has made the point that "the apostle could not do everything." Those who contend that the Lord is committed to invariably healing in response to faith might bear this in mind. The Lord reserves the right to sovereignly grant or withhold healing.

b. As was inevitable, Paul had friends who gave him

pain, and this he felt most keenly at this time. Yet he was no cynic on this account. In this connection Demas must have brought untold sorrow to his heart, for at one time the young man had been one of his closest associates. In Col. 4:14 and Philem. 24 his name is linked with that of Luke, but apparently he had found the demands of being a fellow laborer with Paul too costly.

On the basis of Scripture evidence we cannot say that Demas became an apostate, but there is a later tradition which so describes him. Nor can we determine the identity of Alexander (14) or the nature of his calumny, though some commentators see in verse 15 evidence that he had appeared as a witness for the prosecution against Paul on the occasion of the preliminary hearing referred to in verse 16. In any case, Timothy is warned to avoid him, for "the Lord will repay him for what he has done" (14, NIV). Kelly comments that this "expresses a prediction rather than an imprecation."[33]

We have no means of telling who, besides Alexander, were among the *all men* who had forsaken the apostle "at the first hearing of [his] case" (16, NEB), but, apparently, these "fair weather friends" shrank from any close identification with one who had been put to an open shame for the gospel's sake. Nevertheless, in such an event Paul had come to know the fellowship of his Lord's sufferings when, in the hour of His greatest need, "they all forsook him and fled" (Mark 14:50). Moreover, the Lord had stood with him and strengthened him; and, said he, *I was delivered out of the mouth of the lion* (17).

Several attempts have been made to determine how *the lion* should be understood. Some suggest that Paul had Nero in mind, others believe he was referring to Satan, though the phrase may be a proverbial expression for extreme danger. But as John Stott has said, "At all events Paul emerges from this incident as a New Testament Daniel. In the future, too, Paul goes on confidently, the Lord will also 'save me for his heavenly kingdom'; though Nero may soon dispatch me from my earthly kingdom."[34] In the meantime, as he had admonished Timothy, so he himself had done, for he had preached the word "out of season" (see v. 17). Evidently he had grasped the opportunity afforded by his preliminary hearing to preach the gospel, seeing in this event too good a chance to miss. Alfred Plummer has described how, in that Roman forum, the apostle would face one of the most representative audiences to be found anywhere in the world.

c. As might be expected, Paul longed to have Timothy by his side. Twice he beseeches him, *do thy diligence to come,* with the specially urgent addition in verse 21, *before winter,* this probably because the Adriatic would then be closed to shipping for a period of weeks. This intensely human touch strongly suggests the imminence of the apostle's trial, and it could mean that Timothy's journey had already been planned in principle.

Scarcely less moving is Paul's request that Timothy bring Mark with him. We recall the sharp contention which had arisen between Paul and Barnabas on this young man's account (Acts 15:38). For some reason, at that time Paul had lost confidence in him and had flatly refused to comply with Barnabas' request that he be taken along with the senior missionaries. Judging from Col. 4:10, however, Paul had begun to have second thoughts about young Mark, for he commended him to that church. Now here, in verse 11, we see the breach completely healed and the apostle's confidence fully restored as he writes, "Pick up Mark and bring him with you, for I find him a useful assistant" (NEB).

In contrast, what an unspeakable tragedy it is when disagreements and misunderstandings are left unresolved, so that "winter comes" and death's icy hand forever restrains any hope of reconciliation. One of the saddest epitaphs ever composed was inscribed by Thomas Carlyle over his wife's grave in the old Kirk Yard in Haddington— "Oh, that I had you with me yet for five minutes by my side that I might tell you all." All what? We do not know. Winter came too soon.

The Apostle's Last Word

2 Tim. 4:22

> 22 The Lord Jesus Christ be with thy spirit. Grace be with you. Amen.

This final benediction is in two parts:

1. *The Lord Jesus Christ be with thy spirit.* Here the singular *thy* is employed giving to the words an exclusively personal application. The phrasing is similar to that used by Paul in Gal. 6:18 and Philem. 25, though J. H. Bernard draws a meaningful contrast between the usage there and here. He writes, *"There* the presence of 'the grace of the Lord', *here* the presence of 'the Lord of grace' is invoked."[35]

2. "Grace be with you all!" (NEB). In this case Paul addresses the entire community. So, if 2 Timothy is the lastest of the three Pastorals, as seems most likely, these are the last words to come from the pen of the great apostle. How typical of him that they should be inclusive rather than exclusive.

The Epistle to
TITUS

Topical Outline of Titus

Address and Salutation (1:1-4)
> The Nature and Scope of Apostolic Authority (1:1-3)
> The Character of an Apostolic Deputy (1:4)

The Place and Purpose of Church Organization (1:5-16)
> Church Organization Essential (1:5)
> Church Organization Adaptable (1:6-9)
> Church Organization Disciplinary (1:10-16)

The Province of Pastoral Indoctrination (2:1—3:11)
> Guidance for the Older (2:2-4)
> Guidance for the Younger (2:5-8)
> Guidance for the Christian Worker (2:9-10)
> Theological Basis (2:11-15)
> Guidance for the Christian Citizen (3:1-2)
> Theological Implications (3:3-8)
> Action Against Heretics (3:9-11)

Final Instruction and Salutation (3:12-15)

Address and Salutation

Titus 1:1-4

TITUS 1

The Nature and Scope of Apostolic Authority

Titus 1:1-3

> 1 Paul, a servant of God, and an apostle of Jesus Christ, according to the faith of God's elect, and the acknowledging of the truth which is after godliness;
> 2 In hope of eternal life, which God, that cannot lie, promised before the world began;
> 3 But hath in due times manifested his word through preaching, which is committed unto me according to the commandment of God our Saviour;

This is one of Paul's longer salutations, but in view of its content it is remarkably concise. As is common in his letters, it anticipates the main purpose, in this case "to further the faith of God's elect and their knowledge of the truth which accords with godliness" (1, RSV). Thus, at the outset, he draws a sharp contrast between the high ethical standards of the Christian and the traditional moral turpitude of the Cretan.

In addition, within these opening verses, Paul has defined "more completely than in any other New Testament passage the scope and function of the apostleship."[1] This may seem surprising since the apostle is writing to a close and trusted friend, but the detail is probably included because of the semiofficial character of the Epistle. Furthermore, it was important that Titus, now being authorized to act as an apostolic delegate in Crete, should be reminded of certain responsibilities attaching to his office.

1. *A servant of God.* Barclay describes this as a "title of mingled humility and legitimate pride."[2] It implies a total subservience to God, but it also puts Paul in the select line of patriarchs and prophets, those to whom, and through whom, God spoke to men.

2. *An apostle of Jesus Christ.* This more usual designation draws attention to Paul's right to speak currently on behalf of Jesus Christ. The apostle never forgot, and was constantly amazed, that he should have been chosen to be Christ's ambassador and mouthpiece (2 Cor. 5:20).

3. *The features of an apostolic ministry.* Such a ministry is to be exercised within the context of faith, knowledge, godliness, and hope.

    a. Faith (1). According to the RSV it was part of the apostolic task to "further the faith of God's elect," and here the word is used in the more usual Pauline sense of trust in God. No ministry is more greatly needed for, sadly, in the case of too many Christians, faith has become fixed but not furthered. Yet the just are to live by faith, that is, faith is meant to be the life-style of those who have been justified and sanctified by faith. And faith, to be furthered, must be put to the test. This is a definite spiritual law, as George Mueller of Bristol proved when, at God's behest, he set out to house, feed, and clothe 2,000 orphans with no backing but the promises of God. Many have longed for a like faith but, as Samuel Chadwick used to say, "We sigh for a like faith in our own souls. BUT WE DO NOT TAKE THE ORPHANS. We shrink from the risk."[3]

    b. Knowledge (1). "To further . . . their knowledge of the truth" (RSV). Saving faith must issue in a correct grasp of the apostolic message.

      (1) *Faith is more than "positive thinking."* "This seems to be the confusion made by Norman Vincent Peale. Much of what he writes is true. His fundamental conviction concerns the power of the human mind. He quotes William James that 'the greatest discovery of my genera-

tion is that human beings can alter their lives by altering their attitudes of mind.'... So Dr. Peale develops his thesis about positive thinking, which he goes on (mistakenly) to equate with faith. What exactly is the 'faith' which he is advocating? His first chapter in *The Power of Positive Thinking* is significantly entitled, 'Believe in Yourself.'"[4] Small wonder Adlai Stevenson said, "I find Paul appealing, but Peale appalling!" For never did the apostle imply that faith in self bears any resemblance to faith in God. In fact we do not begin to enjoy the latter until we have abandoned the former.

(2) *Faith is not a substitute for rational thinking.* It has been well said that the day of "consecrated ignorance" is past, if indeed it ever existed. For deliberate ignorance in the guise of a superior sanctity has no place upon the altar of God. One would have to admit that on occasion an overweening intellectual pursuit has been to the detriment of the soul, but this need not be. As proof of this one "need only look at the life of John Baillie, who combined the affectionate faith of a little child with the tough mentality of a highly civilized man. In one of the books which Mrs. Baillie has released since her husband's death, the biographical note tells how three objects in the great man's study were symbolic of the wholeness of his career. One was the desk where he wrote, a second was the chair where he read, and the third was the pad where, daily, he knelt to pray."[5]

(3) *There is a quality of understanding unattainable apart from faith.* Consequently Paul puts his concern for the furtherance of the *faith* of God's elect before their knowledge (1, RSV). No one needs a firmer spiritual grounding than the scholar, but it is no less true that there are realms of understanding which lie forever beyond the grasp of the worldly-wise (see Matt. 11:25). For there is a quality of knowledge which is attainable only under moral conditions. Indeed, the peril in the Cretan churches arose largely from the attempts of the sectaries there to divorce knowledge from morality.

c. *Godliness* (1). So it was that he wrote of the "knowledge of the truth which accords with godliness" (RSV). He will discuss this in some detail in the course of the Epistle, but at this point he introduces yet another basic feature of his apostolic ministry, namely, hope, a feature of which he usually links with faith.

d. *Hope* (2). He speaks of *hope of eternal life*. However, in this particular instance, Paul has linked hope with the person of God rather than with faith though, of course, Christian faith is essentially trust in God. Hope rests upon the following solid foundations.

(1) *The promise of God.* This is a promise which cannot fail for it has been given by a *God that cannot lie.*

(2) *The purpose of God.* And this is a purpose that cannot fail, for it was "promised before the beginning of time" (Phillips and NIV). Some modern translators have preferred the rendering "promised ages ago" (RSV and NEB), but Kelly has expressed doubt as to the accuracy of this interpretation of what is, literally, "before eternal times" (see also 2 Tim. 1:9). He prefers holding to the thought of "God's pre-cosmic resolve."

(3) *The preaching of the Word* (3). "At his appointed season he brought his word to light through the preaching entrusted to me by the command of God our Savior" (NIV). Here Paul has reached the apex of his apostolic ministry, for through his preaching, by divine commandment, God had revealed His eternal purpose on this plane of time.

The Character of an Apostolic Deputy

Titus 1:4

> 4 To Titus, mine own son after the common faith: Grace, mercy, and peace, from God the Father and the Lord Jesus Christ our Saviour.

While we learn very largely from the Corinthian correspondence that Titus possessed qualities of person and skills which ideally fitted him to pursue his difficult and delicate assignment in Crete, it is from this verse that we learn of his true capabilities.

1. *Titus was a "true-born son in the faith"* (NEB). Compare this with 1 Tim. 1:2 (NEB), though here Paul makes a special point of the fact that Titus shares his faith. This ensured the preservation of both the spirit and content of the gospel in Crete, and this was of fundamental importance.

2. *Titus was a capable administrator.* See 2 Cor. 8:6— "Now this has made us ask Titus, who has already done so much among you, to complete his task by arranging for you too to share in this work of generosity" (Phillips). It had been a tribute to Titus' skill in the field of administration that he had been entrusted with a project which lay so close to Paul's heart.

3. *Titus was a capable arbitrator.* See 2 Cor. 8:16-23. In this connection Barclay adds a fitting comment: "There are the people who can make a bad situation worse, and there are the people who can bring order out of chaos and peace out of strife. Titus was the man to send to the place where there was trouble."[6]

The Place and Purpose of Church Organization
Titus 1:5-16

Having expressed greetings in words similar to those addressed to Timothy, the apostle at once reminds Titus of the directions given to him when he had been left in charge of the Cretan work. While this is one of the incidents unrecorded in Acts, there is no reason to doubt that it does belong to the period of Paul's release from his first imprisonment (see Introduction: The Historical Problem). Nor is there any question, judging from these verses, as to what Paul's prime concern had been for the Cretan work.

Church Organization Essential

Titus 1:5

> 5 For this cause left I thee in Crete, that thou shouldest set in order the things that are wanting, and ordain elders in every city, as I had appointed thee:

His direction to Titus had been to "straighten out what was left unfinished and appoint elders in every town" (5, NIV).

1. To some, "organized religion" is a contradiction in terms. The view of such ecclesiastical libertarians would be that religion, like love or art, is not organizable. But nothing, not even the most spiritual brand of religion—nor love nor art, for that matter—can survive for long without some degree of form and order. It must be said that, as a rule, one finds that those who resent church organization are unwilling to accept most other kinds as well. What is more, it is by no means unknown for the unorganizable type, having withdrawn from an existing fellowship, to set up very soon an organization of his own which, not infrequently, proves to be a model of hyper-autocratic government!

2. Church organization is essential to the preservation of order, the cultivation of Christian fellowship and service, the conservation of Christian orthodoxy, and, no less importantly, the widest communication of the Christian gospel. An instance of how this last purpose can be hindered is seen in the Corinthian church. Here was a congregation well endowed with spiritual gifts, by no means lacking in spiritual zeal, yet because, by and large, every man did what was right in his own eyes, Paul had to write and say, "If therefore the whole church come together into one place, and all speak with tongues, and there come in those that are unlearned, or unbelievers, will they not say that ye are mad?" (1 Cor. 14:23). It is possible for unorganized fellowships to enjoy a wonderful time, to be full of fire and enthusiasm, and yet be the last place that needy, lonely,

lost, and confused souls will seek. Needless to say, we must at any cost avoid stumbling into the opposite ditch, finding outselves so hidebound and walled in by the most excellent and, possibly, scriptural forms of organization that the Spirit of true liberty can find no point of entry.

Church Organization Adaptable

Titus 1:6-9

> 6 If any be blameless, the husband of one wife, having faithful children not accused of riot or unruly.
> 7 For a bishop must be blameless, as the steward of God; not self-willed, not soon angry, not given to wine, no striker, not given to filthy lucre;
> 8 But a lover of hospitality, a lover of good men, sober, just, holy, temperate;
> 9 Holding fast the faithful word as he hath been taught, that he may be able by sound doctrine both to exhort and to convince the gainsayers.

There are significant organizational variations in the Cretan situation. For example, whereas in Ephesus Timothy had apparently inherited an existing structure of church officers, Titus was authorized to appoint elders himself. The fact that, in doing so, he was not forbidden to recruit novices, furnishes additional evidence, not only of organizational flexibility, but also of the fact that the Christian communities in Crete were of very recent origin. A further modification, which points to a more rudimentary order in this area, is that no provision seems to have been made for the appointment of deacons.

From verse 5 it is plain that by this time the office of elder had been given authoritative Pauline endorsement. In comparing verses 5 and 7 it is also clear that the terms "elder" and "bishop" had become virtually synonymous. This conclusion is strengthened by the fact that the list of qualifications given in verses 6 to 9 closely resembles that contained in 1 Tim. 3:2-7. We may also judge from a comparison of these lists that, adaptable as the organization of the primitive Church was, there was one vital constant, namely, the high character demanded of its leadership. Indeed, it is significant that, perhaps on account of the relative immaturity of the church in Crete, and the low moral calibre of the Cretan society at large, Paul's directions regarding the children of elders take on an even firmer line.

In this case the elder is to be a man whose children "are believers, who are under no imputation of loose living, and are not out of control" (NEB). When a society is as lax in morals as it was in Crete, and as it is in much of our world, it is imperative that the home be seen as the moral and spiritual training ground that it was originally meant to be. A further stiffening of the detailed requirements laid down in 1 Tim. 3:2-7 is seen in verse 9 of this chapter, for while, in Ephesus, the ability to teach betokened a rather exceptional elder, here it is stated as an essential qualification. The reason for this is probably implied in verse 10 where Crete is shown to be a veritable hotbed of heresy, demanding that every church leader be capable of meeting and refuting it.

Church Organization Disciplinary

Titus 1:10-16

> 10 For there are many unruly and vain talkers and deceivers, specially they of the circumcision:
> 11 Whose mouths must be stopped, who subvert whole houses, teaching things which they ought not, for filthy lucre's sake.
> 12 One of themselves, even a prophet of their own, said, The Cretians are alway liars, evil beasts, slow bellies.
> 13 This witness is true. Wherefore rebuke them sharply, that they may be sound in the faith;
> 14 Not giving heed to Jewish fables, and commandments of men, that turn from the truth.
> 15 Unto the pure all things are pure: but unto them that are defiled and unbelieving is nothing pure; but even their mind and conscience is defiled.
> 16 They profess that they know God; but in works they deny him, being abominable, and disobedient, and unto every good work reprobate.

Verse 9 describes the end product of church organization—a people who know what they believe, who believe the right things, who are able to declare their beliefs cogently and convincingly, and whose behavior matches their beliefs. The situation in Crete cried out for such folk for, said Paul, "there are plenty of insubordinate creatures who impose on people with their empty arguments, particularly those who have come over from Judaism" (10, Moffatt).

Here Paul has unmasked the troublemakers in Crete. Their teaching was akin to that of their Ephesian counterparts but with a strong Judaistic accent (10, 14). They openly flouted authority, they talked "nonsense and yet in so doing . . . managed to deceive men's minds" (10, Phillips). Again, like their colleagues in Ephesus they insinuated themselves into the family life of the community, and their chief aim was sordid gain (11). In short, they were typical "men of Crete . . . always liars, evil and beastly, lazy and greedy" (12, Phillips). Some have felt that while this may well have been a quotation from a Cretan prophet, its use in this context betrayed a most un-Pauline tactlessness, since the letter was intended for public reading. But in dealing with such a peril Paul was not one to mince his words, and the medicine he prescribed was no less strong than his diagnosis—*whose mouth must be stopped.* However, his ultimate objective was remedial—"Don't hesitate to reprimand them sharply, for you want them to be sound and healthy Christians" (13, Phillips).

But, as already noted, such salutary discipline can be effectively administered only by the proper persons.

1. *People who know what they believe.* For only such people can hope to gain a hearing. "There is no doubt that things are as they are in the Christian Church throughout the world today because we have lost our authority. We are faced by the fact that the masses of the people are outside the Church. They are there, I suggest, because the Church has in one way or another lost its authority. As a result, the people have ceased to listen or to pay any attention to its message."[7] And, as a further result, they have been subjected to the most vicious and subversive kinds of propaganda. For while the people of God have been speaking so falteringly, the enemies of God have been sowing their message broadcast. How true are the words of Daniel Webster,

If truth be not diffused, error will be.
If God and His Word are not known and received,
The devil and his works will gain the ascendancy;
If the evangelical volumes do not reach every hamlet,
The pages of a corrupt and licentious literature will;
If the power of the gospel is not felt throughout
    the length and breadth of the land,
Anarchy and misrule, degradation and misery,
    corruption and darkness,
Will reign without mitigation, nor end.

The sentiments in these prophetic lines agree with the mind of the apostle.

2. *People who believe the right things.* In such a day as ours there is absolutely no justification for echoing the parrot-cry of yesterday, "It doesn't matter what a man believes as long as he believes it sincerely." "Little did the assistants in the British Museum who handed out books to Karl Marx know what was going on in his mind."[8] Hence Paul's concern as expressed in verse 9.

3. *People who are able to communicate what they believe.* This is the task of the people, not alone of the bishop. Those who have interpreted the word *bishop,* in verse 7, in the Ignatian sense, have tended to see this officer as an hierarchical figure who acts as the "official guardian of apostolic orthodoxy." Consequently, in such communions, the people have been content to look upon the bishop and the clergy as the spokesmen for the Church. There may have been periods in the Church's history, for example when Gnosticism began to make such an impact upon the Church in the second century, during which it was essential to have an able leader speak on the Church's behalf. And, for a time, until the churches were sufficiently indoctrinated, such a procedure may have been advisable in Crete. But a tremendously important part of the local church leader's responsibility is so to teach his people that, with all speed, they might function as communicators (see Acts 8:1 and 4).

4. *People whose behavior matches their beliefs.* Only such people can effectively "stop the mouths" of those who *profess that they know God; but in works . . . deny him* (16).

But how had these unfortunate people landed themselves in such a moral muddle? Simply by imagining that it is possible to believe wrongly and behave rightly. They had given *heed to Jewish fables, and commandments of men, that turn from the truth* (14). They had multiplied such commandments, compiling in the process endless lists of what they considered to be clean and unclean. Yet, said Paul, "nothing is pure to the tainted minds of disbelievers, tainted alike in reason and conscience" (15, NEB).

Horace, the Roman poet, had taught a century before that "unless the vessel be clean, whatever you put into it turns sour." Though this applies to the orthodox as well as to the heretical, for it is possible to believe rightly and still behave wrongly. In this case it were better to keep quiet until the life has been aligned to the truth.

> *What you are speaks so loud*
>   *That the world can't hear what you say.*
> *They're looking at your walk,*
> *Not listening to your talk,*
>   *They're judging from your actions every day.*
> *Don't believe you'll deceive*
>   *By claiming what you've never known;*
> *They'll accept what they see*
> *And know you to be,*
>   *They'll judge from your life alone.*

Before passing on, it may be well to take special note of the opening clause of verse 15, for these words have been frequently misquoted and even perverted. Paul is not saying here that the pure man may feel free to play fast and loose with things impure on the supposition that his purity will render him proof against contamination; he was simply applying the teaching of Jesus Christ himself (see

Mark 7:15 and Matt. 15:10ff.), thereby arguing that "ritual purity is at best artificial, [whereas] if a man's moral condition is healthy, the distinction of 'clean' and 'unclean' should have no meaning for him."[9]

The Province of Pastoral Indoctrination
Titus 2:1—3:11

TITUS 2

In the conviction that all which God provides is pure, and with perfect naturalness, Paul proceeds to advise Titus of his responsibility to give spiritual direction on personal, domestic, and civic matters. As further convincing evidence that, to the Christian, the whole of human life is sacred, the apostle has interspersed this section on practical guidance with passages which give what Donald Guthrie describes as "the theological basis for Christian living" (2:11-15; 3:4-7), climaxing these with the fifth and final "trustworthy saying" (3:8).

Responsibility to Teach
Titus 2:1

1 But speak thou the things which become sound doctrine:

Since all this stands in such marked contrast to the doctrines of the false teachers, whose heresies have spread spiritual disease throughout the Christian community, Paul opens this section by making the pronoun *thou* emphatic, so admonishing his young deputy to administer to all ages and stations the medicine of sound, wholesome doctrine.

Guidance for the Older

Titus 2:2-4

> 2 That the aged men be sober, grave, temperate, sound in faith, in charity, in patience.
> 3 The aged women likewise, that they be in behaviour as becometh holiness, not false accusers, not given to much wine, teachers of good things;
> 4 That they may teach the young women to be sober, to love their husbands, to love their children,

The word "sober" (Gk., *nēphalos*), used in the more correct sense of "temperate" in the RSV and NIV, may seem a little out of place in a list of qualities expected of the aged. One might expect this to be indigenous in the elderly. Yet, some time ago, when a friend suggested to a man who had lived a long and godly life that he should allow his biography to be written while he was still alive, he refused permission, saying, "I have seen too many fall out on the last lap." The necessity for wise restraints belongs to every age. The word *sōphrōn,* translated *temperate* in the KJV, and, according to Barclay, descriptive of "the man with the mind which has everything under control,"[10] adds emphasis to this fact.

The word "grave" (Gk., *semnos*), refers to that serious disposition which one expects of seniors, though it does not imply a gloomy killjoy. It is interesting to note that these three qualities were expected of the aged pagan. But it is the triad of essentially Christian virtues—faith, love, and stedfastness—which then, as now, gave a light to the countenance of age "not seen on land or sea."

The phrase, *in behaviour as becometh holiness,* applied to the aged women, is most descriptive when viewed in the light of Walter Lock's observation that they were to carry into their daily living the demeanor of priestesses in the Temple. In our day Paul might possibly have used some lines of George Herbert in which he comments on the words "for Thy sake":

> *A servant with this clause*
> *Makes drudgery divine;*

> *Who sweeps a room, as for Thy laws,*
> *Makes that and the action fine.*

At the opposite extreme Titus is told to warn the older women "not to be slanderers or slaves to drink" (RSV). Scott comments that "the coupling of slander and wine-drinking is significant. In ancient times, when wine was the only beverage, it was at their little wine-parties that old women would take their neighbours' character to pieces."[11] If we were to substitute "tea" or "coffee" for "wine," perhaps the situation might sometimes be all too contemporary! The final admonition is that the older women be *teachers of good things*.

Guidance for the Younger

Titus 2:5-8

> 5 To be discreet, chaste, keepers at home, good, obedient to their own husbands, that the word of God be not blasphemed.
> 6 Young men likewise exhort to be sober minded.
> 7 In all things shewing thyself a pattern of good works: in doctrine shewing uncorruptness, gravity, sincerity,
> 8 Sound speech, that cannot be condemned; that he that is of the contrary part may be ashamed, having no evil thing to say of you.

Guidance to the younger women was to be ministered through their godly seniors, and who would be more fitted to teach in the field of marital and domestic responsibilities? That is, so long as they acted as "humble advisers and not interfering busybodies"!

Several editors have made the point that the standards here must be seen in the light of the times, and doubtless Hanson is justified in his comment on the phrase admonishing the young women to be "submissive to their own husbands" (5, RSV), "To westerners this view of woman's status will seem very old-fashioned; to Eastern Christians it will seem perfectly obvious."[12] Yet the overall emphasis upon the woman's responsibility to love husband and children and to be "temperate, chaste, and kind, busy at home" (NEB), is most timely to women in either hemisphere.

Two commentators have supplemented the text by expressing themselves in words which some present-day Christian women might do well to note. Barclay writes, "It is infinitely more important that a mother should be at home to put her children to bed and to hear them say their prayers than that she should attend all the public and Church meetings in the world."[13] Donald Guthrie adds, "Even our modern age is not without instances of professing Christian women lacking true maternal affection. For women who put their careers before the welfare of their own children are displaying a significant symptom of this weakness."[14] It is significant that Paul states as his special reason for this admonition in verse 5, "that the Gospel will not be brought into disrespect" (NEB).

In contrast to the foregoing Paul's advice for the young men would seem, at first reading, to be mild, being limited to one sentence (6). Albeit, it is a pregnant sentence, and carries much greater force when one recognizes that at this point, for the first time in this chapter, the writer has used the imperative—"Likewise urge the younger men to control themselves" (RSV). However, Paul goes on to remind Titus that, as a young man himself, he will teach more by example than by exhortation. If he is a pattern pastor (7), he is more likely to have pattern young people (see also 1 Tim. 4:12). In his behavior he is to be "a model of good deeds"; in his teaching he is to show "integrity and gravity" (RSV). In other words, his actions and his motives must be pure with no desire for gain either in substance or status, and he must maintain a true dignity.

On this we again quote William Barclay, "There is nothing so injures the cause of Christ as for the leaders of the Church and the pastors of the people to descend to conduct and to words which are unbefitting an envoy of Christ."[15] Thus, in his preaching, Titus is to employ "sound speech that cannot be censured" (RSV). By maintaining such a pattern ministry Paul assures his young colleague that he will teach most effectively and preach most convincingly, for as regards both manner and matter he will most clearly reflect the ministry and young manhood of the One "whose he is and whom he serves."

Surely it behooves the modern preacher and pastor to study the Master Pattern with a diligence even greater than that of Titus, for he stood at but one remove from the Master himself. A young Jewess, who became a Christian, asked the lady who had led her to the Saviour to read history with her. The older woman gladly complied but was somewhat curious to know the reason for the choice of subject. The young convert replied, "because I have been reading the Gospels and I am puzzled. I want to know when Christians began to be so different from Christ."

Guidance for the Christian Worker
Titus 2:9-10

> 9 Exhort servants to be obedient unto their own masters, and to please them well in all things; not answering again;
> 10 Not purloining, but shewing all good fidelity; that they may adorn the doctrine of God our Saviour in all things.

The principles laid down in these verses are broadly similar to those in 1 Tim. 6:1, though, as Guthrie observes, the use of the forceful word *hupotassō* ("to be submissive" —RSV), may suggest "a greater tendency on the part of Christian slaves in Crete to abuse their new-found emancipation in Christ."[16] It would be assumed, however, that in this case the injunction would apply more directly to slaves with Christian masters, for no believing slaves could submit to a demand from a heathen master which would prejudice his conscience. Nevertheless, this would not give licence to suspend the general principle of obedience. As we saw from 1 Tim. 6:2, where slaves had believing masters, even a greater sense of obligation was expected.

In the light of such admonitions as these some have attributed "bourgeois" principles to the Pastorals, making the observation that they contain no directives to the masters. But Paul certainly did not neglect to direct the most solemn charges to these elsewhere (Eph. 6:9; Col. 4:1). While modern working conditions are radically different and industrial relations infinitely more complex, this section is certainly not without value to the Christian workman. Still today the Christian's place of work offers one of the most effective backgrounds against which he may *adorn the doctrine of God our Saviour in all things* (10).

Perhaps, in these more strike-happy days, special note might be taken of Paul's reference to *not answering again* (9). Donald Guthrie observes that this phrase should "probably be understood in the wider sense of 'opposition'. The ERV captures this with 'gainsaying', which would involve the thwarting of their master's plans."[17] Needless to say, no Christian would want to defend the exploitation of the worker, but neither can he defend the exploitation of the employer. What a contribution could be made towards the resolving of industrial discord, with all its unbending defence of one's "rights," and with all the swift-tongued attacks and counterattacks of employers and employed, if there were a revival of the spirit which motivated the primitive Church and, as we have seen in our study of 1 Tim. 6:1-2a, sealed the doom of the enormity of slavery.

Theological Basis

Titus 2:11-15

> 11 For the grace of God that bringeth salvation hath appeared to all men,
> 12 Teaching us that, denying ungodliness and worldly lusts, we should live soberly, righteously, and godly, in this present world;
> 13 Looking for that blessed hope, and the glorious appearing of the great God and our Saviour Jesus Christ;
> 14 Who gave himself for us, that he might redeem us from all iniquity, and purify unto himself a peculiar people, zealous of good works.
> 15 These things speak, and exhort, and rebuke with all authority. Let no man despise thee.

The dictum of the Preacher, that "there is nothing new under the sun" (Eccles. 2:9), seems amply borne out in the title of a book, recently off the press, *Theology in an*

Industrial Society. The author is theological consultant on industrial and social affairs to the bishop of Durham and in the North East of England. This is but one evidence of a new concern to seek a theological basis for living, and in this book the author asks, "How is man to understand his own life within our industrial world? What faith can enable him to respond and live as a complete and responsible human being?"[18] Paul has given the broad answer in these verses. In this outstanding passage he gives his reasons why all men should, and may, live according to the will of God.

1. *The epiphany of God's grace* (11); *The grace of God . . . hath appeared.* God's grace is something of which men, unaided, could never have become aware. In this sense the revelation of God's grace was itself an act of grace. Not that God ever was any other than One whose nature it is to bestow unmerited favor upon the undeserving, but there came an historic moment when that grace "dawned upon the world" (NEB). As Alexander Maclaren said, "The same word is used in telling of the stormy darkness when 'neither sun nor stars' had for many days *'appeared'*, and then at last a rift came in the thick cloud, and the blue was seen, and the blessed sunshine poured down. . . . So, by some historical manifestation, this mighty thing, the love of God, has been put into concrete shape, embodied and made a visibility to men."[19] See John 1:14.

> *Beyond compare the Son of God was seen*
> *Most glorious; in Him all His Father shone*
> *Substantially expressed; and in His face*
> *Divine compassion visibly appeared,*
> *Love without end, and without measure grace.*
>   (Milton in *Paradise Lost*)

2. *The saving energy of grace* (11). *The grace of God that bringeth salvation to all men, hath appeared* (quoting the margin of the KJV), as in 1 Tim. 2:4, shows the universal scope of salvation. This is no declaration of universalism,

however, for salvation cannot be flung broadcast and indiscriminately upon all men of all sorts, regardless of their attitude towards God. But it is more than likely that as Paul wrote this all-embracing word he had in mind the slaves whom he had already mentioned, men who were living witnesses to the fact that any one, of whatever class or kind, may personally prove the energy of saving grace.

3. *The teaching ministry of grace* (12). Here we see grace cast in a most unusual role, "training us to renounce irreligion and worldly passions, and to live sober, upright, and godly lives in this world" (RSV). Grace, as it were personified, is presented as exercising an educative, disciplinary ministry. This is an aspect of grace that is too often neglected, for there is nothing cheaply indulgent about it. No sooner does God's grace dawn upon a man's heart than it begins to resolutely change his actions and attitudes. Negatively, it leads him away from "ungodliness and worldly lusts. It teaches us to say 'No' to ungodliness and worldly passions" (NIV). "The decisiveness of this rupture with the past is brought out in the original by the word rendered *renounce,* which is in the aorist participle indicating a once-for-all act."[20] Compare Rom. 6:15. Positively, grace teaches us "to live a life of self-mastery, of integrity and of godliness" (Moffatt). As Scott points out, "The three words describe man's life in its three-fold relation—to himself, to his fellow-men, and to God."[21] So that, in a very practical sense, as would be expected, grace incites a man to live in obedience to the Great Commandment, maintaining a wholesome relationship with God, his neighbor, and himself. Nor does grace postpone this experience to a vague, indeterminate future, it is for the "here and now" (Phillips).

> *It is the now that makes the sinner;*
> *It is the now that makes the saint.*

Consequently, in the meantime, grace alerts us to the grand expectation.

4. *The future appearing of our Savior God* (13). The term which was used in verse 11 in relation to the grace of God is now used of our great Savior God. The divine title used in this verse has caused no little perplexity. Unlike the translators of the KJV, most moderns have rendered the phrase "our great God and Savior Jesus Christ," as in the RSV. Guthrie, after a very full discussion of the problem, opts for this latter.

Incidentally, while the writer presumably now sees little likelihood of his being among the number of those who will be alive at the time of the Lord's return, that blessed hope is still very real and vivid to him and, as always, it is seen as essentially a purifying hope.

5. *The present purpose of the grace of God* (14-15). As Scott observes, verse 14 "is meant to connect the thought of Christ's future coming with that of the Divine grace now operating."[22] That grace operates with a view to redemption, not exemption; for how could God, on the one hand, excuse His people for living much as the heathen around them and yet, on the other, expect them to be peculiarly His? The whole emphasis in this essentially Pauline statement is upon the fact that God's present purpose, through grace, is to "rescue us from all our evil ways and make for himself a people of his own, clean and pure, with our hearts set upon living a life that is good" (Phillips).

With verse 15 Paul ends the chapter as he began it, by heavily underscoring Titus' pastoral duty to speak with all authority in teaching the sound doctrine which had been committed to him. In this verse, however, he is admonished not only to teach the truth but to exhort his hearers to receive it and, in the event of their noncompliance, to reprimand them. Neither his youth, nor any other consideration, was to be allowed to blunt the edge of such a ministry.

Since it is almost certain that the letter was intended for public reading, Calvin had good reason for suggesting that this forthright pronouncement of the apostle was intended more for the Cretan churches than for Titus himself. Nevertheless, authoritarian as it unquestionably is, such a command needs to be heard and heeded, from time to time, by pastor and people alike. For Leonard Griffith has good reason for writing that "some people have a curiously distorted idea of religion. They regard it as the supreme sport for amateurs, the one thing in life where expert knowledge counts for nothing, where one man's opinions are quite as good as the next and where anybody is competent to criticize and pass judgment."[23] Yet there are many people looking and listening for an authoritative word on such a life or death matter as religion, nor are these by any means necessarily people unable or unwilling to think for themselves.

One of the heroes of the Second World War was Group Capt. Leonard Cheshire, V.C. Asked to explain the logic of his faith, he replied, "When I became a pilot I had to learn the laws of aerodynamics and I went to a training school with the authority to teach me. There I expected and found teachers to give me facts—not their own personal ideas. If God exists and has spoken to us, then the facts He has revealed to us are no more capable of private interpretation than the facts, say, of aerodynamics."[24] Hence Paul's justification for writing to Titus, "These, then, are your themes; urge them and argue them. And speak with authority: let no one slight you" (15, NEB).

TITUS 3

Guidance for the Christian Citizen

Titus 3:1-2

> 1 Put them in mind to be subject to principalities and powers, to obey magistrates, to be ready to every good work,
> 2 To speak evil of no man, to be no brawlers, but gentle, shewing all meekness unto all men.

While the apostle had elsewhere discussed the Christian attitude towards the civil power (Rom. 13:1-7; 1 Tim.

2:1 ff.), it is likely that the need for Titus to convey such guidance had a greater urgency since the Cretans had the reputation of being notoriously intractable in such matters. E. M. Blaiklock has remarked that "a passionate independence, with by-products of lawlessness, is often the mark of the population of rugged islands." He goes on to say that "the occupying Nazis in the Second World War found the population [of Crete] impossible to subdue."[25]

Evidently Paul's fear was that the turbulent Cretans might too readily implicate the church in a political agitation that would bring the gospel under suspicion, hence his admonition to Titus, "Remind your people to recognize the power of those who rule and bear authority. They must obey the laws of the state" (1, Phillips). We may be sure that the apostle intended that his words should be read with proper reservations for, as we see from Rom. 13:3, he assumed that the ruler would encourage the good and oppose the evil. Where this did not obtain, Peter and John had shown where the Christian duty lay (Acts 5:29). Nevertheless, in verse 2, Paul added, "Remind them . . . to speak evil of no one, to avoid quarrelling, to be gentle, and to show perfect courtesy toward all men" (RSV). Courtesy may not have been native to the Cretans, indeed, it may not always come easily to any Christian, especially should he be under provocation, but this quality which is in such short supply in the modern world, has never ceased to be a requirement of Christian character.

Writing more positively, Paul commands the Christians to be prepared to "render whatever good service they can" (1, Phillips). This was not a reference to acts of Christian charity, specifically. As E. M. Scott has said, "It was one of the grievances against Christians that they were exclusive, and too often they so interpreted the call to brotherhood as to give color to this charge."[26] This is a form of exclusivism which ill suits those who profess to follow that One who, while separate from sinners, rejoiced to be known as the Friend of publicans and sinners. This is not an easy tension to maintain, but it is an essential part of Christian discipline.

Colin Morris, in discussing the statement of Archibald MacLeish to the effect that "there are only two kinds of people in this world, the Pure and the Responsible," declared that "in that division, the Church stands always amongst the responsible rather than the pure; the engaged rather than the detached."[27] Morris has apparently failed to appreciate Paul's declaration in 2:11, where the apostle emphatically states that the Christian must stand amongst the responsible *and* the pure. Yet it is because some have divorced responsibility from purity, so producing a travesty of sanctity, that men like MacLeish have gained such a jaundiced view of religion.

Theological Implications
Titus 3:3-8

> 3 For we ourselves also were sometimes foolish, disobedient, deceived, serving divers lusts and pleasures, living in malice and envy, hateful, and hating one another.
> 4 But after that the kindness and love of God our Saviour toward man appeared,
> 5 Not by works of righteousness which we have done, but according to his mercy he saved us, by the washing of regeneration, and renewing of the Holy Ghost;
> 6 Which he shed on us abundantly through Jesus Christ our Saviour;
> 7 That being justified by his grace, we should be made heirs according to the hope of eternal life.
> 8 This is a faithful saying, and these things I will that thou affirm constantly, that they which have believed in God might be careful to maintain good works. These things are good and profitable unto men.

As in the previous chapter, Paul now presents a convincing theological argument for the kind of behavior expected of the Christian. As a basis for demanding such a courteous and considerate attitude towards others, he reminds his readers of three things.

1. *The depths into which their old lives had led them* (3). Certainly the picture Paul has given is painted in the darkest colors. Some have commented that while this may have been warranted in the case of the Cretans, in identify-

ing himself with their previous excesses Paul has gone to undue lengths. Nevertheless, Paul's strong revulsion at the remembrance of his former, unregenerate life had already been given forceful expression in 1 Tim. 1:15. He obviously believed that "retrospect is often salutary in helping us to understand the magnitude of God's grace."[28] It behooves us all to remember that "there go I, but for the grace of God." Of all people in the world the Christian should be the most humble, and, therefore, the most patient with the sins and shortcomings of others.

2. *The means by which new life had reached them* (4-7)

   a. Revelation of divine love (4). Once again Paul writes of an "epiphany," this time of the *kindness and love of God our Saviour toward man.* Scott has made the remark that "this Divine grace is described by a vivid and daring word—the 'humanity' (lit. the 'philanthropy') of God."[29] In other words, God has felt for man as if He were a fellowman.

   b. Salvation by divine grace (5a). Stated negatively, "not because of righteous things we had done" and positively, "but because of his mercy" (NIV), this leaves man no vestige of ground for claiming salvation by human merit.

   c. Regeneration by the Holy Spirit (5b). The phrase, *by the washing of regeneration, and renewing of the Holy Ghost,* has occasioned much debate. Many commentators insist that *the washing of regeneration* must refer in some degree to the rite of baptism. Indeed, Scott considers the phrase to be a clear evidence, not only of the non-Pauline authorship of the Epistle, but bearing witness that "since Paul, the Church [had] advanced another step towards sacramental religion." He continues, "The writer of the Pastorals conceives of the mercy of God as acting immediately through the sacred rite. In other words, the Church is now on its way towards a magical estimate of baptism, and this is evidenced by the use of what appears to be fixed ritual terms."[30]

While it might be conceded that this phrase may employ the language of baptismal ritual, Scott has erected a somewhat complicated theory upon a very slender premise. We are bound to say, with Hendriksen, that "the washing referred to is wholly spiritual," even though *loutron* has been rendered as "laver." This is the case in the margin of the ERV. But Simpson insists that this rendering has slight support and is probably influenced by the dogma of baptismal regeneration. Horton has commented that "the passage is parallel to John 3:5 and 8, where our Lord, in coupling the water and the Spirit together, shows that his object is to assert the supremacy of the Spirit, implicitly denying the efficacy of water unless the Spirit be the source of re-birth."[31]

3. *The goal to which new life has brought them* (6-8). "The Holy Spirit, whom he poured out on us generously through Jesus Christ our Saviour, so that, having been justified by his grace, we might become heirs having the hope of eternal life" (6-7, NIV). This does not exclude the present possession of eternal life, but it does anticipate its full and complete realization (see Eph. 1:13-14). "The Christian is the man who knows the wonder of past sin forgiven, the thrill of present life lived with Christ, and the hope of the greater life which is yet to be."[32]

To round off his dissertation in verses 3 to 7, having given his readers such an incentive to apply the standards of a godly life, Paul adds the now familiar formula, *This is a faithful saying.* Consequently Titus is again required to "insist on these things, so that those who have believed in God may be careful to apply themselves to good deeds; these are excellent and profitable to men" (RSV).

Action Against Heretics

Titus 3:9-11

> 9 But avoid foolish questions, and genealogies, and contentions, and strivings about the law; for they are unprofitable and vain.
> 10 A man that is an heretick after the first and second admonition reject;

11 Knowing that he that is such is subverted, and sinneth, being condemned of himself.

This mention of the benevolent outflowing of sound
doctrine serves to remind Paul again of the sheer futility of
the errorists' "stupid controversies, genealogies, dissen-
sions, and quarrels over the law" (9, RSV). Titus is to
avoid these, and he is to admonish those who seek to
propagate them. In this connection it is interesting to note
that the word *heretick,* used nowhere else in the Bible,
had not acquired its present meaning, hence the NIV
translation, "Warn a divisive person." It was not until the
second century that the word *heretic* came to connote a
holder of false doctrine. We may gather, therefore, that
what most disturbed Paul about the Cretan situation was
not so much the existence of false teaching but the way in
which the sectarians were forming dissident groups, thus
dividing the Body of Christ.

The discipline to be meted out upon such persons
appears to have been relatively mild, for heresy had not yet
been rated as a deadly sin demanding the excommunication of the offender. Yet it constituted a grave danger to
the church, so that anyone who persisted in his divisive
activities after a second warning was to be rejected, or "left
out of account." This would certainly mean that such a
person could not be considered for church office (1:9), but
such action would also imply a withholding of any real part
in Christian fellowship. Of such a heretic Paul wrote, "You
can be sure that he has a moral twist, and he knows it" (11,
Phillips); yet insofar as the disciplinary procedure was a
reflection of that taught in 2 Thess. 3:14-15, its aim was
the eventual recovery of the offender.

Referring again to the sectarians' predilection for
argument and discussion, it might be said that Paul did
not in any sense underrate the place of constructive discussion and debate. What is now better known as "dia-
logue" is by no means a 20th-century expedient. It
belonged to the age of Paul who used it to tremendous
advantage, especially during his lengthy sojourn in

Ephesus. We note in Acts 19:8-10, that "Paul . . . held daily discussions in the lecture hall of Tyrannus . . . and continued this practice for two years, so that all who lived in Asia, both Greeks and Jews, could hear the Lord's message." And this in spite of the fact that the discussion sessions were held at a time when the citizens of Ephesus normally enjoyed their daily siesta!

Yet there is nothing more unproductive than the kind of discussions that the heretics of Crete were so fond of. Indeed, these were counterproductive, for "it has been said that there is a danger that a man may think himself religious because he discusses religious questions. . . . There is no virtue in sitting discussing deep theological questions when the simple tasks of the Christian life are waiting to be done. . . . Such discussion can be nothing other than an evasion of Christian duties."[33] This was why Paul set this criticism of the errorists within the context of positive Christian religion (see 3:8).

Final Instructions and Salutation
Titus 3:12-15

Titus 3:12-15

> 12 When I shall send Artemas unto thee, or Tychicus, be diligent to come unto me to Nicopolis: for I have determined there to winter.
> 13 Bring Zenas the lawyer and Apollos on their journey diligently, that nothing be wanting unto them.
> 14 And let ours also learn to maintain good works for necessary uses, that they be not unfruitful.
> 15 All that are with me salute thee. Greet them that love us in the faith. Grace be with you all. Amen.

From verse 12 we learn of Paul's intention that either *Artemas* or *Tychicus* should take over Titus' responsibilities in Crete. Tychicus was the well-proven associate of Paul already mentioned by him in 2 Tim. 4:12, but of Artemas we have no previous knowledge. Nor can we be certain as to the exact location of *Nicopolis,* since there were several cities of that name in the ancient eastern world of New Testament times.

The Nicopolis which Paul probably had in mind, however, was situated on the Greek mainland. Not only was this a fine winter resort but it would also provide a convenient base from which missionary work might be extended into Dalmatia. It would seem possible, therefore, that Titus did reach this city prior to his working in Dalmatia (see 2 Tim. 4:10). *Zenas the lawyer* is also unknown to us, but the scholarly, eloquent *Apollos* we have met both in Acts and 1 Corinthians. Of these latter colleagues Paul wrote, "Do everything you can to help [them] on their way and see that they have everything they need" (13, NIV).

In verse 14 Paul concludes his Epistle by bringing once again into clear focus the essentially practical nature of Christianity. As we have seen, Paul has been scrupulously careful to point out that God's favor cannot be gained by "works of righteousness," but he has occupied the major part of this letter in stressing that those who, through the grace of God, have been granted His favor, must bear witness to this fact by adorning the doctrine of God in practical holy living. One might say that in this Epistle the Christian has been presented as (1) *a person to whom something has appeared* (2:11; 3:4); (2) *a person to whom something has happened* (2:11, 14; 3:5-7); (3) *a person to whom something has been given* (3:5*b*-6); (4) *a person to whom something has been promised* (3:7); and, therefore, (5) *a person from whom something is expected* (3:8, 11).[34]

And so we come to the apostle's final salutation, from himself and all who were with him to all who were bound by love in the faith to him. How very like Paul to give grace the last word—*Grace be with you all.*

Reference Notes

Abbreviations:

BBC   *Beacon Bible Commentary*
BNTC *Black's New Testament Commentaries*
MNTC *Moffatt New Testament Commentary*
NCB   *New Century Bible*
NTC   *New Testament Commentary*
TNTC *Tyndale New Testament Commentaries*

INTRODUCTION AND FIRST THESSALONIANS

1. A. L. Moore, "1 and 2 Thessalonians," *New Century Bible* (London: Thomas Nelson and Sons Ltd., 1969), p. 1.

2. Arnold E. Airhart, "The First and Second Epistles to the Thessalonians," *Beacon Bible Commentary* (Kansas City: Beacon Hill Press of Kansas City, 1969), 9:436-37.

3. Leon Morris, "1 and 2 Thessalonians," *Tyndale New Testament Commentaries* (London: The Tyndale Press, 1967), p. 9.

4. William Neil, "Thessalonians," *The Moffatt New Testament Commentary* (London: Hodder and Stoughton, Ltd., 1965), p. xxvii.

5. W. E. Sangster, *The Pure in Heart* (London: Epworth Press, 1954), p. 124.

6. John Eadie, *A Commentary on the Greek Text of the Epistles of Paul to the Thessalonians* (London: 1877), p. 38.

7. William Barclay, "The Letters to Philippians, Colossians, Thessalonians," *The Daily Study Bible* (Edinburgh: The Saint Andrew Press, 1970), p. 218.

8. J. Agar Beet, *A Commentary on St. Paul's Epistle to the Romans* (London: Hodder and Stoughton, 1900), p. 280.

9. Neil, "Thessalonians," *MNTC*, p. 18.

10. William Hendriksen, "1 and 2 Thessalonians," *New Testament Commentary* (London: The Banner of Truth Trust, 1972), p. 53.

11. Morris, "1 and 2 Thessalonians," *TNTC*, p. 46.

12. Hendriksen, "1 and 2 Thessalonians," *NTC*, p. 63.

13. Leonard Griffith, *The Need to Preach* (London: Hodder and Stoughton, 1971), p. 60.

14. Morris, "1 and 2 Thessalonians," *TNTC*, p. 62.

15. Samuel Chadwick, *Humanity and God* (London: Hodder and Stoughton, 1904), p. 186.

16. Moore, "1 and 2 Thessalonians," *NCB*, p. 53.

17. Hendriksen, "1 and 2 Thessalonians," *NTC*, p. 86.

18. Barclay, *Daily Study Bible*, p. 213.

19. Morris, "1 and 2 Thessalonians," *TNTC*, p. 69.

20. Quoted by Neil, "Thessalonians," *MNTC*, p. 70.

21. W. E. Sangster, *The Path to Perfection* (London: Hodder and Stoughton, 1943), pp. 193-94.

22. Airhart, *BBC*, 9:472.

23. Neil, "Thessalonians," *MNTC*, p. 73.

24. J. A. T. Robinson, *Honest to God* (London: SCM Press, 1963), p. 106.

25. Morris, "1 and 2 Thessalonians," *TNTC*, p. 78.

26. Quoted by Frederick Coutts in *The Call to Holiness* (London: Salvationist Publishing and Supplies, Ltd., 1964), p. 4.

27. Quoted by Neil, "Thessalonians," *MNTC*, p. 85.

28. *Ibid.*

29. Barclay, *Daily Study Bible*, p. 234.

30. John R. W. Stott, *Your Mind Matters* (London: Inter-Varsity Press, 1972), pp. 10-11.

31. Morris, "1 and 2 Thessalonians," *TNTC*, p. 85.

32. Neil, "Thessalonians," *MNTC*, pp. 89-90.

33. Quoted by A. Skevington Wood in *Prophecy in the Space Age* (London: Marshall, Morgan and Scott, 1964), p. 121.

34. Henry Alford, *The Greek Testament*, rev. E. F. Harrison (Chicago: Moody Press, 1958 reprint), 3:276.

35. Wood, *Prophecy in the Space Age*, p. 33.

36. Quoted by Morris, "1 and 2 Thessalonians," *TNTC*, p. 95.

37. Sir Frederick Catherwood, *A Better Way* (London: Inter-Varsity Press, 1975), p. 130.

38. Roy S. Nicholson, "Holiness and the Human Element," *Insights into Holiness* (Kansas City: Beacon Hill Press, 1962), p. 156.

39. Neil, "Thessalonians," *MNTC*, p. 126.

40. *The Letters of the Rev. John Wesley,* ed. John Telford (London: The Epworth Press, 1931), 4:10.

41. Neil, "Thessalonians," *MNTC*, p. 131.

42. Quoted by J. Baines Atkinson in *The Beauty of Holiness* (London: The Epworth Press, 1953), p. 77.

43. Richard E. Howard, *Newness of Life* (Kansas City: Beacon Hill Press of Kansas City, 1975), p. 207.

44. Moore, "1 and 2 Thessalonians," *NCB*, p. 87.

45. Neil, "Thessalonians," *MNTC*, p. 134.

SECOND THESSALONIANS

1. Morris, "1 and 2 Thessalonians," *Tyndale New Testament Commentaries* (London: The Tyndale Press, 1967), p. 116.

2. *Ibid.,* p. 117.

3. A. Skevington Wood, *Prophecy in the Space Age* (London: Marshall, Morgan and Scott, 1964), pp. 122-23.

4. Quoted by Wood, *ibid.,* p. 123.

5. *Ibid.,* p. 124.

6. Quoted by Morris, "1 and 2 Thessalonians," *TNTC*, p. 120.

7. A. L. Moore, "1 and 2 Thessalonians," *New Century Bible* (London: Thomas Nelson and Sons, Ltd., 1969), p. 97.

8. William Neil, "Thessalonians," *The Moffatt New Testament Commentary* (London: Hodder and Stoughton, Ltd., 1965), p. 152.

9. *Ibid.,* p. 153.

10. Moore, "1 and 2 Thessalonians," *NCB*, p. 103.

11. Morris, "1 and 2 Thessalonians," *TNTC*, p. 132.

12. Moore, "1 and 2 Thessalonians," *NCB*, p. 105.

13. Neil, "Thessalonians," *MNTC*, p. 176.

14. *Ibid.,* p. 180.

15. *Ibid.,* p. 182.

16. Moore, "1 and 2 Thessalonians," *NCB*, p. 109.

17. Sir Frederick Catherwood, *A Better Way* (London: Inter-Varsity Press, 1975), p. 77.

18. Kenneth Grayston, *Letters of Paul to the Philippians and Thessalonians* (Cambridge: The University Press, n.d.), p. 108.

Introduction to the Pastoral Epistles

1. E. F. Scott, "The Pastoral Epistles," *The Moffatt New Testament Commentary* (London: Hodder and Stoughton, 1957), p. xxi.

2. William Barclay, "The Epistles to Timothy and Titus," *The Daily Study Bible* (Edinburgh: The Saint Andrew Press, 1956), p. xviii.

3. Donald Guthrie, "The Pastoral Epistles," *Tyndale New Testament Commentaries* (London: The Tyndale Press, 1967), p. 45.

4. J. N. D. Kelly, "A Commentary on the Pastoral Epistles," *Black's New Testament Commentaries* (London: Adam and Charles Black, 1972), p. 23.

5. R. F. Horton, "The Pastoral Epistles," *The Century Bible* (Edinburgh: T. C. and E. C. Jack, n.d.), p. 45.

6. Donald Guthrie, *The New Bible Dictionary* (London: The Inter-Varsity Fellowship, 1962), p. 1282.

First Timothy

1. A. T. Hanson, "The Pastoral Letters," *The Cambridge Bible Commentary* (Cambridge: The University Press, 1966), p. 19.

2. R. F. Horton, "The Pastoral Epistles," *The Century Bible* (Edinburgh: T. C. and E. C. Jack, n.d.), p. 84.

3. J. N. D. Kelly, "A Commentary on the Pastoral Epistles," *Black's New Testament Commentaries* (London: Adam and Charles Black, 1972), p. 44.

4. William Barclay, "The Epistles to Timothy and Titus," *The Daily Study Bible* (Edinburgh: The Saint Andrew Press, 1956), p. 20.

5. *Ibid.,* pp. 18-19.

6. J. A. T. Robinson, *Honest to God* (London: SCM Press, 1963), p. 106.

7. Sir Frederick Catherwood, *A Better Way* (London: Inter-Varsity Press, 1975), p. 13.

8. Donald Guthrie, "The Pastoral Epistles," *Tyndale New Testament Commentaries* (London: The Tyndale Press, 1967), p. 62.

9. J. N. D. Anderson, *Morality, Law and Grace* (London: Tyndale Press, 1972), p. 124.

10. William Hendriksen, "1 and 2 Timothy and Titus," *New Testament Commentary* (London: The Banner of Truth Trust, 1972), p. 75.

11. Barclay, *Daily Study Bible,* p. 32.

12. E. F. Scott, "The Pastoral Epistles," *The Moffatt New Testament Commentary* (London: Hodder and Stoughton, 1957), p. 14.

13. Daniel Steele, *Half Hours with St. Paul* (Rochester, Pa.: H. E. Schmul, reprint, n.d.), pp. 67-68.

14. Kelly, "Pastoral Epistles," *BNTC,* p. 55.

15. W. T. Purkiser, *et al., Exploring Our Christian Faith* (Kansas City: Beacon Hill Press of Kansas City, 1960), pp. 282-83.

16. Scott, "Pastoral Epistles," *MNTC,* p. 14.

17. *Ibid.,* p. 17.

18. Donald Guthrie, *The New Bible Dictionary* (London: the Inter-Varsity Fellowship, 1962), pp. 1282-83.

19. Eberhard Bethge, *Dietrich Bonhoeffer* (London: Collins, 1970).

20. E. K. Simpson, *The Pastoral Epistles* (London: The Tyndale Press, 1954), p. 40.

21. Quoted by Paul S. Rees in *Things Unshakeable* (Grand Rapids, Mich.: Wm. B. Eerdmans Publishing Co., 1950), p. 104.

22. Guthrie, "Pastoral Epistles," *TNTC,* p. 71.

23. Horton, "Pastoral Epistles," *NCB,* p. 97.

24. *Ibid.*

25. *Ibid.,* p. 98.

26. Kelly, "Pastoral Epistles," *BNTC,* p. 64.

27. Scott, "Pastoral Epistles," *MNTC,* p. 15.

28. Hanson, "Pastoral Letters," *Cambridge Bible Commentary,* p. 36.

29. Guthrie, "Pastoral Epistles," *TNTC,* p. 76.

30. Catherwood, *A Better Way,* pp. 24-25.

31. E. M. Blaiklock, *The Pastoral Epistles* (London: Pickering and Inglis, 1972), pp. 32-33.

32. *Ibid.,* p. 33.

33. Scott, "Pastoral Epistles," *MNTC,* p. 30.

34. Guthrie, "Pastoral Epistles," *TNTC,* p. 79.

35. Barclay, *Daily Study Bible,* pp. 54-65.

36. *Ibid.,* p. 65.

37. J. Glenn Gould, "The Pastoral Epistles," *Beacon Bible Commentary* (Kansas City: Beacon Hill Press of Kansas City, 1969), p. 579.

38. Scott, "Pastoral Epistles," *MNTC,* p. 32.

39. Horton, "Pastoral Letters," *Century Bible,* p. 108.

40. Guthrie, "Pastoral Epistles," *TNTC,* p. 84.

41. Kelly, "Pastoral Epistles," *BNTC,* p. 86.

42. Catherwood, *A Better Way,* p. 131.

43. Barclay, *Daily Study Bible,* p. 84.

44. Scott, "Pastoral Epistles," *MNTC,* p. 38.

45. James Hastings, *The Great Texts of the Bible* (Edinburgh: T. and T. Clark, 1946), pp. 112-13.

46. Guthrie, "Pastoral Epistles," *TNTC,* p. 90.

47. Barclay, *Daily Study Bible,* p. 87.

48. Kelly, "Pastoral Epistles," *BNTC,* p. 95.

49. Scott, "Pastoral Epistles," *MNTC,* pp. 47-48.

50. *Ibid.,* p. 52.

51. R. E. O. White, *A Guide to Preaching* (London: Pickering and Inglis, 1973), p. 3.

52. Kelly, "Pastoral Epistles," *BNTC,* pp. 114-15.

53. Barclay, *Daily Study Bible,* p. 107.

54. Scott, "Pastoral Epistles," *MNTC,* p. 60.

55. Guthrie, "Pastoral Epistles," *TNTC,* p. 104.

56. Kelly, "Pastoral Epistles," *BNTC,* p. 121.

57. *Ibid.,* p. 124.

58. Catherwood, *A Better Way,* p. 133.

59. Westminster Chapel, London. Pastored until recently by Dr. Martyn Lloyd-Jones.

60. *Ibid.,* p. 133.

61. Leonard Griffith, *The Need to Preach* (London: Hodder and Stoughton, 1971), p. 20.

62. Barclay, *Daily Study Bible,* p. 121.

63. Neil M. Robertson, "Wine and Its Significance in the New Testament," being an unpublished thesis in partial fulfilment of requirements for the degree of Master of Arts in Theology, Winona Lake School of Theology, June, 1961, p. 74.

64. *Ibid.,* p. 40.

65. *Ibid.,* p. 81.

66. Gould, "Pastoral Epistles," *BBC,* 9:611.

67. F. S. Fitzsimmonds, *New Bible Dictionary,* p. 1332.

68. *Is Revolution Change?* A symposium edited by Brian Griffiths (London: Inter-Varsity Press, 1972), p. 33.

69. *Ibid.,* p. 12.

70. *Ibid.,* p. 40.

71. Scott, "Pastoral Epistles," *MNTC,* p. 73.

72. Kelly, "Pastoral Epistles," *BNTC,* p. 136.

73. Hanson, "Pastoral Letters," *Cambridge Bible Commentary,* p. 70.

74. H. Orton Wiley, *The Epistle to the Hebrews* (Kansas City: Beacon Hill Press, 1959), p. 395.

75. Kelly, "Pastoral Epistles," *BNTC,* p. 141.

76. G. Campbell Morgan, *The Westminster Pulpit,* Vol. 2 (London: Pickering and Inglis, n.d.), p. 16.

SECOND TIMOTHY

1. Samuel Chadwick, *25 Sunday Mornings with Samuel Chadwick,* selected and arranged by D. W. Lambert (London: The Epworth Press, 1952), p. 84.

2. "The Pastoral and Johannine Epistles," *The Speaker's Bible,* ed. E. Hastings (Aberdeen, Scotland: "The Speaker's Bible" Office, 1942), p. 38.

3. J. A. Simpson, *There Is a Time To . . .* (London: James Clarke & Co., Ltd., 1971), p. 94.

4. *Ibid.,* p. 97.

5. J. B. Phillips, *Ring of Truth* (London: Hodder and Stoughton, 1967), p. 33.

6. E. K. Simpson, *The Pastoral Epistles* (London: Tyndale Press, 1954), p. 125.

7. Phillips, *Ring of Truth,* p. 13.

8. Donald Guthrie, "The Pastoral Epistles," *Tyndale New Testament Commentaries* (London: The Tyndale Press, 1967), p. 130.

9. E. F. Scott, "The Pastoral Epistles," *The Moffatt New Testament Commentary* (London: Hodder and Stoughton, 1957), p. 96.

10. C. K. Barrett, "The Pastoral Epistles," *The New Clarendon Bible* (Oxford: Oxford University Press, 1963), p. 97.

11. Guthrie, "Pastoral Epistles," *TNTC,* p. 130.

12. *Ibid.,* p. 136.

13. John R. W. Stott, *Guard the Gospel* (London: Inter-Varsity Press, 1973), p. 43.

14. Leonard Griffith, *The Need to Preach* (London: Hodder and Stoughton, 1971), p. 26.

15. Handley C. G. Moule, "The Second Epistle to Timothy," *The Devotional Commentary* (London: Religious Tract Society, 1905), p. 77.

16. J. H. Jowett, *The Preacher, His Life and Work* (London: Hodder and Stoughton, n.d.), p. 114.

17. A. T. Hanson, "The Pastoral Letters," *The Cambridge Bible Commentary* (Cambridge: The University Press, 1966), p. 85.

18. William Hendriksen, "1 and 2 Timothy and Titus," *New Testament Commentary* (London: The Banner of Truth Trust, 1972), p. 260.

19. William Barclay, "The Epistles to Timothy and Titus," *The Daily Study Bible* (Edinburgh: The Saint Andrew Press, 1956), p. 180.

20. Scott, "Pastoral Epistles," *MNTC,* p. 109.

21. Guthrie, "Pastoral Epistles," *TNTC,* p. 147.

22. Barclay, *Daily Study Bible,* p. 179.

23. Stott, *Guard the Gospel,* p. 87.

24. Guthrie, "Pastoral Epistles," *TNTC,* p. 158.

25. E. M. Blaiklock, *The Pastoral Epistles* (London: Pickering and Inglis, 1972), p. 114.

26. Murdo Macdonald, *The Need to Believe* (London: Collins Fontana Books, 1964), p. 112.

27. Guthrie, "Pastoral Epistles," *TNTC,* p. 164.

28. Phillips, *Ring of Truth,* p. 14.

29. Stott, *Guard the Gospel,* p. 104.

30. R. E. O. White, *A Guide to Preaching* (London: Pickering and Inglis, 1973), p. 3.

31. Guthrie, "Pastoral Epistles," *TNTC,* pp. 166-67.

32. J. Glenn Gould, "The Pastoral Epistles," *Beacon Bible Commentary* (Kansas City: Beacon Hill Press of Kansas City, 1969), 9:655.

33. J. N. D. Kelly, "A Commentary on the Pastoral Epistles," *Black's New Testament Commentaries* (London: Adam and Charles Black, 1972), p. 216.

34. Stott, *Guard the Gospel,* p. 124.

35. Quoted by Guthrie, "Pastoral Epistles," *TNTC,* p. 179.

Titus

1. J. N. D. Kelly, "A Commentary on the Pastoral Epistles," *Black's New Testament Commentaries* (London: Adam and Charles Black, 1972), p. 225.

2. William Barclay, "The Epistles to Timothy and Titus," *The Daily Study Bible* (Edinburgh: The Saint Andrew Press, 1956), p. 239.

3. Samuel Chadwick, *Humanity and God* (London: Hodder and Stoughton, 1904), p. 169.

4. John R. W. Stott, *Your Mind Matters* (London: Inter-Varsity Press, 1972), p. 28.

5. Quoted by Elton Trueblood in *A Place to Stand* (New York: Harper and Row, 1969), p. 29.

6. Barclay, *Daily Study Bible,* pp. 245-46.

7. D. Martyn Lloyd-Jones, *Authority* (London: Inter-Varsity Fellowship, 1966), p. 7.

8. R. J. McCracken, *Questions People Ask* (London: SCM Press, 1952), p. 136.

9. Kelly, "Pastoral Epistles," *BNTC,* p. 237.

10. Barclay, *Daily Study Bible,* p. 262.

11. E. F. Scott, "The Pastoral Epistles," *The Moffatt New Testament Commentary* (London: Hodder and Stoughton, 1957), p. 164.

12. A. T. Hanson, "The Pastoral Letters," *The Cambridge Bible Commentary* (Cambridge: The University Press, 1966), p. 113.

13. Barclay, *Daily Study Bible,* p. 267.

14. Donald Guthrie, "The Pastoral Epistles," *Tyndale New Testament Commentaries* (London: The Tyndale Press, 1967), p. 193.

15. Barclay, *Daily Study Bible,* p. 270.

16. Guthrie, "Pastoral Epistles," *TNTC,* p. 196.

17. *Ibid.,* p. 197.

18. Margaret Kane, *Theology in an Industrial Society* (London: SCM Press, 1975), p. 1.

19. Quoted in *The Great Texts of the Bible,* James Hastings, ed. (Edinburgh: T. and T Clark, 1946), p. 253.

20. Kelly, "Pastoral Epistles," *BNTC,* p. 245.

21. Scott, "Pastoral Epistles," *MNTC,* p. 168.

22. *Ibid.,* p. 170.

23. Leonard Griffith, *Barriers to Christian Belief* (London: Hodder and Stoughton, 1967), p. 71.

24. Andrew Boyle, *No Passing Glory* (London: Collins Fontana Press, 1959), p. 328.

25. E. M. Blaiklock, *The Pastoral Epistles* (London: Pickering and Inglis, 1972), p. 90.

26. Scott, "Pastoral Epistles," *MNTC,* p. 172.

27. Colin Morris, *Mankind My Church* (London: Hodder and Stoughton, 1971), p. 16.

28. Guthrie, "Pastoral Epistles," *TNTC,* p. 203.

29. Scott, "Pastoral Epistles," *MNTC,* p. 174.

30. *Ibid.,* p. 176.

31. R. F. Horton, "The Pastoral Epistles," *The Century Bible* (Edinburgh: T. C. and E. C. Jack, n.d.), p. 189.

32. Barclay, *Daily Study Bible,* p. 282.

33. *Ibid.,* p. 283.

34. Adapted from R. E. O. White, *Sermon Suggestions in Outline* (London: Pickering and Inglis, 1965), pp. 31-32.

Bibliography

(Books cited in text or suggested for further study)

1 and 2 Thessalonians

Airhart, Arnold E. "The First and Second Epistles to the Thessalonians," *Beacon Bible Commentary*. Kansas City: Beacon Hill Press of Kansas City, 1969.

Alford, Henry. *The Great Testament*. Chicago: Moody Press, 1958 reprint of rev. ed.

Atkinson, J. Baines. *The Beauty of Holiness*. London: The Epworth Press, 1953.

Beet, J. Agar. *A Commentary on St. Paul's Epistle to the Romans*. London: Hodder and Stoughton, 1900.

Bicknell, E. J. "The First and Second Epistles to the Thessalonians," *The Westminster Commentaries*. London: Methuen and Co., Ltd., 1932.

Buckland, A. R. "St. Paul's First Epistle to the Thessalonians," *The Devotional Commentary*. London: The Religious Tract Society, 1906.

Chadwick, Samuel. *Humanity and God*. London: Hodder and Stoughton, 1904.

Coutts, Frederick. *The Call to Holiness*. London: The Salvationist Publishing and Supplies, Ltd., 1964.

Denney, James. "Commentary on 1 and 2 Thessalonians," *The Expositor's Bible*. London: Hodder and Stoughton, 1892.

Eadie, J. *A Commentary on the Greek Text of the Epistles of Paul to the Thessalonians*. London: 1877.

Frame, J. E. "Commentary on First and Second Thessalonians," *The International Critical Commentary*. London: T. and T. Clark, 1912.

Griffith, Leonard. *The Need to Preach*. London: Hodder and Stoughton, 1971.

243

Hendriksen, William. "I and II Thessalonians," *The New Testament Commentary* (Reprint). London: Banner of Truth Trust, 1972.

Howard, Richard E. *Newness of Life*. Kansas City: Beacon Hill Press of Kansas City, 1975.

Lightfoot, J. B. *Notes on the Epistles of St. Paul*. London: Macmillan, 1895.

Milligan, A. *Commentary on 1 and 2 Thessalonians*. London: Macmillan, 1908.

Moore, A. L. "1 and 2 Thessalonians," *New Century Bible*. London: Thomas Nelson & Sons, Ltd., 1969.

Morris, Leon. "1 and 2 Thessalonians," *Tyndale New Testament Commentaries*. London: The Tyndale Press, 1967.

Neil, William. "Thessalonians," *The Moffatt New Testament Commentary*. London: Hodder and Stoughton, 1965.

Nicholson, Roy S. "Holiness and the Human Element," *Insights into Holiness*. Kansas City: Beacon Hill Press, 1962.

Sangster, W. E. *The Path to Perfection*. London: Hodder and Stoughton, 1943.

———. *The Pure in Heart*. London: The Epworth Press, 1954.

Steele, Daniel. *Half Hours with St. Paul*. Reprint. Rochester, Pa.: H. E. Schmul, n.d.

Stott, John R. W. *Your Mind Matters*. London: Inter-Varsity Press, 1972.

Wood, A. Skevington. *Prophecy in the Space Age*. London: Marshall, Morgan & Scott, 1964.

Pastoral Epistles

Alford, H. *The Greek Testament,* Vol. 3. 4th ed. London: Rivington, 1865.

Anderson, J. N. D. *Morality, Law and Grace*. London: Tyndale Press, 1972.

Barclay, William. "The Epistles to Timothy and Titus," *The Daily Study Bible*. Edinburgh: The Saint Andrew Press, 1956.

Barrett, C. K. "The Pastoral Epistles," *The New Clarendon Bible*. Oxford: The University Press, 1963.

Bethge, Eberhard. *Dietrich Bonhoeffer*. London: Collins, 1970.

Blaiklock, E. M. *The Pastoral Epistles*. London: Pickering and Inglis, 1972.

Boyle, Andrew. *No Passing Glory*. London: Hodder and Stoughton, 1967.

Calvin, John. *The Epistles of Paul to Timothy and Titus*. London: Oliver and Boyd, 1964.

Catherwood, Sir F. *A Better Way*. London: Inter-Varsity Press, 1975.

Chadwick, Samuel. *Humanity and God*. London: Hodder and Stoughton, 1904.

―――. *25 Sunday Mornings with Samuel Chadwick*. Selected and arranged by D. W. Lambert. London: The Epworth Press, 1952.

Fairbairn, P. *Commentary on the Pastoral Epistles*. London: Oliphants, 1956.

Gould, J. Glenn. "The Pastoral Epistles," *Beacon Bible Commentary*, Vol. 9. Kansas City: Beacon Hill Press of Kansas City, 1969.

Griffith, Leonard. *Barriers to Christian Belief*. London: Hodder and Stoughton, 1967.

―――. *The Need to Preach*. London: Hodder and Stoughton, 1971.

Griffiths, Brian, ed. *Is Revolution Change?* A Symposium. London: Inter-Varsity Press, 1972.

Guthrie, Donald. "The Pastoral Epistles," *Tyndale New Testament Commentaries*. London: The Tyndale Press, 1967.

Hanson, A. T. "The Pastoral Letter," *The Cambridge Bible Commentary*. Cambridge: The University Press, 1966.

Harrison, P. N. *The Problem of the Pastoral Epistles*. Oxford: Oxford University Press, 1921.

Hastings, E. *The Pastoral and Johannine Epistles*. Aberdeen, Scotland: "The Speaker's Bible" Office, 1942.

Hastings, J. *The Great Texts of the Bible*. Edinburgh: T. and T. Clark, 1946.

Hatch, E. *The Organization of the Early Christian Churches*. London: Longman's, Green and Co., 1901.

Hendriksen, William. "I and II Timothy and Titus," *The New Testament Commentary*. Reprint, 1972.

Horton, R. F. "The Pastoral Epistles," *The Century Bible*. Edinburgh: T. C. and E. C. Jack, n.d.

Jowett, J. H. *The Preacher, His Life and Work*. London: Hodder and Stoughton, n.d.

Kane, Margaret. *Theology in an Industrial Society*. London: SCM Press, 1975.

Kelly, J. N. D. "The Pastoral Epistles," *Black's New Testament Commentaries*. London: Adam and Charles Black, 1972.

Lloyd-Jones, Martyn D. *Authority*. London: Inter-Varsity Fellowship, 1966.

Lock, W. "The Pastoral Epistles," *The International Critical Commentary*. Edinburgh: T. and T. Clark, 1924.

Macdonald, Murdo E. *The Need to Believe*. London: Collins Fontana Press, 1964.

McCracken, R. J. *Questions People Ask*. London: SCM Press, 1952.

Morgan, G. Campbell, *The Westminster Pulpit,* Vol. 2. London: Pickering and Inglis, n.d.

Morris, Colin. *Mankind My Church*. London: Hodder and Stoughton, 1971.

Moule, H. C. G. "The Second Epistle to Timothy," *The Devotional Commentary*. London: The Religious Tract Society, 1905.

Phillips, J. B. *Ring of Truth*. London: Hodder and Stoughton, 1967.

Plummer, A. "The Pastoral Epistles," *The Expositor's Bible*. London: Hodder and Stoughton, 1888.

Purkiser, W. T., *et al. Exploring Our Christian Faith*. Kansas City: Beacon Hill Press of Kansas City, 1965.

Rees, Paul S. *Things Unshakeable*. Grand Rapids, Mich.: Wm. B. Eerdmans Publishing Co., 1950.

Robertson, Neil M. "Wine and Its Significance in the New Testament." An unpublished thesis in partial fulfillment of requirements for the degree of Master of Arts in Theology, Winona Lake School of Theology, June, 1961.

Robinson, John A. T. *Honest to God*. London: SCM Press, 1963.

Scott, E. F. "The Pastoral Epistles," *The Moffatt New Testament Commentary*. London: Hodder and Stoughton, 1957.

Simpson, E. K. *The Pastoral Epistles*. London: The Tyndale Press, 1954.

Simpson, J. A. *There Is a Time to . . .* Cambridge: James Clarke and Co., Ltd., 1971.

Stott, John R. W. *Guard the Gospel: A Study in Second Timothy*. London: Inter-Varsity Press, 1973.

———. *Your Mind Matters*. London: Inter-Varsity Press, 1972.

Trueblood, Elton E., *A Place to Stand*. New York: Harper and Row, 1969.

White, N. J. D. "The Pastoral Epistles," *The Expositor's Greek Testament*. London: Hodder and Stoughton, 1910.

White, R. E. O. *A Guide to Preaching*. London: Pickering and Inglis, 1964.

———. *Sermon Suggestions in Outline*. London: Pickering and Inglis, 1965.

Wiley, H. Orton. *The Epistle to the Hebrews*. Kansas City: Beacon Hill Press, 1959.